The IT Manager's
Survival
Guide

The IT Manager's Survival Guide

Rob Aalders and Peter Hind

JOHN WILEY & SONS, LTD

Copyright © 2002 by John Wiley & Sons, Ltd,
Baffins Lane, Chichester,
West Sussex PO19 1UD, England

National   01243 779777
International   (+44) 1243 779777
e-mail (for orders and customer service enquiries): cs-books@wiley.co.uk
Visit our Home Page on http://www.wiley.co.uk
or http://www.wiley.com

Other Wiley Editorial Offices

John Wiley & Sons, Inc., 605 Third Avenue,
New York, NY 10158-0012, USA

Wiley-VCH Verlag GmbH, Pappelallee 3,
D-69469 Weinheim, Germany

John Wiley & Sons Australia, Ltd, 33 Park Road, Milton,
Queensland 4064, Australia

John Wiley & Sons (Asia) Pte Ltd, 2 Clementi Loop #02-01,
Jin Xing Distripark, Singapore 129809

John Wiley & Sons (Canada) Ltd, 22 Worcester Road,
Rexdale, Ontario M9W 1L1, Canada

British Library Cataloguing in Publication Data

A catalogue record for this book is available from the British Library

ISBN 0-470-84454-X

Typeset in 10/12pt Garamond by Dorwyn Ltd, Rowlands Castle, Hants
Printed and bound in Great Britain by T.J. International Ltd, Padstow, Cornwall

This book is printed on acid-free paper responsibly manufactured from sustainable forestry, in which at least two trees are planted for each one used for paper production.

I have but gathered

a posie

of other men's flowers

and nothing

but the thread that binds them

is mine alone.

John Bartlett[1]

Contents

Contents

Foreword

Rob Aalders was CIO and General Manager of Corporate Services for Tyndall Australia Ltd, which was one of GPG's most successful investments. Rob was responsible for ensuring the company had a well run IT department—a critical component in maintaining and enhancing the value of the business.

Rob also helped develop many staff members, both in and outside IT, to achieve higher management positions. His approach to teaching those staff sound skills was both sensible and pragmatic.

I believe he has recaptured that shrewd, down-to-earth streak in this book. This is not another technical academic study for industry specialists but a really practical guide to what happens in the IT department on a daily basis. If you are a newcomer to IT management you would do well to read carefully and apply Rob's recommendations.

Sir Ron Brierley
Chairman, Guinness Peat Group plc
Sydney, 2002

Preface

God is not on the side of the heavy battalions, but of the best shots. (Voltaire)

The siege of Leningrad in the Second World War lasted for 900 days from September 1941 to January 1944. It has been described as one of the most horrible, most heroic episodes in human history. An oft-quoted statement is that the average life span of a senior IT manager is also about 900 days, and, like the siege, it often represents a heroic stand against horrible odds, with *the best shots* outside of IT.

This book aims to improve your chances of survival. It provides a number of practical housekeeping recommendations as well as approaches to solving perennial management issues. It is not a replacement for the numerous publications that provide advice on information technology strategy or the myriad technical issues that plague the managers of information systems. Neither does it deal with the wider processes of budgeting and financial planning or the detail of human resource management practices. There are a wide number of excellent books on these subjects and the prudent manager will seek specialist help from the appropriate departments. Instead, the book aims to ensure that you cover those chinks in your armour that have led to so many IT managers being mortally wounded by unhappy business colleagues.

If you are new to the role or a hardened veteran you should find answers to these two persistent questions:

- *What do I do first?*
- *What do I do next?*

The first chapter introduces you to the changes required to transform yourself from being a technical professional to a manager. Immediately following are chapters dealing with a common challenge for technical managers—managing people. The body of the book then covers typical issues facing IT managers. This part ends with a series of chapters on planning, architecture and preparing for the future. Anecdotes from practising IT managers and business executives are scattered throughout the book.

The second part of the book contains essays on what is wrong with IT management. These contributions from leading managers and academics illustrate what others think of IT managers—allowing you to "know your enemy" so to speak.

The book closes with a number of short chapters summarizing the work of a number of management theorists. These provide a useful backstop if you are ever faced with attacks on your management methods.

The book does not have to be read in a linear fashion and most chapters are freestanding, though they may direct you to related topics.

At this point you may be wondering what prompted such a treatise. The trigger was twofold. The first was the view that there is little in the way of management advice published for IT professionals, many of whom were given little if any exposure to management techniques during their formative years. The second was an e-mail from my co-author, Peter Hind. Peter, who interviews upwards of a thousand IT managers each year as part of his research work, made the following observation.

> I feel from running InTEP that there are some basic parameters for effective IT management. Good IT operations have a number of consistent variables. These are things like: a belief in operational benchmarking to understand best practice and what is feasible; . . . a sense of cooperation between the business and IT cultivated by things like SLAs, IT steering committees, IT business account management, business ownership of projects etc.; an appreciation of the project management discipline so projects have deadlines, KPIs, milestones etc. Often this manifests itself in a strong commitment to a programme or project office. I also see issues around IT staff management and career modelling. There's much more . . .

We would like to make a contribution to effective IT management, so we set out to provide a reference book for IT managers, both old and new, with the aim of improving their 900-day survival rate.

The IT Manager's Survival Guide addresses a range of common issues and provides a number of suggestions and techniques for management. The list of potential inclusions was endless. It would not be possible to deal with them all without writing an encyclopedia.

We offer no silver bullets, no holy grails, no one-size-fits-all answer. What is offered is a path that can be followed by motivated and intelligent people, adapting as they go to suit their circumstances.

Acknowledgements

Thank you to those who kindly allowed us to re-use material from their work, and in particular:

- John Thorpe and DMR's Centre for Strategic Leadership and their publishers McGraw-Hill Ryerson Ltd for use of material from *The Information Paradox.*
- Elliot Jacques and his publisher Cason Hall for use of material from *Requisite Organization.*
- The Australian Graduate School of Management Studies for use of the material in Chapter 2.
- Gary Yukl and Prentice Hall for the permission to use material from *Leadership in Organizations*

Thank you also to those who contributed by writing the essays which appear in this book, in particular; Kate Behan, Anna Hinder, John Oleson, John Smyrk and Jeremy Tozer.

I especially thank Diane Taylor, Senior Publishing Editor (Business and Management), Anne Flynn, Editorial Assistant, Vivienne Wickham, Senior Production Editor and Peter Hudson, Marketing Executive of John Wiley & Sons Ltd for the support, advice, patience and encouragement they have given to me as a writer. I add the praise that every person to whom I have talked, written, e-mailed or spoken at John Wiley & Sons has been unfailingly helpful.

I also thank Angela E Grant, my friend from ages past and the most excellent editor for her keen eye and sensitive surgery on my clumsy writing.

Those familiar with *The IT Outsourcing Guide* will recognize the fine work of Jane Canfield and Sue Cannon who again produced the illustrations.

The final thanks go to Margaret, Julian and Gemma for encouraging and supporting this work.

Introduction

Initiative consists of doing the right thing without being told. (Irving Mack in *Forbes Business Quotations*)

What do I do once the induction, introductions and housekeeping of taking up the new position are complete? Every manager faces this question sooner or later. The options might appear to be:

- React to the first crisis that hits your desk and go forward from there.
- Be a sponge, absorbing all around you until you are ready to act.
- Call in the consultants.
- Manage!

The first may satisfy a craving for action and the need to be seen to be doing something. But it will be one of many crises. You will have no idea of its relative importance and it will shortly be followed by another crisis, and another and another, until you are no longer managing but firefighting.

The second option, the waiting game, may erode your credibility and fail to satisfy your new employer's pressing need for you to correct what they will see as the endless wrongs of the IT unit—unless you are the exception that inherited a paradisiacal IT unit.

The third works, if they are good *management* consultants. If they are mainly technology technicians, then you are unlikely to be provided with *management* solutions.

We suggest a fourth option, which is the self-help approach. This guide aims to provide you with the tips and techniques for better managing your IT unit—and your business colleagues.

The self-help approach is based on one critical belief. You must set sound rules of engagement with the business in order to be successful. These principles must underpin your every action (see Figure 1.1). If you do this you will almost inevitably follow up by implementing other sound practices including good corporate governance and service level agreements. If you fail to introduce sound rules of engagement your time as an IT manager may well be spent in an unpleasant management maelstrom with its inevitable consequences.

While this important concept is covered in an early chapter, the remainder of the guide is not a chronological step-by-step approach to surviving as an IT manager. Instead it aims to be a handy reference book of ideas and tips that you can apply as you choose.

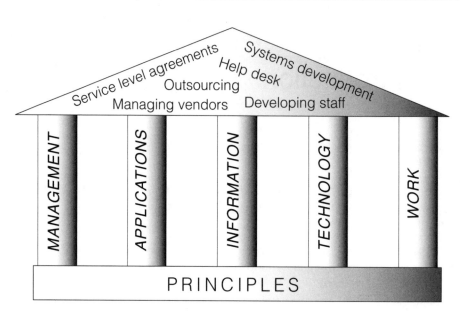

Figure 1.1—The pillars of principles.

Before going any further, however, you should be aware of the belief system that underpins this survival guide.

The first is a belief that IT managers are there to manage, not to be the chief technical guru in management clothing. For this reason the next chapter deals unashamedly with "Becoming a manager". If you are a deeply experienced, well-trained *professional manager* you may find this no more than an interesting revision before you dig into the practical parts of the book. If you are a recent graduate from the ranks or have previously managed by intuition then you may find it enlightening.

The second belief that should shine throughout the book is that IT is not isolated from "the business". Developing and operating a sound IT unit requires the active participation of both *IT and business managers—for they must be jointly involved in the process to share in the outcomes.*

One of the most difficult jobs you face will be convincing both your staff and your colleagues in other business areas that you sink or swim together. The people of the business cannot sit on their hands waiting for technology miracles, nor can your staff afford to ignore the fact that the research, development, production, marketing and customer service staff are the key to earning the company income which pays their wages.

Third is the belief that IT units have three key characteristics:

- The IT unit is a *supply* unit that provides outputs to other business units in the form of effective and efficient automated business processing.

- The IT unit is a *commercial* unit, and should only supply those outputs where it is commercially appropriate to do so.
- The IT unit also acts as a *logistics* unit, undertaking the detailed coordination of process, people and technology.

The last article of faith is probably the most critical and derives from the belief that unless the appropriate Business, Technology, Organization, Process and People (BTOPP)[2] are properly coordinated in technology-based projects, failure will certainly follow. A derivate BTOPP model is shown in Figure 1.2. BTOPP reappears time and time again in this book. It is worth while making yourself familiar with the model and description now.

Finally, this work aims to pass on the experience of others in dealing with a number of critical issues that typically face IT managers.

Some chapters are brief and to the point. The aim is to provide crisp, succinct ideas rather than an extensive discourse on every subject. Gartner, Seybold, Meta and other research and consultancy companies can direct you to their reference files if you do wish to study the extensive body of knowledge in each area.

You may also find it worth while to read material that lies outside the traditional sphere of information technology if you wish to be thoroughly informed. For example:

- Texts on purchasing and vendor management.
- Books on human resource management and the psychology of change.
- Books and reference material on managing projects.
- Guidelines on disaster recovery planning and business continuity.

The list is endless. A quick search of any on-line reference will illustrate the extent of published work on these topics.

The aim here is to provide a useful and informative text that time and time again provides you with support in your role as an IT manager. A brief summary of the book now follows.

Becoming a manager

This chapter highlights the personal challenge that faces those moving from being technical experts to becoming managers. It offers some tools for evaluating your competencies and position. Abraham Maslow wrote "Proper management of the work lives of human beings; of the way in which they earn their living, can improve them and improve the world . . ." The IT manager's job is to manage and manage well. This chapter gives you some hints as you move along that path.

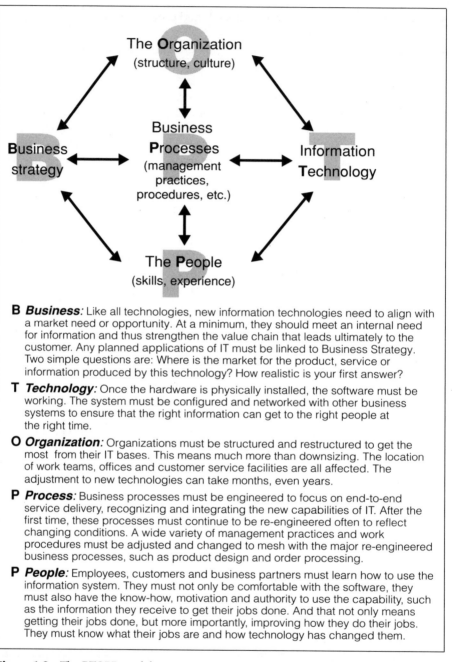

The Organization
(structure, culture)

Business
Processes
(management
practices,
procedures, etc.)

Business
strategy

Information
Technology

The People
(skills, experience)

B Business: Like all technologies, new information technologies need to align with a market need or opportunity. At a minimum, they should meet an internal need for information and thus strengthen the value chain that leads ultimately to the customer. Any planned applications of IT must be linked to Business Strategy. Two simple questions are: Where is the market for the product, service or information produced by this technology? How realistic is your first answer?

T Technology: Once the hardware is physically installed, the software must be working. The system must be configured and networked with other business systems to ensure that the right information can get to the right people at the right time.

O Organization: Organizations must be structured and restructured to get the most from their IT bases. This means much more than downsizing. The location of work teams, offices and customer service facilities are all affected. The adjustment to new technologies can take months, even years.

P Process: Business processes must be engineered to focus on end-to-end service delivery, recognizing and integrating the new capabilities of IT. After the first time, these processes must continue to be re-engineered often to reflect changing conditions. A wide variety of management practices and work procedures must be adjusted and changed to mesh with the major re-engineered business processes, such as product design and order processing.

P People: Employees, customers and business partners must learn how to use the information system. They must not only be comfortable with the software, they must also have the know-how, motivation and authority to use the capability, such as the information they receive to get their jobs done. And that not only means getting their jobs done, but more importantly, improving how they do their jobs. They must know what their jobs are and how technology has changed them.

Figure 1.2—The BTOPP model.

From THE CORPORATION OF THE 1990s: INFORMATIONAL TECHNOLOGY AND ORGANIZA-TIONAL TRANSFORMATION, edited by Michael Scott Morton, copyright © 1991 by The Sloan School of Management. Used by permission of Oxford University Press, Inc.

Knowing your customer

Your customer *is* the business. The first rule of business survival is to *know your customer.* How often have you heard the criticism that IT does not understand the business? This chapter points the way to ensuring that criticism is not directed at you or your staff. This process of discovery can identify opportunities for IT.

Our greatest asset

Imitation is said to be the sincerest form of flattery. This chapter suggests you imitate the methods employed by recruitment consultants to better determine, document and identify the myriad skills at your disposal both inside and outside your domain.

Developing staff

One of your primary tasks is to make sure that you have adequately trained and experienced resources to meet future needs. Staff development must be targeted to the future demands of the business. This chapter suggests a useable and useful approach.

Supporting roles

There are jobs that make the difference between an effective and efficiently functioning IT manager and a dysfunctional one. What roles are required? What skills are needed in them? How can they make a difference?

Managing recruiters

With typical staff turnover rates reaching between 20% and 30% per annum, recruiting staff is a part of life in IT. Make the process rigorous and effective by following certain steps.

The rules of engagement

Without rules, anarchy rules. The most important thing an IT manager can do is reach agreement with fellow company officers on how technology is to be managed. This chapter provides a simple and effective approach to achieving this critical goal.

Establishing sound corporate governance

If you fail to perform, the judges on the governing body can sign your death warrant. This will happen, and for all the wrong reasons, if you don't ensure they are properly informed and focused. We show you how to ensure that the IT Steering Committee concentrates on the right things and takes responsibility for their role in your success.

Establishing service level agreements

Service level agreements are an established approach to agreeing performance levels. However, numerous mistakes have been made in selecting, measuring and reacting to performance measures. In this chapter you will learn how to identify the things that IT must do well if it is to be a responsive unit within the business organization.

Dealing with hot spots

You rarely have to seek these out! Your new colleagues will be only too quick to tell you what needs fixing *now!* This chapter provides some tips and techniques for managing hot spots.

Tips for quick-wins

Everyone wants them. They can build instant credibility for a new IT manager. They can also become instant disasters. This chapter suggests some hints for making sure they become wins, not losses.

Living with legacy systems

These will not go away. Today's technological breakthrough is tomorrow's legacy system. This chapter proposes ways of dealing with legacy issues including some replacement and re-engineering strategies.

Managing vendors

The verdict of most observers is that IT managers do this badly. Find out how to bring vendors under control. Make sure they know their responsibilities and your expectations. Despatch the time-wasters. Try external service level agreements.

Using consultants

It is a rare IT manager who does not use numerous consultants today. Managing them can be a nightmare. Here is how to simplify the process and make the consultants more responsive to your needs.

Business process re-engineering

This is a tricky topic that can improve or thwart the best-laid plans of mice and IT managers. The experiences of others may help you avoid some of the pitfalls.

Benchmarking

Along with service level agreements, benchmarking is a seductive topic for those that manage you. What can you do to make sure that your operation is benchmarked in an appropriate way? This chapter gives some indicators.

Managing the desktop

Someone said desktop management was an oxymoron. Most who have been involved with it might agree. This chapter offers some suggestions that go beyond the obvious.

Disaster recovery planning

Many countries now demand that substantial business organizations have a formal disaster recovery plan. Find out some of the pitfalls and opportunities that DRP offers.

Managing change

This chapter does not concern itself overmuch with software change management. It instead directs you to the broader issue which underpins the failure of so many IT projects—business change management.

Outsourcing

If you haven't done it already, you may be doing it soon. How do you avoid joining the list of the unsuccessful? Discover some basic steps in this chapter.

Information management

It is the twenty-first century and we are a quarter of a century into the widespread use of information technology—and the lack of understanding by business people about information management continues. We provide some simple guidelines for educating the masses.

Planning for the future

This chapter does not tell you how to execute a strategic planning exercise. Instead it suggests things you should consider and ensure are covered in your strategic plan to put you a step ahead of the average IT manager.

Understanding architectures

Enterprise architectures (EA) are often poorly understood and even more poorly used. Understand architectures and turn your EA into a functioning tool. If you don't have one, you need to get one.

Take stock of your assets

Do you really know where all the licences, maintenance agreements, servers and contracts signed over the last twenty years are hidden—and what they commit you to? Do you really know how many printers and servers you are responsible for managing? Research suggests the answer is probably a blunt "No". Worse still, the gap between what IT managers think they have and what actually exists is often huge.

Structuring the IT organization

Are there any empirical rules for setting organization structure and reporting lines? Yes—Elliot Jacques has written widely on the subject. Discover a well-researched basis of organization structure.

Where to next?

Telecommuting, wireless connectivity, externally sourced workers and the virtual company all spell change for the business. You, as IT manager, will be expected to support it all. This chapter raises some emerging issues and gives food for thought.

Anecdotes

These are scattered throughout the book. Their aim is quite simply to offer a human perspective on the trials and tribulations of IT managers. There is a message in each one.

Part B   What is wrong with IT management?

What do your customers think? These essays are contributions from managers, consultants and practitioners on what they think is wrong with IT management. They show that dissatisfaction is widespread and that it has a number of core components. The IT manager who ignores them may not be a manager for long!

Part C   Management theorists

Professionals such as IT managers, engineers, actuaries and others are not exposed to orthodox management theories as part of their professional training. This leaves us vulnerable to criticisms of our management approach. These short chapters introduce you to the thinking of some management theorists.

There is some bad news. The role of IT manager requires that you inject significant effort, in analysis, design, development and maintenance of your IT department—in the same way that significant effort is required in all these processes when developing robust, reliable computer systems.

In closing this introduction, you should know that despite our occasionally light-hearted approach, both Peter and I subscribe to the view expressed by Professor Fred Hilmer of the Australian Graduate School of Management.[3]

The essence of management is the skilful application of sound and proven ideas to particular situations facing managers, not dogma, jargon or quick-fix fads.

PART A
MANAGE YOUR WORLD

2 Becoming a manager

The test for any person is—that you want to find out if he's an apple tree or not—Does He Bear Apples? (Abraham H. Maslow in *Maslow on Management*)

The above quotation can be paraphrased to ask the same question about managers. Managing is very different from being the technical guru. A key aspect of becoming an effective IT manager is recognizing how the perspective and behaviours required of a manager differ from those of a technical expert.

Changing your frame of reference

As a professional specialist you made your *distinctive* contribution by using your *specialist* skills in dealing with the complex and often ambiguous problems in information systems. For example:

● Assessing whether potential solutions fit certain kinds of technical problems.
● Skilfully implementing your selected solutions to efficiently rectify the problems.
● Bringing order to situations of ambiguity, complexity and uncertainty.

As an IT professional, you will have spent many years of theory and practice developing these skills and you will have developed specific ways of addressing these issues. You have a particular focus and distinct way of looking at problems. You see problems from a perspective developed to suit your profession. You are observant, and you will have noted that the accountants see everything in dollar terms, the human resources people see things as people issues, and as Packard said: "Law students are trained in the case method, and to the lawyer everything in life looks like a case.[a]"

This perspective can lead to a failure to see problems from other viewpoints. This in turn can limit the number and types of solutions to problems. Your training will have predisposed you to see, collect and analyse information in a certain way and overlook information that does not fit your *frame of reference*.

---

[a] Edward Packard Jr, "The world: law: attorneys and the practice of law", *Columbia Forum*, Spring 1967

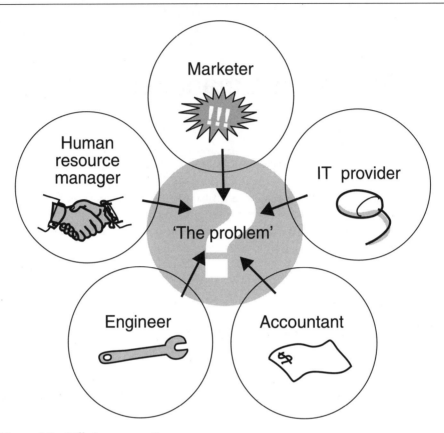

Figure 2.1—Differing perspectives.
Reproduced by permission of the Australian Graduate School of Management's MBA (Executive) Programme, *Managing People and Organizations (2000)*, AGSM, Sydney, 2000.

To be an effective IT manager you will need to develop a broader frame of reference, admit information you might otherwise ignore and consider the other professional viewpoints as if they were your own! The Australian Graduate School of Management[4] believes:

> When excellent professionals become poor managers, a failure to transcend their functional perspective is often a prime cause. In general, the incorporation of a full range of professional perspectives is usually required to make good managerial decisions. Effectiveness at managing and incorporating the ideas of people with different paradigms is therefore a crucial factor in being an effective manager.

One technique that is most useful is to cultivate the habit of putting yourself in the shoes of your fellow executives. Ask yourself how each affected executive may see the problem and the solution.

Make this more than a good resolution. Take action now. Take an outstanding issue and a piece of paper and write down how you think your colleagues may view it from their frame of reference. Make it a habit to analyse problems from the broader perspective. You will stand out as an IT professional and a manager if you can do this one thing effectively.

Spending your time

Mintzberg's[5] work on how managers spend their time revealed the following:

- Managers work at a relentless pace, seldom taking a break. Upper level managers often take their work home.
- Managers typically spend brief amounts of time on fragmented activities and are frequently interrupted. These characteristics are even more pronounced at lower management levels.
- Managers tend to direct their attention to concrete issues and to the most current information, rather than reflective planning.

This has significant implications for information systems professionals reared on focused work on a single activity such as programming which is in turn directed to ephemeral mental models of the finished system. The only item in common is the relentless pace of work.

Activities of a manager

Changes may also be expected in the activities you will undertake as a manager, for instance, Gary Yukl identified the following things as typical management activities:[6]

- Making decisions
- Giving and seeking information
- Influencing people
- Building relationships.

The typical IT professional is often limited to making closely bound technical decisions and seeking related information. They can be lacking in people related skills and communication.

These behaviours are illustrated in Figure 2.2 and described in Figure 2.3. Study these carefully: it is what your job entails from now on.

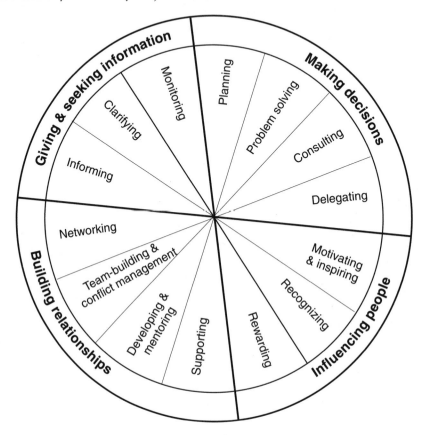

Figure 2.2—Management behaviours.
Reproduced by permission of the Australian Graduate School of Management's MBA (Executive) Programme, *Managing People and Organizations (2000)*, AGSM, Sydney, 2000.

I'm good at some things and not so good at others

Take a highlighter and work down the list in Figure 2.3 and mark those things you are not very good at. If you fit the typical preferred work type[b] for IT professionals

---

[b] Isabel Myers and Katherine Briggs wrote an excellent analysis of personality types and work. Managers are encouraged to take a Myers–Briggs type indicator test (or similar) so that they have an objective definition of their own personality. This will also provide cues for building on strengths and overcoming weaknesses in dealing with people. See Myers I and Briggs K, *Gifts Differing*, Consulting Psychologists Press, Palo Alto, CA, 1980.

Planning and organizing. Determining long-term objectives and strategies, allocating resources according to priorities, determining how to use personnel and resources to accomplish a task efficiently, and determining how to improve coordination, productivity, and the effectiveness of the organizational unit.

Problem solving. Identifying work-related problems, analysing problems in a timely but systematic manner to identify causes and find solutions, and acting decisively to implement solutions to resolve important problems or crises.

Clarifying roles and objectives. Assigning tasks; providing direction in how to do the work; and communicating clear understanding of job responsibilities, task objectives, deadlines, and performance expectations.

Informing. Disseminating relevant information about decisions, plans and activities to people that need it to do their work; providing written materials and documents; and answering requests for technical information.

Monitoring. Gathering information about work activities and external conditions affecting the work, checking on progress and quality of the work, evaluating the performance of individuals and the organizational unit, analysing trends and forecasting external events.

Motivating and inspiring. Using influence techniques that appeal to emotion or logic to generate enthusiasm for the work; commitment to task objectives; compliance with requests for cooperation, assistance, support or resources; setting an example of appropriate behaviour.

Consulting. Checking with people before making changes that affect them, encouraging suggestions for improvement, inviting participation in decision making, incorporating the ideas and suggestions of others in decisions. Allowing subordinates to have substantial responsibility and discretion in carrying out work activities, handling problems, and making important decisions.

Supporting. Acting friendly and considerate, being patient and helpful, showing sympathy and support when someone is upset or anxious, listening to complaints and problems, looking out for someone's interests.

Developing and mentoring. Providing coaching and helpful career advice; doing things to facilitate a person's skill acquisition, professional development and career advancement.

Managing conflict and team building. Facilitating the constructive resolution of conflict; encouraging cooperation, teamwork, and identification of the work unit.

Networking. Socializing informally; developing contacts with people who are a source of information and support; maintaining contacts through periodic interaction, including visits, telephone calls, correspondence, and attendance at meetings and social events.

Recognizing. Providing praise and recognition for effective performance, significant achievements, and special contributions; expressing appreciation for someone's contribution and special efforts.

Rewarding. Providing or recommending tangible rewards such as a pay increase or promotion for effective performance, significant achievements, and demonstrated competence.

Figure 2.3—Yukl's definition of management practices.

you will have fewer ticks in the relationship material (the sensing stuff) and more ticks in decision making (judging competency). If your profile is the reverse then you are an unusually extroverted and congenial IT manager!

Your career development task will be to seek *help* on building those missing skills because wishing to have them or making good resolutions will not change your spots.

In addition, you may require support staff to be more effective. Refer to Chapter 6 for insight into this pernicious failing of IT managers to appreciate that they are not all competent in all matters.

People and work

One of the first difficulties in becoming a manager is learning how best to manage people. Your approach will be influenced by your preferred work type, previous training, personal belief system and frame of reference. The management theorists in Part B of this book offer some guidance. However, there are some good, basic practices which are common to many theories and are worth adopting if you want to run an efficient unit.

First, if you believe in authoritarian management, then, think again, you need to learn that treating people with consideration is more profitable, both profession- ally and personally.

Maslow, McGregor, Yukl, Mathews, Herzog and others all come to one basic conclusion that is best summed up by Yukl:[7]

> A manager who is considerate and friendly towards people is more likely to win their friendship and loyalty. The emotional ties that are formed make it easier to gain cooperation and support from people the manager must rely on to get work done.

He adds:

> Do be aware that as a manager you hold a position of power and people below you are very sensitive to how you treat them. Whether you are polite, supporting, whether you listen, mentor and reward or whether you are rude, uncaring self-centred and grasping.

If you doubt his wisdom, think about the people you least liked working for and which of the above traits they demonstrated.

Second, being a mentor and developing others to realize their potential can be one of the most rewarding experiences for a manager. It can also pay off in ensuring you have a well trained, soundly developed, loyal team. Mentoring can extend beyond competencies and skills, and take in the whole gamut of human development, for both immediate work and non-related issues.

Problems will occur from time to time, and you will need to tactfully guide people to make a self-assessment of their weaknesses. Encourage them to probe why something didn't work and ask if they'd like help or development in the area.

Third, recognizing contributions is another important aspect of good management. Don't sit passively waiting to be told of achievements. Walk around, look, observe, and listen. Recognize achievements at home, work and play. When someone has done something special, recognize it immediately. Make an informal announcement, send an e-mail, let their boss know, let the chief executive know, give them a dinner voucher, a box of chocolates. Do something!

Finally, much of your time will be spent in conflict resolution between your department and business colleagues, vendors, personalities and even between outsiders. It goes with the territory in management. You will have to resolve conflicts you didn't start, want or even know existed. Training in mediation, negotiation and conflict resolution would be most useful.

A complete list of guidelines on sound management behaviours can be found in Appendix A.

Are you ready to manage?

Before we turn to our first Checklist you may find it useful to track where you believe you are positioned on the chart shown in Table 2.1.

This is not a trite exercise. Titles are often misleading or misunderstood both by those appointing and those receiving. The nature of your managerial role may also depend on your company's size and the scalar location of your title.

A common trap for IT managers is to act as operating-level managers when the managing director or chief executive intends them to act as top-level managers.

This chapter calls for more job analysis and self-analysis than any other does. It offers you an opportunity to reflect on the role change implied by the change to management and your readiness for the role. It offers you the chance to quietly identify your strengths and the areas that need attention. It promotes good people skills.

Now go forth and manage.

Checklist

The checklist (overleaf) demands careful reflection rather than a swift box-ticking response. Think about it.

Table 2.1—Transformation to management

	Operating-level managers	Senior-level managers	Top-level managers
Changing role	From operational implementers to aggressive entrepreneurs	From administrative controllers to supportive coaches	From resource allocators to institutional leaders
Primary-value added	Driving business performance by focusing on productivity, innovation and growth within front-line units	Providing the support and coordination to bring large company advantage to the independent front-line units	Creating and embedding a sense of direction, commitment and challenge to people throughout the organization
Key activities and tasks	Creating and pursuing new growth opportunities for the business	Developing individuals and supporting their activities	Challenging embedded assumptions while establishing a stretching opportunity horizon and performance standards
	Attracting and developing resources and competencies	Linking dispersed knowledge, skills and best practices across units	Institutionalizing a set of norms and values to support cooperation and trust
	Managing continuous performance improvement within the unit	Managing the tension between short-term performance and long-term ambition	Creating an over-arching corporate purpose and ambition

1. Have you identified the competencies that you have?
2. Have you identified the competencies that you need to build?
3. Have you enlisted professional help in building those competencies?
4. Have you implemented a system for ensuring you always develop alternative views of problems?
5. Do you know which managerial style you favour?
6. Do you need to modify it to be effective?
7. Who in your department will you mentor and have you developed a schedule that allows you to mentor?
8. Do you have a means of recognizing and rewarding achievements?
9. Have you taken or enrolled in a conflict resolution or mediation class?
10. Have you examined and made a point to regularly review the guidelines in Appendix A?

3   Knowing your customer

. . . the few customers who actually pay for our products will return them by throwing them at employees. (Scott Adams in *The Dilbert Principle*)

The cynical but perceptive comment by Scott Adams is retiterated by the GartnerGroup[8] who stated "The most frequently cited disconnect is the lack of business unit knowledge by [IT] relationships manager . . . knowledge specific to the business unit, its needs and its processes are missing or inadequate". IT managers the world over work with people that single out IT for special criticism in this regard.

Give yourself a fighting chance. Get to know your "customer" so well that you know more about them than they do themselves.

Here's how

Some steps you can and should take are to identify:

- The company's business model including customers, markets and financial history.
- The key business processes and in particular those that are *or may become* technology dependent.
- The background, skills and competencies of the key people in the business.
- The organization structure and the rationale that underpins the structure.
- The technologies used by the business including production and logistics plant and equipment that falls outside the scope of IT.

You should have established some picture of these aspects of the business in the job interviews. A prudent person might also examine the company's public records. The more sophisticated will do as Peter Hind suggests in his essay, "Finding the Right Job", later in this book and that is make an effort to contact the person who previously held the IT management role and obtain their views on the business, organization, technology, processes and people.

Implications

If you don't know your organization well, then you may fall foul of some or all of the following.

- Serious errors of judgement including:
  - Approval or support of misdirected investments in information technology.
  - Failure to properly deploy staff and resources to support the right parts of the business.
  - Proposed investments that do not make sense or that are outside the company's financial or cultural capacity to manage.
- Failure to identify information technology investment opportunities in support of the key business processes.
- Misunderstanding the real corporate power structure, thereby over-reacting to the demands of some, and conversely, ignoring the advice of the key executives.
- If you fail to understand the premise on which the organization is structured and sets pay and conditions, you may make commitments to your new staff that cannot be kept. This is an easy trap to fall into in the first few nervous weeks in a new job.

Benefits

The benefits of knowing the business are many and largely self-evident. In several instances, they are counterpoints to the implications listed previously.

- A proper knowledge of the businesses' products and markets enables you to assess where IT investment should be directed. It enables you to determine whether the current budget is directed to propping up moribund products or supporting high-profit lines.
- Proper knowledge of the lines of business and related financials will help you better identify opportunities and quick-wins.[c]
- Another benefit of understanding and preferably *documenting* processes is that you can start to weed out or to prevent investment in redundant processes.
- Importantly, you can also participate fully in executive discussions and meetings from a business perspective rather than just from the passive role of technology management.

---

[c] Quick-Wins are short projects with high payback. Quick-Wins are covered in Chapter 12.

- Proper knowledge of the organization alerts you to cultural behaviours, risk-taking profiles and the nature of the formal and informal management paths through the company. It will help you establish the organizational dependencies and links. It may very well identify business units and locations you were not previously aware of.
- Another benefit of mapping the informal organization structure is that it focuses on *people* who make strategy, decisions, rules and conceive, produce and sell product. Without people, there is no company. If you know their skills, background, work-styles, preferences, competencies and relationships, you are better placed to manage effectively. You can frame recommendations in the most appropriate manner for the intended audience. You will understand what changes the company is capable of and not capable of making.
- Understanding the culture—preferably before you make a final commitment to accept the role—will enable you to assess the match between your personality and the dominant company culture. If you are a highly innovative maverick and you join a hidebound risk-averse organization, neither you nor they will be happy.
- Knowing the types of technology that exist in the business and who controls it enables you to take cognizance of potential systems and infrastructure that lie outside the IT domain. In some companies, particularly those that are engineering based, you may find a number of "quasi-IT" units operating in conflict or competition with the central IT unit.

It is clearly impossible to deliver services effectively if you do not know the business. Yet time and time again IT managers fail to take concrete action to understand these critical aspects, hoping to survive and develop their role by some combination of osmosis and perception. The IT manager needs to know about the whole business. Divisional managers may survive within the limits of their business unit's speciality, but not the IT manager. You need to know every aspect of the business!

Start to build your knowledge of the business in general and the role of IT within the business from the moment you decide to apply for the role of IT manager. If you are an external appointment you should start before you apply for the job. Much company information is available publicly in the form of annual reports, brochures, public-access records and other records filed with government agencies controlling company registrations.

Two other rich sources of information are former employees and suppliers. You may know some of the new company's suppliers from business dealings in your previous jobs. Ask them about the company you are thinking of joining. You usually find out quite a lot and it may not all be good.

As a newcomer to the company you will be in the enviable position of a general acceptance that the process of discovery is an acceptable first step. Your research will be welcomed as someone getting to know the business.

The bad news for an incumbent IT manager—or one appointed from within—is that they are expected to "know" all this information and they may quickly find they do not. Many IT units, unfortunately, operate in isolation from their companies and their introverted and insular culture works against building key *management* knowledge. It is easy to make the mistake of thinking you know all about the company because you have been employed there a few years.

Some guidelines for building up management knowledge for both new appointees and internal promoted staff follow.

Corporate entity

Inquire and document what you can about the business. You must be able to answer the following questions with absolute confidence:

- What were the company's establishment date, parentage, financial performance and growth over the past ten years?
- How many employees does it have and in which locations? Has this changed much in the past five years?
- What are the broad employee classifications, for example production workers, clerical staff, engineering, technology and finance?
- What products and services does it offer?
- Which of these are profitable and which less so? Has there been any shift in the past five years?
- Who are the customers for each product? What socioeconomic class do they fall into? Why do they buy this company's products?
- Does the company have any significant potential liabilities, for example, outstanding product litigation?
- What are the company's vision, mission and values or its goals and objectives?

You should have an interesting time doing this research. You may even be surprised to find several other executives "Don't know the business" either.

Business processes

The best way to get to the heart of what the business does is to document the company's business processes. Your staff can do the documentation and walk you through it.

It will provide valuable insight into the quality and appropriateness of what is being done, the proper application of technology and help you identify quick-wins. The processes are what the business *does*. If you don't understand the process you can only react and do as others demand.

Make sure that you have a fairly good idea of the answers to these questions:

- What are the key processes of the business?
- What are the triggers that start and stop the process?
- What are the key steps in each of these processes?
- What are the dimensions of the process, input, duration, output, throughput, and cost?
- What skills and competencies are required and deployed to carry out each process?
- Which processes are most troublesome and why?
- Which business division owns each process?
- What technology supports or could support the process?

Yes, it is tough. Yes, it is necessary. You as IT manager must *insist* on having the key processes documented to a level of detail where you can re-use that information and knowledge within IT. Your team must know these processes. They offer the key to understanding the business and ensuring the proper deployment of IT resources. They are also a very useful source of quick-win opportunities and long-term business improvement.

Organization

Organization charts are highly misleading when it comes to identifying the importance of various people and the *real* power structure in the business. First, organization charts are frequently out of date. Second, they represent a formal structure which is usually misleading in practice. Organization charts often imply common levels of authority and responsibility that are not comparative in practice. They may not include countless consultants, temporary workers, associate companies or subsidiaries. Probe the real extent of the company. Some questions you will need to seek answers to include:

- Does the chart include all consultants, temporary employees and the like?
- Does it include subsidiary companies or affiliates?
- Which employees sit on the executive committee or its equivalent?
- What are the professional qualifications of the key employees?
- What are the skills and competencies of the remainder?

- Who are the board members and how much do they influence the running of the company?
- What is the staff turnover and is it comparable to other companies in the industry?
- If not, what are the triggers for the variation in turnover?
- What is the dominant culture?[d] (See Figure 3.1.)

Entrepreneurial	**Conservative**
Risk encouraging	Risk averse
Informal	Formal
Decisive	Deliberate
Results oriented	Process oriented
Aggressive	Defensive
Clear authority lines	**Ambiguous authority**
Functional or divisional	Matrix
Profit and loss responsibility	Cost and revenue centres
Hierarchical	Consensual
Cooperative	**Competitive**
Team oriented	"Macho"
Collaborative	Individualistic
Reward oriented	Censure oriented
Merit based	Power based
Led	**Managed**
Long-term goals	Short-term objectives
Clear, enduring mission	Mixed messages
Big picture oriented	Detail oriented
Creative	Analytical
Ethical	**Amoral**
Visible ethics and policies	Tacit acceptance of unethical behaviour
Ethical leadership and supervision	Hiring for cultural fit between systems
Internal checks and balances	

Figure 3.1—Contrasting cultural dimensions.

Note: There are many other models and dimensions to culture, *Few* organizations will be totally entrepreneurial or conservative and will have a mixture of these dimensions. The above provides many clues for identifying organizations' behavioural traits.

From *Computerworld* (Australia) 23 September 1985. Reproduced by permission of IDG Communications.

- Are there multiple cultures or only one company-wide culture?
- What does the culture (or cultures) imply for IT?
- Who are the key players and how are their ambitions fulfilled?
- Which key staff are IT literate and illiterate?
- Are there any groups with unique technology requirements?

---

[d] A culture map is shown in Figure 3.1. It should provide some prompts to help you classify your organization's dominant traits in those five dimensions.

Answer these and you will start to develop a picture of the environment you need to manage within. This will include the decision makers as well as the unofficial power groups.

Personalities

You may learn much of the information below as you trawl through the organization's history. However, you must discover the following:

- The few key people with whom you will work with outside the information technology unit and their personality types, likes, dislikes, previous IT experiences, level of IT literacy and pet projects and hates.
- The key staff who work within the IT domain. You may have to limit yourself to the top ten or twenty, but do not limit yourself to direct reports.
- Try to avoid the temptation to discover the above attributes through experience over time. The gaining of experience can be painful: better to ask questions first.

Knowing the people who matter is essential. Don't trust the views of others. Carry out your own research. Ask around. Now test yourself against the checklist below.

Checklist

Do you have adequate knowledge of:

1. **The business**
    1.1 Locations
    1.2 Location budgets
    1.3 Location business plans
2. **Customers and markets**
    2.1 Customer types and socioeconomic categories
    2.2 Products and services
    2.3 Key customer interactions
    2.4 Current and future markets

3. **Key business processes**
    3.1   Management
    3.2   Product development
    3.3   Marketing (if not included in product development)
    3.4   Manufacturing
    3.5   Product administration (for example, insurance policy or bank account administration)
    3.6   Finance payable and receivable
    3.7   Service delivery and/or customer relationship management
    3.8   Logistics and supply
    3.9   Archiving/waste removal
    3.10 Records management
    3.11 Procurement
    3.12 Contract management
    3.13 Information technology management
    3.14 Information technology operations
4. **Organization**
    4.1   Formal organization charts
    4.2   Informal organization map
    4.3   Key players and influencers
    4.4   Culture imprint.

4   Our greatest asset

Behind an able person there are always other able people. (Chinese proverb)

I'm on first-name terms with everyone

Yes, but do you know them? Do you have a complete inventory of their capabilities beyond their obvious technical skills? Do you know who has a major in accountancy, who has well-developed human resource management skills, who is a qualified mediator, how well they rated in their last three performance appraisals, or what their peers think of them? This chapter is about recording *complete* information covering your staff.

You should have ready access to their:

- Professional and technical qualifications.
- Managerial or organizational competencies.
- Experience both in the company and prior to joining.
- Previous performance appraisals and job history.
- Preferences and ambitions.
- Interests outside work.[e]

Build a human resources database

IT managers should never be afraid to borrow another person's good idea. The business expects you to be smart and innovative, so build a database of your human resources skills and make sure that it extends beyond the limits of technology skills, and enrich it with scanned CVs, interviews, peer reviews and personal observations.

---

[e] Be careful not to invade personal privacy or transgress privacy laws.

Most of us display a touch of cynicism when we see the company slogan "People are our most important asset". The truth is they usually are but are rarely treated that way. A significant part of treating people well is knowing them well and deploying them effectively.

This chapter encourages you to know your people more effectively than is typical for a manager—any manager. Companion chapters are Chapter 5, "Developing staff", and Chapter 26, "Structuring the IT organization". The chapter on developing staff reiterates the need to model future demand and develop skills to meet those needs. Chapter 6, "Supporting roles", deals with a common weakness among IT managers, that is, the failure to ensure they employ appropriate support staff in contract administration, human resource management, project office management and the like.

Keeping your staff

How can you keep highly skilled IT staff without being held hostage to their pay demands? With a worldwide shortage of many IT skill sets there will always be someone prepared to offer higher wages than you. This confronted Martin Telfer when he moved from Britain to take over the IT reins at Mallesons Stephen Jaques, one of Australia's leading legal practices. Martin appreciated that it was unreasonable to expect to retain staff forever. Instead he saw his challenge was to increase the tenure of their employment in his department. His approach was to interview each staff member to understand both their career aspirations and what motivated them as individuals. He then strove to ensure that the tasks he assigned helped staff embellish their résumés towards these long-term career goals. He knew there would come a point when he had nothing more to offer some staff. For example, there can only be one CIO in a company so someone with this ambition will eventually need to look elsewhere. However, when they did move on both parties knew that their work up to then had helped them progress towards their long-term goal.

Process

As elsewhere in this book, what follows is not prescriptive. Instead it is a series of possible steps to help you do your job more effectively. You may need to add additional steps or remove steps. The numbers of people, their locations and your available time will force you to rationalize the process. However, you should ensure you carry it out for your direct reports and managers once removed[f]—in simple terms, the next level down.

---

[f] Manager Once Removed (MOR) is a term coined by Elliot Jacques in *Requisite Organizations*, Cason Hall, VA, 1988. His definition is: "The manager of a subordinate's immediate manager is that subordinate's manager-once-removed."

- Define what you need to know to make sound decisions about the deployment of your staff. Consider technical, personal and business skills.
- Define the *other* information you need about your staff for professional development, for example: performance appraisal records, résumés, peer reviews, personal observations, personal preferences and ambitions.
- Establish whether the corporate Human Resources Management Systems (HRMS) can record all the information you need.
- Create the means to record and retrieve both competencies and related data. This could mean purchasing a system developed for staff recruitment agencies, modifying your HR system or building a simple internal database, hopefully linked to your HR system.
- Collate and enter *all* the information that you require.
- To collect the data you will need to:
  - Obtain personnel files, read and extract useful data.
  - Review CVs and identify other useful skills or experience.
  - Review performance appraisal records and establish track records.
  - Talk to staff and probe around technical, business and other skills such as formal negotiation and financial modelling.
  - Ask them about their plans and preferences—what they want to do and why.
  - Talk to their peers and managers where appropriate and probe their perceptions of their colleague's strengths and weaknesses.

Populating the database and matrices will be tiresome work. So consider what help you can enlist on the project. If you are running a sizeable IT unit you may wish to recruit your own HR specialist.

Now, to make your job just a tiny bit harder, but far more rewarding, consider adding basic information on people outside IT that may prove useful now or in the future, for example:

- Staff in other parts of the business with useful IT-related skills.
- Staff outside IT whose skills can enhance your department, for example financial modellers, project managers, mediation experts, writers, graphic artists. These staff may be employed:
  - In your company
  - By suppliers or consultants
  - By your competitors.

Don't doubt you will find people outside IT but in the company who have specialist IT skills. They will often be hidden in engineering or actuarial departments. They may be specialists in programmable logic controllers or sophisticated spreadsheet development. A leading research company[9] observed:

> [The] Line of business view . . . is that more than 20 percent of IT resources will come from within business units but the CIO sees no resources coming from this group.

Take the initiative by bringing people who perform IT functions in the business unit into IT. If you can't have them on your team, then at least make sure you know what they are capable of so you can access them when you need to.

Checklist

1. Have you made an inventory of the current technical skill set in your department?
2. Have you included the current business skills, for example budgeting, planning, financial modelling, legal, negotiation, mediation and the like?
3. Have you included the current support skills such as contract management, human resources, project office administration?
4. Have you reviewed staff résumés to identify skills or experiences that may prove useful now or in the future?
5. Have you checked performance appraisal documents and undertaken peer or managerial reviews of your staff?
6. Do you have a reliable and effective way of recording and retrieving this information?
7. Have you widened your net to include details on staff outside of IT and outside the company?
8. Have you considered a career transformation process to bringing business people into IT?
9. Have you enlisted appropriate help to execute the process?
10. Have you taken due note of privacy laws to ensure you don't fall foul of the law?

5 Developing staff

Treat people as if they were what they ought to be and you help them become what they are capable of becoming. (Johann Wolfgang Von Goethe)

Developing staff is a task that requires professional support from the Human Resources Department. If your IT unit is large it may extend to appointing a dedicated resource within your department. The previous chapter recommended the creation of a comprehensive database on your staff. This chapter focuses on enhancing that database to include *future* needs to guide staff development.

What's the problem?

The single greatest issue is that *future* competency analysis is not done and staff development sees tens of thousands of dollars spent aimlessly funding attendance at irrelevant conferences, courses and seminars.

There is a reasonable chance that you will find some of the following unpleasant manifestations of this in your IT unit.

- Little more than an intuitive knowledge of the gap between the current and required skills pool.
- Career development that is driven by personal preference rather than corporate need.
- Extensive junketing disguised as training, including course attendance given as a reward for good performance rather than need.
- Limited or altogether absent in-house information systems training programmes.
- An absence of resources to support individual directed self-training.

It may take a moment of reflective honesty to admit these things exist. You are not being asked to share them publicly.

The alternative

If, on the other hand, staff development and training are run professionally, you may experience the following pleasing results:

- Improved morale in the department.
- Lower recruitment costs.
- Improved staff retention.
- Shortened time span between needing a skill and acquiring it.
- Lower corporate training costs.
- The department becoming more attractive to potential employees.

Identifying current and required staff competencies is a critical component of well-directed career development.

The major tasks

The following statement summarizes the process:

> The skills management process links the enterprise vision to a technology forecast, the technology forecast to an enterprise's required skills, the required skills to an IT skills inventory, the skills inventory to the IT staff's competency levels, and the competency levels to gaps and timeframes during which those gaps need to be filled.[10]

Please use your HR unit to assist you in this job. They are a very important team that are only too happy to ensure IT staff development becomes a composite part of corporate training—which it should be. Ask them to assist you to:

- Establish a competency matrix for your department's required skills. A competency matrix defines the skill levels required in each job type. It should form part of the database described in Chapter 4. An example competency matrix for project management is illustrated in Table 5.1.
- Analyse the immediate needs of the business to identify current gaps. This task is explained more fully later in this chapter.
- Analyse the future needs of the business. This task is also explained further. A companion to this is Chapter 23, "Planning the future".

Table 5.1—Project management competency matrix

Competency matrix—project management stream

Competencies	Stratum II	Stratum III	Stratum IV
Project management	Project span less than 1 year. Competent MS project. Completed Stage 1 internal PM-01	Project span up to 2 years. Advanced MS project. Completed Stages 2 and 3 internal PM-03	Project span up to 5 years Diploma Project Management
Budget and expenditure	Expense spreadsheet span 1	Cost, amortization, expense multi-year	Cost, amortization, expense and ROI
People management	Competent counselling	+ Termination and counselling	+ Industrial relations Stage 2
Data architecture	Department scale	Up to 4 interlined departments	Corporate scale model
Process modelling	Single department	Location (multi-department)	Corporate
Technical architecture	Single department	Location (multi-department)	Corporate
Program architecture	Simple single function application	Multi-function application	Interfaced applications
Indicative education	MIS degree—entry level Project Manager	As II with three years' practical experience and coursework	As III with Diploma PM and more than three years' experience

Indicative requirements for each stratum

Competencies	Stratum II	Stratum III	Stratum IV
Project management	Mandatory	Mandatory	Mandatory
Budget and expenditure	Mandatory	Mandatory	Mandatory
People management		Mandatory	Mandatory
Data architecture	⇑		Mandatory
Process modelling	Any of three	⇑	⇑
Technical architecture		Any of two	Any of two
Program architecture	⇓	⇓	⇓
Indicative education	MIS degree—entry level Project Manager	As II with three years' experience and coursework	As III with Diploma PM and three years' experience

- Determine the gap and work with HR on an upskilling strategy including individual career development plans. This may be achieved through a combination of:
  - Externally provided courses from colleges, universities or technical educators.
  - Internal courses delivered by *trainers* who are knowledgeable about the subject matter.
  - Self-training courses including the often-overlooked, inexpensive and flexible concept of programmed reading guides, with texts supplied through a company library.
  - Recruitment of new staff. Ensure that profiles covering *every* aspect of the required skill set form part of the statement of requirements.

Developing the current competency matrix

This takes a substantial amount of analysis and questioning. You must:

- Analyse the business processes[g] internal to IT to determine the competencies and numbers required to run the department.
- Analyse service level agreements to determine the competencies and numbers to deliver your commitments.
- Analyse business processes external to IT to determine competencies that are or may be required to support them.
- Talk to people inside and outside IT and ask them about the skills and competencies currently required of IT.

These steps may show a gap in competencies required to meet current demands. Expect to find serious gaps between the inventory of current staff skills described in the previous chapter and these current demands.

Identify future needs

If you have no plan or architecture for the future then it is plainly impossible to do anything more than guess at the needs. Victor Hugo[11] said ". . . where no plan is

---

[g] This will often have a beneficial side effect. It may lead to improvement and elimination of substandard or unnecessary processes.

laid, where the disposal of time is surrendered merely to chance or incident, chaos will reign'. The steps required to avoid chaos follow.

Examine architectures and plans

The recommended approach is to analyse the strategic plan or architecture and map the competencies and numbers of people required to deliver, operate and maintain future systems and services onto a timeline. If the plan was well executed, this data should be available and the task easy. This will show you both what you need and when you need it.

If the architecture is limited to technology and applications or the strategic plan did not include business, organizational, people and process change considerations, then you may need to think more broadly about the demands that will be placed on IT competence.

If you have no future plans

If you do not have a strategic plan or architecture then you will need to analyse and interview the executive staff and others to determine where the company is heading. Turn to Chapter 23 for further guidance. It recommends that you:

- Interview the chief executive and other key executives.
- Examine marketing documents, annual reports, anything that may hint at the future.
- Read and analyse the company's past to build a picture of how it is likely to behave in the future.
- Document these findings and test them with your colleagues.

This should give you a faint view of the distant needs. Use them to map out a time-line of competency requirements and numbers. This approach is weaker, less stable and lacks the preferred rigour. Nevertheless it does give sense and direction to career development. Comfort yourself with the thought that: "half a loaf of bread is better than nothing at all."

The deliverable

You should now produce a required competency matrix. This should list all the *roles* required by the department, the *required competencies* and the *numbers* in each role. It should also indicate *when* those competencies are required. There should be no names at this stage. An example is shown in Table 5.2.

Table 5.2—Required competencies matrix

Role	Stratum	Year 1	Year 2	Year 3	Year 4
Project manager	IV	—	1	1	2
Project manager	II	3	2	1	
Data architect	III	1	1	1	1
Wireless specialist	II	2	2	3	4
"C" programmer	I	1	2	1	1
COBOL programmer	II	1	1	0	0
Financial planner	II	1	1	1	1
Contract manager	IV	1	1	2	2
LAN manager	II	1	1	2	2

Don't overlook non-technical competencies

Ensure that other requisite skills such as budget development and management, human resource management skills and negotiation skills are included in job profiles. Do not assume that a new employee holds these skills because he or she has filled certain roles. It must now be obvious to anyone who has done a significant amount of recruiting that a new employee's previous role title is no guide to whether the person has the *appropriate* skills and experience in using them.

Include support competencies

A second common oversight in IT units is the failure to define the full range of skills required to run the unit. The typical IT human resource inventory listing will be 100% IT skill based.

How do I retain them?

How can you train staff in the latest IT skill sets when you know that as soon as the training is finished these people are liable to be poached on the open market? This was a concern that confronted Peter Dazeley when he was CIO at RGC, the former Australian mining company, in the mid-1990s. Peter was implementing an ERP solution at the time. He took a radical alternative approach to this problem. He challenged the perception that training was best offered to the young because they were the most adaptable. He saw that these people were also the most mobile. Instead he preferred to invest in the training of older workers who more valued continuity of employment. However, he also found these people were delighted to be invited to grow their skill sets and were more business cognizant about how and where the application of their training could benefit the business.

However, a review of other departments will show that they often include a wide range of skills such as marketing, finance, relationship management and others. Technology professionals alone imagine that they have the wonderful facility to do these things without expert help.

Do not overlook the possible need for the following support competencies in your department.

- Financial planning and accountancy
- Contract management
- Librarianship and knowledge management
- Project office administration
- Customer relationship management.

This topic and these roles are further discussed in the following chapter on "Supporting roles". Having these skills available may be more important to your success than hiring an assistant whose skills are limited to diary, phone and correspondence management.

The competency matrix must identify *all* the skills required to effectively manage the IT unit, not just the obvious and unimaginative range of analysis, programming and operations related skills.

Checklist

1. Have all the skills existing in your department now been recorded?
2. Have they been rated according to levels of competence?
3. Have you identified current competency demand?
4. Have all the competencies required in your department in the future been identified?
5. Do those matrices include non-technical skills required by people to be effective in their jobs?
6. Have you mapped the current skill base to the future skill set?
7. Do you have people who can be trained and developed to fill those roles?
8. Do you have a process for closing the gap?
9. How are you going to implement and monitor the skill-upgrading process?
10. Should you have a dedicated HR person to assist you?

6 Supporting roles

We cannot exist without mutual help. All therefore that need aid have a right to ask it from their fellow-men. (Sir Walter Scott in *Forbes Business Quotations*)

The issue is so pervasive and destructive of so many promising IT managers that it merits a brief chapter of its own.

The conundrum

IT would not let an accountant reconfigure a UNIX system so why do IT people think they can do accounting, human resources, contract administration, training or legal work? The demands on IT managers are large enough in a rapidly changing business and technical environment without trying to do work best done by other professionals.

IT managers alone seem imbued with this short-sightedness in defining a requisite administration team. Other business units generally, but not always, have a more comprehensive and appropriate administration structure. The simple issue is that IT managers too often try to do too much that should be done by other more appropriately qualified staff.

DIY

The undesirable effects are frequently painfully obvious and manifest themselves in the short career spans of IT managers and the grey-faced haggard survivors in IT management roles. The characteristics are:

- Overworked IT managers taking charge of non-critical administration processes.

- Poorly let and managed contracts. The vendor's contract, drawn up to protect the vendor, is too often signed without negotiation over anything but price. Contract management is non-existent and the IT manager's faith is rarely matched by the vendor's charity.
- Pricing negotiation is often naïve and fails to use the tools and techniques of the professional purchasing officer. Asset management is sloppy and asset disposal fails to recover retained values.
- Program and project oversight is poor. The IT manager is relying on weekly meetings with project managers to determine progress. It is invariably "on track" and customer feedback on projects which almost invariably is in contrast with the project manager's self-deception.
- Dismal human resource management and development. Too often the IT manager does unto others what was done unto him by a manager equally poorly skilled in people management.
- Financial modelling in business cases and procurement proposals is outstanding simplistic.
- The facets of Business, Organization, People and Process that surround the IT programs are ignored as the project team focuses solely on delivering the technology project component.
- Timesheet management, periodic reports, arranging training and other administrative roles consume valuable management time.
- Procurement requests clog the manager's desk and negotiations with vendors over trifling purchases fill the workday.
- Customer relationship management is restricted to facing summonses to explain IT failures to business colleagues. IT marketing is non-existent and the profile of the IT department is often appalling.

The list is endless. The key lesson which emerges from this tale of woe is that IT units often fail to adequately define their administrative requirements and fill them.

Use a specialist

Whether the task is plumbing, carpentry, electrical work or painting, the experienced tradesman will do it better than you can. Likewise contract management, financial modelling and budgeting, and human resource management. Support staff can be deployed as follows:

- Financial analysts or accountants to undertake financial modelling of investments, identify better financial models for infrastructure acquisition and maintenance, review business cases, develop budgets and control and monitor IT-directed expenditure.

- Contract managers to undertake direct control of all major contracts and vendor relationships, including focusing contract adherence, price and service negotiation and maintenance agreements. This role can also manage all procurement standards and purchasing.
- Project office staff to prepare reports, reviews, presentations and the like as well as project report consolidation, investigation and control. This can extend to contractor time-sheet management as well.
- Customer relationship staff to deal with your internal customer base, review satisfaction, guide business people and promote awareness of technical opportunities.

Too often the IT manager tries to be contract manager, purchasing clerk, project office manager and customer relationship manager—doing none well and at the same time failing to manage IT properly.

The first reaction when this concept is pointed out to managers is a rebuff that: "That there is no way the company will let me hire all those *extra* people". There are at least three responses to this.

- The first is that this work is now done badly by inadequately trained staff. If that work is shifted to professionals in these fields then you must be able to free up what are often much more expensive and rare skills.
- The second is that you may also be able to shed some expensive IT staff if you gain a contract manager, financial analyst, procurement officer or project office administrator.
- The third is that when you explain these issues and benefits to your chief executive, and show good cause including the financial benefits, you may be pleasantly surprised.

Most CEOs want a well-managed IT unit. Show them you intend to manage it well and you will find them surprisingly supportive! Apart from the benefits of reversing the above failings you, as an IT manager, will:

- Gain valuable time to review, consider and deliberate on demands that have a high value or impact or both.
- Build much better business relationships with your colleagues and suppliers who will appreciate these things being well managed. IT is often the broker in the middle of the supply chain and failings affect both the inputs and outputs.
- Gain credibility as a manager rather than merely a high-ranking propeller head.
- Provide a means for knowledge transfer from these professionals in purchasing, finance and relationship management to your technical team.

- Improve staff morale as the overall level of disturbance and difficulties drops away and the work environment becomes more stable and less hostile. But above all, you will have time to manage.

Approach

Chapter 5 describes the approach. The summarized steps include:

- Define the tasks and processes that must be carried out by IT and don't overlook procurement, contract management, financial modelling, budgeting, reporting, and the myriad administration tasks including sub-contractor administration.
- Define the skills and competencies required to carry out those processes.
- Examine the gap that currently exists between the skills and resources you need to run the IT unit and those that are currently employed.
- Develop a strategy for filling the gap. This may be based on a combination of:
  - Recruitment of new skills and competencies.
  - Upgrading existing skills and competencies.

The expectation is that this should be done in conjunction with your HR unit acting as a specialist consulting service to guide and support you. Few things will improve your life as an IT manager—and the lives of those around you—as much as appropriate support staff in your department.

Checklist

1. Have you listed all the support processes that are or should be done within your IT unit?
2. Are there any being done by external parties that would be improved by full time attention within the IT unit?
3. Have you covered all these facets:
   3.1 Contract administration
   3.2 Vendor relationship management
   3.3 Customer relationship manager—with your customer
   3.4 Human resource management (not personnel administration)

    3.5   Training
    3.6   Financial modelling and budgeting
    3.7   Librarian
    3.8   Records maintenance including licences, assets and people?

4. Are there any processes within IT that properly should move outside?

5. Have you determined how much time and money is misspent by technical people doing clerical or unrelated jobs?

7   Managing recruiters

*Agents of disruption, subversion, sabotage and disinformation . . . tunnellers and smugglers, listeners and forgers, trainers and **recruiters** and talent spotters and couriers and watchers and seducers, assassins and balloonists, lip readers and disguise artists.* (John le Carré in *The Perfect Spy*)

It is hardly surprising that John Le Carré lumped recruiters with the seducers, balloonists, lip readers and disguise artists. There appears to be a vast number of people who label themselves IT recruitment specialists who would have difficulty spelling UNIX.

This chapter is focused largely on the methods to extract the maximum value from your recruitment agent. The methods can be applied equally well to managing recruitment through your human resource department.

Your goals

Your goals and those of your subordinates should be only to interview those few people who are competent to do the job you have on offer. The points of rejection should merely be one of degree of fit and your intangible "gut feel".

You should not be involved in weeding out clearly incompetent or unsuitable applicants. That is what you pay your recruitment people to do, and you pay them well. If your recruitment agency cannot meet these goals, discard them. Recruiting can be an expensive and tiring business.

The cost of recruiting

Your local human resources management association will usually hold well-researched data on the cost of replacing staff.

The figures in Table 7.1 are an amalgam and approximation. They have been derived from examining published research and conducting interviews with recruitment and Human Resource Management specialists. They are given both as a percentage and as a proportion of a notional salary of US$100 000.

Table 7.1—The costs of recruitment as percentages and proportions of salary

Item	Percentage of salary	Indicative cost ($)
Salary increase to attract new recruits	10	10 000
Fee paid to recruitment agency	15	15 000
Induction and training for new recruits	5	5 000
Opportunity cost of interviews and briefings	1	1 000
Temporary staff during recruitment period (1 month)	10	10 000
Opportunity cost due to lower efficiency for first three months	5	5 000
Total	**46**	46 000

The percentage and notional salary will vary by location. Some will argue that some rows are merely the sunk costs of doing business. Other people might regard them as avoidable. The costs of replacing staff are immense, regardless which view you take.

Consider that in many countries annual IT staff turnover ranges between 20% and 30% of the IT staff establishment. On this basis a medium-sized IT unit of 100 people may expect to spend over US$1 000 000 a year in up-front and hidden recruitment costs, with a large percentage of that cost winding up in the recruiter's pocket. So there is no need to be timid in making demands of recruitment agencies.

Before you leap

Before you start a recruitment campaign you should consider alternative ways of bridging the gap. Some possible options include:

- Outsourcing the IT process rather than hiring an employee.
- Employing an externally sourced worker which is the new term for contractor or consultant.
- Process engineering of the process which may eliminate it, or reduce it sufficiently to be absorbed by current staff.

- Entering into a telecommuting agreement with a former staff member or with a current staff member if appropriate.
- Job sharing—that is, splitting the task over two or more existing employees.

If you must hire, then make sure that recruitment is done well.

Recruitment campaigns

You will have to recruit people, of that there is no doubt. This section contains some tips on recruiting.

- Enter into a service level agreement with your recruiter.
    - Define their accountabilities and responsibilities, and your own.
    - Define the performance measures and criteria under which they will be judged. This will help them to focus on *your* needs instead of theirs.
    - Include time measures for recruitment, interviews, letters of offer and fee scales.
    - Don't hesitate to introduce a reward and punishment scheme. For example, a better than expected crop of recruits in a shorter than average time span may merit a higher fee. Poor-quality candidates over a lengthy duration will result in a lesser fee.
- Provide them with role descriptions that include the competency levels and skills required for each job.
- Define the *potential* you seek in the candidate for further development and growth.
- Give them your competency matrix that should spell out the criteria that define which level each applicant must reach.
- Commit them to matching the competencies of the applicants to the defined competencies in each role.
- Be specific about the level or degree of fit you will interview. It is unrealistic to only interview those with 100% fit. Show the recruiting agency how the fit is determined.
- Be accurate and honest in describing your company's culture and *your* management style.
- Ask them about their interview techniques. Test their methods if necessary with a role-play in which they interview you or some of your staff.
- Prepare your own set of interview questions, competency and profile tests if appropriate.
- Arrange for company information brochures, including personnel practices for the candidates to be given to selective candidates.

- Organize interview rooms, time slots and back-up interview staff should some-one not be available.
- Make sure that your HR unit is similarly contracted to support you—service level agreements can be used by IT as well!

Think outside the box

Jim Hepburn was a successful farmer in New Zealand when the reality of a decade of economic restructuring finally dawned upon him. Jim came to the conclusion that life on the land was going to get more and more precarious. Appreciating that IT skills were likely to be in demand for the foreseeable future Jim took himself off to the Auckland University of Technology to study IT. Three years later at forty-something he emerged with a degree to pursue a new career in IT. However, this was easier said than done. He endured over forty rejections before he encountered someone at the AGC Finance company who was prepared to look outside the nine dots to give him a chance as a junior on the IT Help Desk. Five years later he's now IT Manager at AGC in Auckland. Perhaps unwittingly the company found it had hired in Jim someone with the management skills from running his own farm for many years as well as the latest IT skills from his recent university degree. Moreover, it also had acquired someone keen to show forty other organizations just what they missed out on. If your company has difficulty attracting and keeping its IT staff perhaps what you need to do is to think outside the nine dots when interviewing potential staff.

There are a number of sound texts and guidelines on recruiting available at any large bookstore. If this fails, try contacting your local Human Resource Management Association. Make yourself familiar with good practice. This is one job you cannot afford to do badly. Consider the long-term implications of each hire and ensure they will suit your current demand and can change or grow to meet future demand.

Induct new staff

New staff frequently become demoralized with their choice of employer. After the excitement of recruitment, the stirring tales of opportunity and the morale-boosting introductions, they are left to sit and rot, their days occupied with menial tasks. While this chapter is mainly concerned with managing recruitment agents, do make sure you keep what you found.

> Nothing frustrates new employees more than having two days' enterprise orientation and then having to fend for themselves.

New recruits, especially those under the age of 35, seek quick access to meaningful work, yet many enterprises do not know what to do with new recruits.[12]

Good assignments do not happen magically, and a number of facets will determine whether the bright-eyed new recruit is given dumbed-down work or whether a company has the management skills and risk profile to give meaningful work to the new.

Do at least arrange the following things when new staff join:

- Make sure their desk and telephone are set up and a PC is ready for them to sign on.
- Provide them with a standard pack[h] of stationery items. This can include directions to public transport, shops and facilities.
- Provide them with their copies of the corporate history, annual reports, policy manuals and the like. These can also be packaged or shrink-wrapped.
- Ensure security is aware they are joining and passkeys, passwords and the like have been set up.
- Buddy them with someone who is charged with their oversight for the first two weeks at least.
- Plan and define the first job they are to undertake and assign a mentor to help them execute it. People want to make a contribution from the very first day.
- Introduce them to their peers and the other people in the business with whom they will come in contact.
- Ensure that they are enrolled in the full formal corporate induction programme if one exists.
- Set a regular review schedule for the first three months until they have settled in.
- Assign them to meaningful work!

It is easier to keep people than to recruit and induct them. The above will help encourage newcomers to stay!

Checklist

1. Do you have a competency matrix that illustrates the skills and experience needed?
2. Have you established market rates for these skills and competencies?

---

[h] Ensure that shrink-wrapped packages of notepads, pencils, erasers, rulers and the like are arranged for all new starters.

3. Are you going to pay above or below market rates?
4. Have you given the recruitment agency a clear and accurate profile of your target staff?
5. Have you considered pointing the agents to potential candidates who may be interested in an indirect approach?
6. Have you got a sound basis for carrying out your interviews?
7. Are other staff who will interview properly trained in interview techniques?
8. Have you informed the recruitment agency of your company's culture—warts and all?
9. Have you got a sound induction process for new recruits?
10. Can you assign the new recruit to meaningful work as soon as they commence?

The rules of engagement

Your prayers shall be answered . . . if you will obey me, and are willing to put in hand the remedy your distress requires. (Oedipus in *Oedipus Rex*)

The single most important action an IT manager can take in order to survive is to agree the principles under which IT will be managed with senior business colleagues.

What are principles?

Principles[i] are simple statements of policy on how the various aspects of information technology will be managed in the corporation. They are set and agreed by you as the IT manager and your senior business colleagues.

Why?

Without some rules on managing IT you wind up with an anarchic relationship—a relationship where anything goes and you are always the fall guy. Make life easier for yourself and everybody else in the company by establishing how corporate priorities will be defined, how budgets will be managed and who owns and manages the various aspects of IT projects as early as you can. Extend the scope of the rulebook to define who does what and to whom with equipment, data and applications.

The benefits

The benefits of principles extend beyond creating a simple internal rulebook. Well-formed principles inform clients, suppliers, consultants and others of the

---

[i] See also *The IT Outsourcing Guide* which contains more information on this topic.

business view on key technology issues. Further, when dealing with consultants or outsource providers they can help protect you against "opportunistic acts of a transient organization."[13]

Above all, principles rationalize and simplify the decision making, permit broader delegation and *give the business and you a framework* within which to manage IT. In summary, principles can:

- Ensure that you take decisions within a considered framework.
- Ensure that the framework is internally consistent which leads to better decisions.
- Remove the need to micro-manage every decision.
- Allow you to focus on controlling the broad strategy and direction.
- Communicate the rules of engagement to all in the IT unit and the business.
- Reduce the probability of issues and disputes.
- Protect against arbitrary decisions made out of context.
- Support the proper execution of the service level agreements.
- Inform the peripherally involved, e.g. contractors, auditors, suppliers and consultants of the IT management framework.
- Provide a framework for future service level variances or increases/decreases in scope.
- Principles also lead business staff into considering their requests more thoughtfully and those that do not comply are still-born rather than "rejected" by what is seen as an "uncooperative IT manager."

Properly developed they will be limited in number yet cover the whole scope of management. Principles are key, if not *the* key to success in the interface between you and the rest of the business. Without them you are likely to:

- Manage in a vacuum.
- Be out of tune with the legitimate[j] preferences of the business.
- Fail to establish guidelines for your subordinates.
- Become involved in the minutiae of each decision rather than delegating effectively.
- Lack consistency and focus in decision making.
- Be subject to the whims of individuals or consultants who determine strategy and tactics according to *their* beliefs and external goals.

Without laws there is no civilization, only barbarism and anarchy. Without principles you will experience the technology equivalent! So start setting the principles with your business peers as early as possible. Don't procrastinate.

---

[j] Not all business preferences will be logical and sound. The IT manager as a professional must challenge these and show cause why inappropriate preferences cannot be sustained in a well-managed environment.

Further background on principles

Paul Strassman is, we think, the father of principles. He wrote at length on the concept in his book, *The Politics of Information Management*. In it he described a number of approaches for improving the management of IT. At the time his concern was with the management of the US Defense Department—so it makes interesting reading.

He recommended the creation of an IT constitution together with policies to guide the CIO and business. He suggested it be kept short, sweet and to the point noting that: "The simplicity of the US Constitution has much to offer as a template for information policy guidance. It represents a point of view that addresses the governance of complexity by concentrating only on the fundamentals while leaving everything else for resolution by means of due process wherever that is deemed appropriate."[1]

The great military strategist Moltke would have agreed with him. "Moltke believed in a few fundamental principles to guide the army's conduct of war"[2] while leaving day-to-day initiatives in the hands of subordinates.

Strassman[3] was adamant that "When you redistribute responsibility and control to others, you must also reallocate accountability and expertise for taking action." Principles are the key to sound delegation. They give the delegate a framework in which to operate and free you from involvement in repetitious low-level decision making.

If you read Strassman you will note we don't use the same terms on this subject. Strassman seems to prefer the term *policies* but we do not. The selection of the word is more than merely pedantic. The two words carry quite different connotations.

Principles are defined in the *Oxford English Dictionary* as "general law as a guide to action" and come from the old English word for foundations. Principles define the foundations of acceptable behaviour in the agreement.

Policy is a word more often associated with contract, as in *Insurance Policy*, and is associated with the French word *police* that carries with it rigidity and exactness we do not seek to achieve with *principles*.

Simply put, *principles* provide a guide to action and incorporate the concept of flexibility and adaptation to circumstances. *Policy* suggests detailed and precise instructions from which deviation is not permitted, and indeed non-adherence will result in punishment.

If you wonder if there is anything worse than no principles the answer is yes. The only thing worse than no principles is inappropriate principles. At least when principles are absent there is a probability that someone will ask you what the appropriate standard is for acting on a requirement. Of course they may not. Whatever happens we don't think asking people to operate in a vacuum is a good survival tactic.

[1] Strassman P, *The Politics of Information Management*, Information Economics Press, New Canaan, 1995 (p.46).
[2] Hughes DJ (ed), *Moltke on the Art of War*, Presidio Press, Novato, CA, 1993.
[3] Strassman P, *The Politics of Information Management*, Information Economics Press, New Canaan, 1995 (p.79).

Define your principles before you find yourself under pressure to agree production targets and supporting service level agreements.

Some background

Principles are usually defined in short statements, as with the three examples below.

> All systems will be developed to the rules of the APT methodology. This principle will apply to internal, contractor developed and user developed systems of any scale, no matter how small.

or

> We will source hardware from one preferred supplier even though this may not always prove cheapest or most effective.

or

> All business cases for future systems development must include the tasks, costs and timing of the effort required for the accompanying business, organization, people and process change, as well as the technology component.

Establishing principles is simple and as is often the case, doing simple things well brings the highest rewards.

However, the principles cannot be just dreamed up in isolation. They must be the outcome of clear and rational thinking of the senior executives as a group. "The most senior executives, as a group, should conceive of and preferably author the fundamental statements of information policy themselves."[14] Strassman goes further to advise against using consultants for this important task, as they will be seen as a proxy for the hirer. However, do use consultants to *facilitate* the process—they bring with them no baggage of the past. Do not delegate this task nor should you permit your fellow executives to assign delegates. Lower-echelon staff will lack the necessary authority and the wrong people may create obstacles that hinder progress.

You might like to suggest the company consider this as an opportunity to introduce the concept of principles on a broader scale covering things outside of IT. There is no reason why principles cannot be developed and applied to any area of the company, for example:

- Marketing
- Distribution or
- Short-term projects where they can be used to nail down in advance how key issues will be addressed.

Scope

Principles should be developed to cover at least the following six areas:

- *Organization* laying out the general rules on organization, accountabilities, employment, human resources, and adherence to host company house rules where appropriate.
- *Technology assets* including procurement, vendor relationship management discounts commissions and disposal.
- *Software assets* including licence management, maintenance agreements, renewals and terminations.
- *Service levels* including authority to vary, compliance, dispute resolution and change management.
- *Data* including ownership, management, standards and archiving.
- *Software development*, including project accountability, approval processes, issue recording and resolution, change management and intellectual property.

Principles are part of your contract with the business. Indeed, once you have agreed the principles that are most critical, they should be reproduced on large laminated cards and strategically distributed throughout the organization, on notice boards and office walls. Don't overdo it or you may appear obstinate and obstructive. However, ensure that staff know of their existence and what they say.

Template

It is important that each principle and all the options and implications of adopting the principle be well considered. For this reason we recommend that each principle be developed within a standard framework or template. You must define and agree the principles with your fellow senior executives as a group.

The proposed template consists of five sections. An example of the template and a completed principle are shown in Figure 8.1. A suggested process for agreeing principles and completing the templates follows.

Process

Our preferred approach to developing principles is:

1. Define the areas that principles need to span. These could include management processes, hardware, projects, operations, network, reporting, staffing, and others.

Principle Number
Issue: A statement, usually in the form of a question, of the scope of the issue that the Principle seeks to address.
Options: Alternative means of addressing the issue, any of which could be selected as the Principle.
Principle: The selected option which now is a Principle.
Rationale: The justification for selecting the particular Option as a Principle.
Implications: A short list of the potential positive and negative implications of the adopted Principle.
Approval: The signature of the authorizing body.

Principle #1
Issue What methodologies and standards will apply to systems development in the outsourced environment?
Options: 1. We will use our existing methods and standards. 2. We will adopt the service provider's methods and standards. 3. We will mix and match to suit each individual situation.
Principle *(2) We will adopt the service provider's methods and standards.*
Rationale The task of training the service provider's staff in our standards will be much greater than the task of training our staff in theirs. The service provider's methods are an industry standard. Our methods and standards are unique and have previously failed us.
Implications *Our systems development will be to industry standards.* +   Our systems development should be of a higher quality. +   We limit dependency on in-house expertise and the service provider by adopting an industry standard. –   We will have to purchase license rights to use the methodology. –   Staff may find the new methods more onerous than the in-house methods.
Approval: (signature) *For the Executive Committee 07 Oct 2000*

Figure 8.1—Template and example of a principle

2. Populate the templates.
3. State an issue, for example, *What standards will apply to hardware purchases?*
4. Offer options to control the issue, for example:
    - Option 1. *We will purchase at the lowest cost, with quality as a secondary issue.*
    - Option 2. *We will tender on each major purchase, seeking a balance between cost, performance and consistent standards.*
    - Option 3. *We will purchase all hardware from a preferred vendor unless it is clearly unable to supply the required items.*
5. Circulate the templates to the senior executive.
6. Workshop with the senior executives to select the preferred option (see below).
7. Document the *rationale* behind the decision in one or two sentences.
8. List the 5 ± 2 positive and negative implications attached to the selected option, for example, if Option 3 were selected, one of the implications might be *We will need to go through a substantial process to select a preferred vendor.*
9. Circulate the selected principles for final ratification by all those who attended the workshop and, if appropriate, the chief executive.
10. Circulate the principles to key staff and to external service providers so they understand your rules.

The last point is crucial. The principles are of no use as shelf-ware, and should be available and known to all that use them. As Strassman says, "To manage information technology successfully, policy makers must set forth explicit policies for information governance and secure cooperation by engaging everyone in a discussion as to their implications".[15]

To make the workshop effective, ensure that your fellow executives both understand the purpose of the meeting and have given the issues and options some consideration before the meeting. Two useful techniques are to:

- Issue a briefing paper with the agenda. This should cover both the concept and benefits of principles.
- Pre-populate the templates with *Issues and Options*. This tends to attract people's attention. (Leave all else to be completed at the workshop.)

Remember Strassman's view that: "The most senior executives, as a group, should conceive of and preferably author these fundamental statements of information policy themselves."[16] Do not allow the process to be delegated to a sub-committee of mid-level managers.

Good practice

The following items will help you ensure that your principles are well made.

- Define a principle only when there is a clear issue to be addressed. Do not define principles for which there is no issue, where the correct path is clear and obvious to all.
- Keep the principles focused on the few fundamental things that need to be defined in advance.
- Limit the principles to a small manageable number so they can be "front-of-mind". Keep them at a high level.
- Ensure the principles are developed at the highest level in the organization. Do not delegate the responsibility to a junior staff member, or worse still a consultant.
- Include reference to appropriate principles in service level agreements as they provide critical insight to staff on how the business expects them to deliver the service.
- Circulate the principles widely including to external parties such as contractors and suppliers, where appropriate.
- Review the principles at least once a year for relevance and currency.

Develop a framework for changing principles and settling disputes or doubts about the application of a principle.

Change control

You will need to consider this from the outset and incorporate change control into the management framework. The primary considerations in change control for principles are that they are the considered opinion of the senior executive on how the information technology service should be managed. Then it goes without saying that the same people who made the decision to adopt the principle should in turn be asked to approve any alteration or amendment.

The second consideration is that the principle may be linked to business goals and objectives. Ensure that any change to a principle does not now conflict with goals, objectives or planned future initiatives.

The third consideration is that the change control process must be undertaken with sufficient rigour to ensure:

- All copies of the obsolete principle are retrieved and destroyed.
- Appropriate staff receive copies of the revised principles.
- The reasons (rationale) for modifying the original principle are recorded.

The *rationale* on the new template must also inform staff *why* the change was made.

Disputes

Disputes will arise. Some may make well-intentioned decisions to sidestep a principle. Others may find it convenient to ignore a principle (and the IT manager) to further their own objectives. Staff turnover and ordinary human frailty and forgetfulness will ensure that some, and hopefully few, occasions will arise when the principle gives rise to a dispute.

Every company is different and yours may already have well-established procedures for dispute resolution. It is not possible to offer a single prescription for setting a dispute-resolution process. However, do give the following aspects proper consideration.

First, the most frequent source of dispute seems to be that those executives who made the rules appear to feel most free to break them. For this reason it may not be easy to resolve an issue without an appropriate internal independent arbitrator— such as the managing director or chairman of the IT Steering Committee.

Second, if the dispute involves an outside party, then favour an honest broker or independent third party to oversee dispute resolution. Dennis Wood of Cathay Pacific Airways said: "We used an independent third party and found it very valuable. It provided a buffer between the contractor and us and removed the emotion from the issue."

Third, if possible train those staff that most deal with internal disputes in the process of negotiation and commercial mediation. These are useful skills to have within the IT fold and may be used in many guises!

Finally, remember the dispute may arise many years after the principle was developed. Those who set and agreed the principle may well be long gone. This is why it is important to record the rationale for setting the principle in the first instance. As our now old friend Strassman said: "Any conflict resolution process must have a legitimate forum for interpreting the *original* intent of the approved policies [principles]".[17]

Rationale can prove exceptionally useful at a later time when someone seeks to understand the thinking that lay behind the adoption of the preferred principle. Those that still doubt the value of the rationale should consider the US Constitution's provision to allow the "bearing of arms" and the self-serving arguments that have been advanced for this provision by those supporting and those opposing gun control.

Drawbacks

We must recognize, however, that principles have some limitations, though many of these can be avoided by appropriate high-level supervision. The drawbacks include:

- Danger of abrogation, substituting principles for oversight and supervision.
- Overdevelopment so they become a form of constrictive micro-management.
- Inconsistencies between principles, for example between quality-based and cost-based principles.
- Overly liberal interpretation as they do not define *Policy* in tight and restrictive terms.
- Blind adherence in circumstances where the principle is inappropriate.
- Abrogation by the IT manager of responsibility for supervision of the activities of staff.
- The development of principles may generate as much corporate discord as unity.

The benefits far outweigh the limitations. The drawbacks can be limited by adhering to good practices. Key among them is to keep the principles at an appropriate level, as described in the analogy at the beginning of this chapter on the model of the US Constitution as a guide for developing IT policy guidance.

Conclusion

You can manage without principles if you enjoy frustration, conflict, confusion and the minutiae of management. If you enjoy those things and like being kicked in the head for making decisions that fly in the face of preferred business direction, then this chapter was not for you. If you wish to introduce stability, direction, robustness and continuity in your management then establishing a sound set of principles will go a long way towards this.

This chapter closes with something that we hope will help you establish a sound foundation for your role as IT manager. It is a checklist for establishing principles. We have also included some example principles in Appendix F.

Checklist

1. Principle Scope
    1.1 Responsibilities and Accountabilities at the Executive.
    1.2 Responsibilities and Accountabilities of Operating Managers.
    1.3 Responsibilities and Accountabilities of Planning and Finance.
    1.4 Responsibility and Accountability for IT Strategy.
    1.5 Sub-Contractors.
    1.6 Problem Resolution.
    1.7 Help Desk Management.
    1.8 Data Management.
    1.9 Geography (Centralization and Decentralization).
    1.10 Personnel Development.
    1.11 Systems Design and Construction.
    1.12 Technology Advancement.
    1.13 Telecommunications.
    1.14 Risk Management.
    1.15 Technology Acquisition.
    1.16 Security.
    1.17 Administration.
    1.18 Asset Management.
    1.19 Human Resource Management.
    1.20 Planning and Scheduling.
    1.21 Network Management.
    1.22 Performance Monitoring.
    1.23 Capacity Planning.
    1.24 Preventative Maintenance.
    1.25 Software Upgrades.
    1.26 Software Licensing.
    1.27 Inventory Control.
    1.28 Media and Storage Control.

2. Are the answers to any identified issues self-evident? If so this is a self-evident truth and does not need a principle.
3. Has more than one option for dealing with each issue been proposed? If only one option is offered, then this is probably a self-evident truth and does not need a principle.
4. Has a briefing paper been prepared for the Executive so they understand the concept of principles?
5. Has the rationale been defined for each adopted principle?
6. Does the rationale still seem sound three days later?
7. Have the implications been considered and documented?
8. Do any of the implications suggest the rationale is weak or the principle wrong?
9. Have all staff and contractors been handed a copy of the principles?
10. Has the legal department reviewed the principles?
11. Has a change control process been documented and agreed by the executive?
12. Has the change control process been agreed with the service provider?
13. Have you checked the principles do not conflict with business goals?

9   Establishing sound corporate governance

It is the duty of government to make it difficult for people to do wrong, easy to do right.
(William Gladstone)

Why establish governance?

The formal answer is that a sound governing body will ensure IT is aligned with the business and that **all** parts of the business take ownership for their role in making technology successful. The unofficial answer is that if the IT manager does not establish an effective process of corporate governance, colleagues in the business may at some time form a mob, legitimised by a title such as "The IT Steering Committee", and lynch the IT manager.

The traditional IT Steering Committee

Most are familiar with the traditional IT Steering Committee. Many will agree that it is rarely a useful body and too often exists as a forum for complaints and criticism instead of guidance and governance.

The members often fail to bring their influence and power to bear on the four facets that are critical to technology success, namely business, organization, people and process alignment. Few committees are established in a manner that ensures investment decisions are continually re-evaluated.

If you are burdened with stultifying oversight by a committee of complainants you must change it quickly!

It will often pay to change the name of the governance group to more properly reflect its role. The term used in this chapter is the Investment Committee.

Characteristics of poor governance

The implications of having a poor IT governance process include:

- Poor or limited strategic direction from your peers.
- Poor investment decisions that result from the above.
- Continued investment in doomed projects—doomed by any of business, technical or market changes.
- Frustrating delays in approval of mission-critical projects.
- Increasing risk of exposure to legal liability by the company officers for maladministration[k] of company resources.
- A failure to align the business, technology, organization, people and process (BTOPP) changes required to ensure technology dependent projects successful.

Demanding and ensuring BTOPP alignment is the biggest single contribution that the governance group can make to corporate IT success.

Benefits

The benefits that accrue from sound governance include:

- Clear strategic direction coupled to balanced investment decisions for technology-dependent projects.
- Proper direction and oversight of the other four facets of BTOPP as well as technology. These are critical to your success.
- Review and oversight of existing investment programmes to ensure that they still make sense and that you are not being driven to develop systems that are no longer of major value.
- Thoughtful guidance to you in the selection of further investment programmes.

Be aware that there are aspects of SLA management that have the potential to cross the boundary of corporate governance of IT. You may have to expend some effort to keep tactical monitoring of SLAs separate from oversight of investment and direction. Do remember, SLA oversight is the province of the department manager, not the Investment Committee.

---

[k] Class actions by disgruntled shareholders show that governance of IT is an integral part of overall corporate governance, and this is the prime duty of management and the board.

The role of the corporate governors of IT

Corporate governance of IT means ensuring that the *organization* is managing its information systems portfolio to ensure that the *organization* is doing the correct things in the correct manner.

The IT manager in isolation cannot do this. The major consultancies will all recommend some form of IT Steering Committee to oversee the IT activity. Unfortunately, many such committees act as a forum for managers to complain about trifling issues, while the real aim of providing investment guidance and strategic direction fall by the wayside.

You may find that one of the best forms of governance is promoted by John Thorpe in *The Information Paradox*. This chapter is not a condensed version of that text. Those seeking to understand the whole concept of benefits realization and the proposed system of governance should read John Thorpe's book.

An illustration of Thorpe's preferred governance model is shown in Figure 9.1. Table 9.1 is the accompanying accountability matrix.

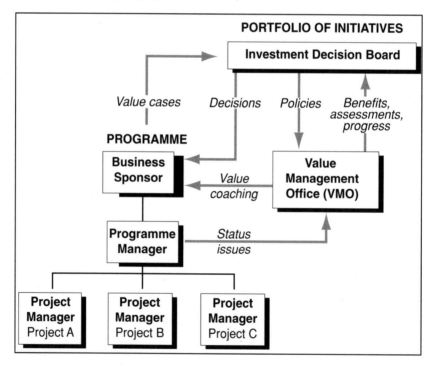

Figure 9.1—Governance model.

Thorpe JM, *The Information Paradox*, copyright © 1996 McGraw-Hill, Montreal. Reproduced with permission of McGraw-Hill Ryerson Ltd.

Table 9.1—Governance accountability matrix

Function	Decision board	Value Management Office (VMO)	Business sponsor	Programme manager	Project managers/ delivery teams
	Accountable through portfolio management for the value of IT investments and the achievement of the associated business benefits	*Accountable for the progress of the initiatives through properly founded and funded programmes*	*Accountable for the achievements of the agreed business benefits of the programme*	*Accountable for overall programme management and the combined results of the projects within the programme*	*Accountable for timely delivery/ implementation of the agreed deliverables*
Portfolio management	owns and manages the portfolio	provides planning and support to the IDB, business sponsors and the programme managers	provides recommendations on the programme provides status on achievement of benefits	has a consultation role provides programme status and facts to VMO	N/A
Business plans	sets annual planning guidelines approves annual plans	proposes and structures programmes formulates value cases prepares annual plans	confirms programme requirements negotiates priorities with IDB	prepares the programme plan in support of programme requirements	prepares project plans
Programme budgets/ funding	approves the budgets and sources of funding for programme commitments	facilitates the budget process prepares funding recommendations	confirms project benefits and costs for next commitment phase negotiates cost and time frames with programme manager	prepares consolidated budgets for the projects allocates funding to projects	provides project schedule and cost information
Programmes	monitors status and resolves major issues/ conflicts recruits business sponsors	facilitates the value (business) cases monitors progress and budgets of programmes	is the business owner of the programme is responsible to IDB for the achievement of business benefits recruits programme manager	directs and coordinates the programme is responsible to the business sponsor for the success of the programme recruits project managers	is accountable to the business sponsor for the project deliverables is accountable to the programme manager for the project execution

Thorpe JM, *The Information Paradox*, copyright © 1996 McGraw-Hill, Montreal. Reproduced with permission of McGraw-Hill Ryerson Ltd.

You will find strong parallels in *The Information Paradox* and the recommendations of this chapter. The key messages are that:

- *Technology*-focused project progress reviews are out, and investment *programme* reviews covering business, technology, organization, people and process change are in.
- The governance group must assign accountability and responsibility to *all* parties involved in investment programmes especially those outside of IT.
- The governors should measure Thorpe's 4Rs—which are described later.
- The governance group must insist on a progressive process that limits investment commitment up to pre-defined "gates".
- The governance group must ensure programmes have well-defined milestones and proper risk management and contingency *plans* that go well beyond the traditional and pointless contingency of 10% of project budget for over-runs.

The structure of this chapter includes further explanation on each of the above, followed by a proposed review process and review group.

BTOPP

As IT manager, seek to ensure that your company accepts as a given that managing the five dimensions below is crucial to ensuring programmes are successful. The dimensions are:

- The **business** component of the programme which raises the question of the commercial value of the investment. How and where does it fit in the value chain?
- The **technology** aspect which covers construction, testing and deploying the system to deliver the process when and where it is required.
- The **organization** which must be organized to make best use of the initiative. This can affect location, offices, fittings, and support tools.
- The **processes** of the business which will almost definitely need review, re-modelling and re-engineering.
- The **people**—employees, customers and business partners who may need induction, training and support to follow the new processes.

The Investment Committee must ensure that all these items are satisfactorily considered and accounted for.

The governors must ensure that each BTOPP task is assigned to a relevant person *and* that the SLA for delivery of those outputs calls out each individual's accountability and responsibility for delivery.

Start by ensuring that the business initiative proposal (or business case) defines and assigns the accountability and responsibility for all the BTOPP components in a programme. An example business initiative proposal is shown in Appendix B.

Accountability and responsibility

The example of an Accountability and Responsibility chart in Figure 9.2 may prove useful. A similar document should form part of the service level agreement for the programme and must be specific in regard to measures and time for new programmes.

It is crucial that the responsibilities are defined and called out, and that the individuals and the programme sponsor[l] sign up to them. Bear in mind that this approach will be a surprise for those who believe that in IT projects, the IT manager is responsible for everything.

The Investment Committee may need guidance on how they measure the current state of programmes. John Thorpe suggests they measure his 4 Rs.

Measuring the 4 Rs

Thorpe stresses the importance of asking four key questions. They are reproduced[m] below. You may like to give the prompt list to the governors. That way you will know what questions will be addressed to you—and hopefully the right answers!

- *Are we doing the right things?* Are we clear what benefits we are seeking? Are the end benefits in line with our organization's goals and easy priorities? Will they remain so over the life of the programme?
- *Are we doing them the right way?* Will the programme comply with all necessary technical and quality standards? Will it reinforce the general direction of

---

[l] The person in the business responsible for delivering the overall benefits.
[m] Thorpe JM, *The Information Paradox*, McGraw-Hill, Toronto, 1998, p. 75; reproduced with permission of McGraw-Hill Ryerson Ltd.

PROGRAMME RESPONSIBILITIES

Marketing	Field Test Agent Attitude	17th Oct
I D B	Decision to Stage 2	20th Oct
Marketing	Prepare/Distribute Agent Pack	1st Dec
H R	Modify Role Descriptions/Competencies	1st Dec
Pensions	Prepare Test Packs	17th Jan
Pensions	Test and Report Inconsistency	20–25th Jan
Training	Prepare Training Packs	1st Dec

PROCESS RESPONSIBILITIES

Pensions	Report Bugs using 'System Failure Form'
Pensions	Test Unit and System in Test Environment
Pensions	Log-Off all Users by 19:00 each night
Pensions	Maintain User Performance Measures Register
IT Unit	Respond to Systems Failure Form within 1 hour
Pensions	Retrieve incorrect output, register details and destroy
IT Unit	Provide hourly status on Class 1 Failures
Pensions	Develop contingency plan for Class 1 exceeding 12 hours
IT Unit	Provide four-hourly status on Class 2 Failures
IT Unit	Activate Monthly Tape Run
Pensions	Deliver Tape to Bank within 2 hours of receipt
H R	Modify recruitment profiles for Pension Clerks
Training	Modify Training Packs to reflect changes (monthly)
Pensions	Unit Manager provide Quarterly report on benefit realized

This extract shows the assignment of accountability and responsibility in a detailed Business Initiative Approval. It is a partial selection and is intended to illustrate:

1. The concept of allocation accountability to all involved in a business program (pre-implementation) and ongoing business process (post-implementation).
2. It stretches beyond project task to incorporate ongoing responsibilities.
3. Each individual Unit Head is responsible for meeting the measures.

Figure 9.2—Accountability and responsibility—extract

other work in the area? Do all the elements of the investment (business, technology, organization, process and people) blend well together?

- *Are we getting them done well?* Have we identified all the work and have all the players accepted responsibility for their part in this work? Are there sound delivery plans and well-designed projects in the programme? Is the project work achievable with the planned resources? Will there be adequate quality assurance? Can the entire "soft" organization, people and process initiatives be completed in time to take full advantage of the technological changes?

- *Are we getting the benefits?* Do the prospective benefits justify the costs? How certain are we about the estimates of these benefits? Is there a solid business sponsor, ready, willing and able to deliver the benefits? How much could the benefits be affected by factors outside the organization's control?

Thorpe gives further invaluable advice on measuring and modelling the programme in order to ensure that every aspect of the programme is clear. His technique has the added benefit of showing alternative paths that may exist to achieve the benefit, and allows some rationalization along the way. Thorpe's 4 Rs Report Card recommendation is shown in Appendix C.

Business cases and gates

Your company probably has its own form or template for seeking investment approval. It was probably designed by an accountant and has a single focus— return on investment. You will need to introduce an Investment instrument that forces the proposer to define the whole of the programme, including all aspects of:

- Business implications and change and who will manage them.
- Technology change and accountability.
- Organizational change and how it will be effected.
- Process change and how it will be handled.
- People change.

You should ensure they call out the costs and risks associated with all these as well. You may like to suggest your new business initiative proposal should be adopted by all facets of the business for all investments, not merely IT.

A template for a business initiative proposal is illustrated in Appendix B. This template forces the proposer to consider strategic alignment, clear scope, benefits definition and measures, state BTOPP implications, state assumptions and risks and identify means to manage them.

Finally the document prompts the manager to add a contingency *plan* that is based on the most probable disasters that may befall the programme. It is not perfect or complete but should point the way for you to model something for your own Investment Committee.

The book, *The Information Paradox*, contains the description of an excellent approach called the ResultsChain™ that provides a sound means for defining the scope in a business initiative proposal. It has the advantage of clarity and compactness that makes the scope readily apparent with minimum confusion. It reinforces the often-quoted saying that a picture is indeed worth a thousand words.

The ResultsChain™ is referred to again in Chapter 23. For more details about the ResultsChain™ refer to *The Information Paradox*.

If the Investment Committee resists including all aspects of the programme in the existing business case or investment template, then encourage them to at least add the four following components to attachments:

- Business, organization, process and people change requirements or implications. (One assumes the technology component will be there.)
- Major process steps including the above.
- Risks with appropriate contingency plans for the programme should the most probable disasters occur.
- Progressive programme investment approval gates.

It is to the last item we now turn.

Programme-approval gates

This concept has been in vogue for some time. The underlying principle is simple; never give any programme *carte blanche* approval from concept to completion. Instead, approve the programme in stages, reviewing it for completeness at each step before approving the next stage.

Ensure that the Investment Committee schedules the reviews for the following gates:

- Business case submission for investment approval.
- Feasibility study completion when further analysis and study have further supported, or disproved, the concept.
- Design stage where the detailed technical modelling is complete and the extent of commitment is refined.
- At various milestones in the build phase, usually based on the acceptance and cost of key modules.
- On user acceptance which is often confused with implementation.
- At implementation, which in a well-considered business case that follows the BTOPP model, may well be where the bulk of the costs fall.

You will also find that the more complete Business Investment Proposal coupled with the definition of BTOPP responsibilities has a sobering effect on new IT initiatives. Now that all parts of the business have accountability and responsibility for the programme success, you may find:

- The **B**usiness rejecting programmes because of the analysis and research now required to justify the investment. (*Most IT managers will know how rarely any real analysis or market research underpins technology related business proposals.*)
- The **O**rganization restructuring component bringing to the surface significant conflict or overlooked costs in redundancy, fit-out or new office buildings.
- The **P**rocess engineering requirement revealing the proposed project is unnecessary or requires unacceptable process change.
- The **P**eople segment revealing training, motivation and staff numbers that cannot be met with present resources.

It goes without saying that the Committee must ensure the stage gate review covers all B(T)OPP progress, not merely the technology development progress that has so far been the focus of most IT governors.

As IT manager it will be necessary to direct the governors' attention to different things. It is also critical that IT-based project managers now also monitor how these "non-IT" things are progressing. Make sure that all understand that programme reporting will be wider than number of software programs written or dollars expended on the technology component alone.

The Investment Committee

If possible avoid the term IT Steering Committee which calls to mind misdirected souls who believed their role was to harangue the IT manager over service difficulties. Propose an alternative name, such as Investment Decision Board or Investment Committee which infer a broader view of the governance of technology-based business programmes.

Limit the number of governors. Keep the committee small. It should consist of those few key people who can take a sound overview of the investment implications.

Permanent governors should include:

- Chief financial officer to review the budget, funding implications, cash-flow implications and revenue-related benefits.
- HR director to review the people and organization implications and progress.
- The IT manager to review the technology-related components.
- Secretariat to maintain calendars, diaries, records and arrange reviews.

Visiting members, called to answer on individual programmes must include:

- Business sponsor.
- Programme manager who is responsible for oversight of each BTOPP project.

Possible specialist help and *ad-hoc* members, called when required, may include:

- Business process engineering specialists.
- Business risk and continuity management specialists.

The role of the Investment Committee is to give initial approval and maintain continuous oversight of all programmes. They must also ensure that all programmes are reviewed at the appropriate gate, and no investment is committed beyond those gates until authorized to do so.

Do not overlook the potential workload that may fall on the secretariat. Coordinating the meetings, gathering information, following up minuted action items and other tasks will make this a full-time job, possibly for more than one person. As IT manager you will probably be expected to provide the resource to carry out that function. Chapter 6 makes some recommendations on support people. You might find it useful.

Checklist

1. Does the corporate investment proposal or business case now include the BTOPP implications?
2. Does the above process include a means of clearly assigning responsibility to people for their roles in the five dimensions?
3. Have milestones been set in the project schedule that reflects critical achievements in all five dimensions?
4. Has the role of the investment committee been formally documented?
5. Has each committee member been given a formal "role description" covering the work of the investment committee?
6. Has a process been established to ensure *all* programmes are reviewed at *all* checkpoints?
7. Have the criteria for judging which then permits progress to the next step been defined and agreed?
8. Has some formal process been agreed to compare the programme position to the required checkpoint hurdles?
9. Has the committee been given a set of questions to help probe the 4 Rs?

10. Have you established a means to measure the following: risk, expense and rewards?
11. Have you established how and when and who will measure rewards (benefits)?
12. Has the concept of a secretariat been considered?
13. If so, has its role and accountabilities been defined and agreed?
14. Does every programme have a formally committed programme owner who is fully aware of their role in coordinating and ensuring the execution of the tasks under BTOPP?
15. Does the IT side have a clear project owner who clearly understands the need to achieve logistical completeness through the BTOPP model?

Establishing service level agreements

10

Stop up the openings,
Close down the doors,
Rub off the sharp edges,
Unravel all confusion.
(Lao Tzu)

Introduce service level agreements!

If, as IT manager, you haven't heard this catch-cry, be assured that you soon will. There is misconception current among many users that service level agreements (SLAs) offer a panacea to all IT-related issues.

They do not! Not at least unless they are surrounded by other good practices such as proper principles, sound corporate governance and underpinned with proper human and technical resources.

What are SLAs?

SLAs are the supply agreements between the IT unit and the remainder of the business. While principles define *how* information technology will be managed, SLAs define *what* outputs IT must deliver. The outputs will be couched in quantitative and qualitative terms. SLAs are in essence contracts between business units for delivery of supplies required to operate the business.

If you are keen to survive as the IT manager you will support the concept because without them you may:

● Face unreasonable demands made without regards to resource constraints or reality. This will guarantee a "failure" to meet someone's measures—however impractical.

- Fail to establish the complementary obligations the business unit must undertake in contributing to the fulfilment of requirements, thus making IT the scapegoat for all failures.
- Make serious mistakes about priorities and what should be done when.
- Base the department's organization and resource inventory on criteria that are little more than guesswork.
- Fail to meet the real needs of the business simply because they have not been properly determined, defined and agreed.
- Not know what the IT department is expected to deliver, how and when and in what quantities.
- Become answerable to the whims and demands of transient individuals rather than corporate requirements.
- Fail to spell out the reciprocal obligations and responsibilities of the units serviced by your department.
- Lack any basis for establishing what constitutes an acceptable level of performance in the delivery of product or service to the business "customers".
- The IT department will lack any *sound* basis for establishing and defending the required budgets to deliver an appropriate service.
- Business colleagues will not be guided towards understanding the relationship between costs and service levels, particularly for the emotive issue of desktop support.

Running an IT department without service level agreements is analogous to running a restaurant where you hold out the promise to serve anything to anyone at any time. This is simply not possible. If IT managers fail to define what is expected of them, they must eventually fail—unless they possess most excellent crystal balls!

Benefits

The benefits of service level agreements include:

- Establishing formal agreement with business colleagues on the key outputs from IT.
- Reaching agreement with business colleagues on their obligations and responsibilities.
- Clearly communicating their obligations and responsibilities to IT staff.
- Establishing a sound basis for determining resource requirements covering hardware, software, people, process and organization.
- Having objective measure of the IT unit's success in meeting its charter.

The process of setting service level agreements can lead towards a reappraisal of services and products demanded from IT. This frequently leads to a reduction in demand and a proper focus on the important.

The process can also be used to inform and educate business colleagues about the costs and implications of their service demands. This too can lead to a swift review and reduction in "nice to have" demands.

Finally, SLAs clarify what the business expects the IT manager to do *now*. It is common for head-hunters and interviewers to dwell on future opportunities for a new appointment—but remember—you will be first measured and succeed or fail on how well you manage the things that *are needed today.*

The key to success is to define those few things that must be the focus of the IT unit if it is to be successful. Take heed of what Guibert[18] said about the French army of 1773: "We have created a uniform which obliges the soldier and the officer to spend three hours a day on their *toilette*, which has turned men of war into wig brushers, shiners and polishers". Similarly, today, many IT units have their fair share of wig brushers and polishers rather than men of action.

SLAs for what?

There is an analogy which compares running an IT unit to driving a car. Generally, you only need to know fuel remaining, oil pressure, water temperature and current speed to proceed with confidence. It is not necessary to know the temperature of the wheel bearings, the rotations of the rear axle or the minute-to-minute wear on the crankshaft. Indeed, if you had to scan all that information, you could not watch the road ahead.

So it is as IT manager you need to know two things:

- What few things, done well, will lead to success in the eyes of the business.
- What few things are for you, as the IT manager, a sound measure of smooth running.

Analysis and research in the field suggests that other business units will measure the IT department's success by the extent to which it facilitates their success. That is logical and understandable.

So the task you face is to determine those few things that IT provides that business values. There will be two categories.

- Maintenance or improvement of current business outputs.
- Technology contribution to new business initiatives.

The first task

The first task is to determine which are the current outputs that the business most values. Be assured of three things:

- They will not be MIPS, bandwidth or programmer productivity.
- They will include technology-facilitated business processes such as insurance policy issuance, commission payments, billings or electronic service delivery to suppliers and customers.
- They will be difficult to measure effectively. There will be a number of contributing factors outside the direct control of IT that affect achievement of these measures. These may be determined by considering the business, technology, organization, process and people (BTOPP) demands that surround the delivery of each measure.

The IT manager **must** work with his business colleagues to identify these outputs and agree the performance measures *within the framework of the principles and commercial realities*.

It is not a simple task to produce perfect service level agreements. It is an iterative process and a negotiation process and will take both time and effort. The process becomes iterative because it often raises hidden obstructions that must be overcome if the outputs are to be delivered in a timely and cost-effective manner. A process of negotiation is required because all concerned will experience difficulty in marshalling the right resources, at the right time, and in the right quantities. These shortages may be lengthy and trade-offs may need to be made. It is probable that the SLAs will also throw up people and technical resource conflicts, whether they are printer, hardware, process-timing or similar resource contention.

This chapter covers a number of practices that together should improve the chances of getting it right. It is suggested you:

- Scope the service level agreements
- Set out the measures
- Agree reporting on measures
- Define remedial or corrective action
- Institute a change management process
- Agree how issues will be managed

The *current* performance measures for the newly defined outputs must also be measured and recorded as part of the process. Be mindful of the advice given by John McNally of VicRoads: "Catalogue all in-house services and assess how well each of these is delivered . . . [and] understand the cost of these services."[19]

Michael Wilkins[20] of Royal and Sun Alliance and Tactitus[21] both warned about the risk of staff later reinventing the past and claiming a superior level of performance that never existed. "Everything was not better in the past," though many would like to imagine it was so.

Agreeing current performance levels will often prove tricky and debatable. The IT department may not have a current methodical approach to measuring outputs. Make sure that you determine and agree the existing baseline measures with business colleagues *before* making any commitments to future targets. Chapter 17 provides a more detailed coverage of the subject of benchmarking and performance measures.

Remember that the SLAs are a single most critical determinant of what the remainder of the business expects *you* to deliver.

Scoping the SLAs

Experienced companies are increasingly shifting to the view that the focus of service level agreements should be on measuring a few essential business outputs. Measures such as MIPS, bandwidth and programmer productivity are of no direct relevance to a manager concerned with paying commissioned agents or issuing drivers' licences.

This evolution from purely technical measures to business outputs has taken place for a number of reasons, including:

- The realization that the business units can compromise their position by dictating inputs to the IT department. Most IT units are smart enough to work out they cannot be held to account for failures in which the business unit dictated the quality, quantity and management of the inputs.
- The growing appreciation that managing the inputs consumes a disproportionate amount of management time—including the IT manager's.
- The number and variety of inputs usually far exceeds the number of outputs. Experienced companies now understand that if a few key business outputs meet performance criteria, then by inference the inputs are of proper quantity and quality.
- By focusing on business outputs, the business can concentrate on the "real" business rather than covertly trying to do your job as IT manager.

Gay and Essinger[22] also point to this stating: "Organizations are more likely to meet their commercial objectives and maximize their success if they direct management control not so much towards controlling inputs, but rather towards focusing on the finished output."

Charge your team tasked with developing the SLAs to *ask the business users* what they think are the important outputs. Technical people are poor at double-guessing the business and frequently select the wrong outputs.

Limit SLAs to ten or fewer things that matter most to the business. It will not be easy to limit the SLAs. At the outset of the process, there will be a large number of candidate areas for improvement and you will need to cull them. Some tips on culling are given later in this chapter.

Do not make the mistake of wrongly focusing SLA performance on the IT unit itself. SLAs may be set for internal IT processes that are no longer the direct concern of the business. However, management of performance within the IT unit is the business of the IT manager. The business unit's concerns should be that the outputs are of appropriate quality and cost.

Here are some checks that can ensure that the candidate pool of SLAs is appropriate:

- Review the business goals and objectives and current initiatives and see that the SLAs are in support of them. If they are not, then you must question why they are key outputs.
- Question the rationale for measuring each proposed item. This should separate the nice-to-know from the things that matter. Some further questions for testing the rationale appear in the next section.
- Consider contributing factors, such as organization, people and processes which must be carried out outside IT that contribute to the performance measures. These will form the basis for accountability and responsibility statements in the agreement.

If you find the idea of a small number of SLAs challenging, consider the words of John McNally[23] who said: "Instead of reviewing systems issues such as availability and response times it would have been preferable to have monitored things like the average time to process a license. It was appreciated this [measuring performance on outputs] was challenging as non-IT factors could affect these outcomes."

Defining SLAs

The IT manager should ensure that the process is focused and pertinent. Ask these questions of every SLA:

- What is being measured, and is it a business output? Users are not interested in bandwidth utilization, they are interested in how long it takes them to issue an insurance policy, or process a bank deposit.
- Why is it being measured? Give some rationale for selecting this particular item for measurement. This step is most useful as it usually leads to a vigorous culling of the list of potential SLAs.

- How will measurement be done? Many organizations have little history of performance measurement and the complexities and costs involved. It is important to define how measurement will be done at the outset.
- When will the measurement take place? Will the process or output be measured daily, weekly, monthly? Will the measure be made at peak times, or at random times during the period?
- What is the current performance level for the item? This should be based on some statistical method. Averages are dangerous. A set of measures that give ranges (lowest and highest measures), modes (most frequent measures) and means (average measures) is more likely to provide a sound basis for judging improvement or failure than a single percentage.
- What are target performance levels? How were they determined?
- When are these levels to be reached? Demand some statistical probability of meeting them.
- Have the accountabilities and responsibilities of business unit and IT unit been defined?
- Do those accountabilities cover the BTOPP aspects of the SLA?
- Will remedial action be taken to correct a failure to meet a SLA, or if a failure to meet the SLA appears *imminent*?
- Will punishment follow a failure, or repeated failure to meet the SLA?
- Is there any value added by over achieving on this SLA?
- Do dependencies flow *from* or *to* this SLA?
- Who owns this SLA in the business and in IT?

This last point is critical. If no one in the business wishes to take ownership of a SLA, it may be because it is unimportant, or it may be because it is absolutely critical! Find out which.

Do not forget to determine how the intangible but nevertheless important measure called *satisfaction* will be measured. There is a clear distinction between "meeting the measures" and "satisfaction". Satisfaction is nevertheless a valid measure.

There is a lengthy definition of "satisfaction" in the *Oxford English Dictionary*, including "fulfilment of one's wishes, expectations, or needs or the pleasure derived from this". The dictionary gives a later example under the heading "satisfactory" that seems closer to the conundrum facing measurement. The example is the "brakes are satisfactory but not particularly powerful". That is, the requirements were met but some unease remains.

You must expect widely differing views of what constitutes a satisfactory experience. The team must obtain agreement from the users that not only do they agree on the objective measures for the output, but also that they agree how this important intangible will be measured.

Colgate-Palmolive also considered the difficulty of measuring internal customer service. In the end they "settled on Quality Function Deployment (QFD)". QFD was developed by the American Supply Institute and is a technique that helps to assimilate the "voice of the customer" into products and services.[24]

Finally, it is important to gain commitment from the business unit to take part-ownership for monitoring the performance of each measure. The business unit cannot abrogate all responsibility for measuring to the IT unit.

Setting measures

The topic of benchmarking and setting measures is covered in Chapter 17. It is important, however, to remember that for SLAs the focus must remain on business output measures rather than technology performance benchmarks. The performance in delivering outputs should be the only determinant from the point of view of the business manager. Managing the input benchmarks is the job of the IT manager and should not be confused with SLA output performance measures.

Motivation

Both the business unit and your department should be motivated towards meeting SLA targets.

- The business unit should be penalized for shortcomings in areas such as user testing or business process support.
- The IT unit should be penalized for its failings.
- Both key IT staff and business unit staff should have some component of their remuneration at risk.

Neither form of compensation is easy to structure or free of subjective judgements. One approach that ensures the pain is equally shared is, depending on who is at fault, to diminish either the IT unit's "bonus pool" or the business unit's bonus pool. However, both penalties and rewards should also reflect that intangible measure—satisfaction.

The task of motivation is challenging. The literature on individual motivation is wide and varied. I suggest that you seek the help of Human Resource experts in structuring the at-risk compensation for both parties. Indeed both parties should ensure that their incentive packages are complementary and consistent. Significant differences between the triggers and quantum of rewards for achievement between the parties may lead to unnecessary friction. The factors that govern the at-risk remuneration need to be equivalent on both sides.

Finally, and importantly, it is critical that the business unit staff are rewarded for the process success, not for their ability to abuse and terrorize IT staff (now isn't that a novel idea?). Failure should benefit no one.

Do not, however, place too much emphasis on personal motivators. Paul Omerod[25] noted: "After all . . . there is such a thing as society, and human welfare is not maximized by the ruthless pursuit of individual self-interest."

Two final rules in establishing SLAs are:

- Address any service shortfall immediately. Kym Norley of Booz·Allen and Hamilton[26] observed that "companies need to make hard decisions, to draw the line when things go wrong, otherwise you abrogate your responsibility for performance".
- Extend the SLA performance model down the food chain to IT vendors. Enter into back-to-back SLA measures, with appropriate punishment and reward mechanisms. These SLAs should ensure that the IT unit receives adequate attention and influence with the companies supplying technology. Chapter 14 reiterates this point.

Measuring achievement

A frequent problem experienced with SLAs is that after all the effort of setting them, no one bothers to measure performance achievement. Watch out for this and make sure that both the IT department and the business units understand that responsibility for measuring achievement sits on both sides of the fence. The business unit must maintain measures over output performance, and IT staff must measure the IT inputs to ensure that they are achieving the goals set for them.

In Chapter 17, we suggest it may be prudent to "outsource" output measurement to an independent third party that specializes in such measures, the benefits being:

- It will be done, as the third party's income is likely to depend on it being done.
- The measures are likely to be more objective. Alternatively, an audit team or other individual removed from the day-to-day issues of the contract can do the measurement.

Do not be surprised at the expense involved in taking regular performance measures. Domberger and Hall offer an explanation why businesses are commonly shocked at the cost of measurement:

Provided performance evaluation can be implemented in a systematic way, the costs of monitoring need not be higher than monitoring in-house operations . . . the reason why it often appears monitoring costs are so high [after contracting] is that either little or no monitoring was previously undertaken or that its costs were not fully assessed.[27]

In addition:

- Review performance against these SLAs at least monthly, preferably using an independent third party.
- Review all SLAs for continued relevance, and cull those past their useful life.
- Add new SLAs where appropriate, bearing in mind the guidelines provided earlier.

If performance is constantly above or below target, then make an effort to understand why. In some cases it may be necessary to revise the measures.

Further considerations

Some steps that you can take to make SLA achievement less of a contentious issue are:

- Ensure performance targets are based on formal statistical method, selecting the best measure (range, mean, mode and acceptable deviations).
- Seeing that performance measures are cumulative or based on an "average" result. For example, a company may set a monthly range that lies at a minimum or 93% and a maximum 97% expectation. However, it may demand that the average over any six-month period never drop below 95%.
- Making penalties small and frequent. It appears that a large number of small penalties are more likely to bring about desired improvements than a savage penalty that is seldom or never applied.

Reward is equally difficult to manage effectively. Typical encouragement offers include bonuses for achievement of targets at an earlier date than envisaged in the service level agreement, or early delivery of major system development projects. However, if these bonuses are known in advance, there is a danger that your project managers will ensure that the projected delivery dates are well within their comfort zone.

Change

Businesses change, and service requirements change. That which was important yesterday is often no longer important today. Accept that SLAs can change or become redundant, and review the SLAs periodically for continued relevance.

Allow both parties to recommend additions, changes and deletions to the port-folio of SLAs. In each case the new SLA should be defined in the manner set out earlier in this chapter. If a SLA is removed from the portfolio, the rationale for its removal should be documented.

Issues

The issues with SLAs are spread throughout this chapter. The list below provides a summary.

- Failure to link the SLAs to business outputs that usually results in other issues below.
- Low-level technical performance SLAs that are only indirectly linked to outputs.
- SLAs that concentrate entirely on management of IT performance, for example, network packet collision, bandwidth usage, number logged-on users, etc.
- Measures set without regard to implications and dependencies. Upgrading or maintaining performance may be impossible without upgrades to CPUs, mem-ory, disk-farms, network bandwidth and even desktop PCs.
- Lack of visibility is another issue that plagues SLAs. It has been known for both IT and business managers to neglect to share the details of the agreement with the very staff responsible for delivering them!
- Ridiculous demands are another common failing. Ask the "Why?" questions included in the checklist to weed out irrelevant SLAs. Typical demands include 24-hour day, seven-day week coverage when the company only operates from 8 a.m. to 6 p.m. Monday to Friday. Another common request is a demand for reports "first thing Monday"—incurring weekend operations cost—for output that is not utilized until much later in the week.
- Ignoring poor performance and laying the foundation for continued poor achievement. The SLA may be ignored for months at a time but is then dredged up as a political weapon.

Tips

Some things that can improve the SLA development, measurement and manage-ment process are:

- Jointly developing the SLAs with the business in a workshop where the parties are forced to change sides and develop the SLA from the opposing perspective.
- Using external parties such as Gartner Measurement to define benchmarks.
- Contracting an external "honest broker" to take monthly measurements on SLA performance and ensure both parties are adhering to the agreed obligations and responsibilities.
- Including such items as vendor management within the SLA framework where the company sees continued good relationships with suppliers as critical.

Some or none of these may work for you. However, it is worth exploring all avenues in the struggle to define those few things that must be done well to achieve success.

Checklist

1. Are you using an independent expert to develop SLAs?
2. Have you scoped the area to be covered by SLAs?
3. Does the SLA consider BTOPP implications?
4. Have the outputs for those areas been defined?
5. Do they tie back to the business objectives?
6. What is being measured?
7. Why is it being measured?
8. How will measurement be done?
9. Has the current performance level been agreed?
10. Has the current performance environment been documented?
11. What are the new measures?
12. Are the costs of achieving the new measures commensurate with the benefits?
13. What changes are required to the environment to achieve these measures?
14. What changes may take place that will alter these proposed measures?
15. What changes may take place in the environment between now and the achievement date?
16. Have you defined the accountabilities and responsibilities of both parties?
17. Has "satisfaction" been considered as a SLA component?
18. Are the measures statistically sound?
19. What rewards and punishments attach to this measure?
20. What dependencies does this SLA have on other people or things?

21. Has change control process been defined?
22. Has a dispute resolution mechanism been agreed?
23. Has an "at risk" remuneration package been agreed for both teams?
24. Have the SLAs been circulated to appropriate staff in the business and IT?

11 Dealing with hot spots

Touch a thistle timidly, and it pricks you;
grasp it boldly, and its spines crumble. (William F Halsey in *Forbes Business Quotations*)

Issue

Hot spots are the highly visible, sometimes intransigent, but minor things that are annoying some vocal member of the business. You may have been alerted to a number of them at the job interview.

The problem with hot spots is that they distract you from your key role as leader, planner and organizer. Instead you are misdirected into a furious round of fire-fighting on minor, though intractable, problems inherited from your predecessor.

Many IT managers embrace this downward-swirling whirlpool that allows them to flex their technological skills and ignore their new responsibility to lead and manage. Jeremy Tozer discusses this failing in his excellent essay, "Leadership weaknesses in IT management", later in this book.

The unhappy outcome for many embryo IT managers is that those things that make for sound IT management, namely knowledge, principles, structure, process and leadership, are abandoned in search of some techno-orgasm.

The problem with hot spots

The problem with hot spots is that they won't go away by themselves. So you have to deal with them effectively. If you don't you run the risks of:

- Lapsing into the role of technology expert who gains credence with the pro-peller heads and gets sucked into the vortex of technical advice that is not an IT manager's role.

- Losing the opportunity to establish credence as a *manager*. Marc Antony's adapted words say it all: "The condemned IT manager rich in his technical honour, creeps apace into the hearts of those that have thrived upon the earlier state, while the rest, grown sick of poor IT management, would purge him by any desperate change."[28]
- The honeymoon period in which you could introduce welcomed sweeping change passes.

However, if you do not attend to these problems and decide whether they are commercially significant, solvable or intractable then you also run a risk of undermining the confidence of your business colleagues. The best solution is to quarantine and deal with hot spots in a structured, limited way. You cannot operate effectively if you are surrounded by minor but very visible technical problems that consume your valuable time, attention and resources.

Below are some benefits to be derived from attending to hot spots in an effective manner:

- Each hot spot is placed in its proper *management* perspective. It is astounding how often what are viewed as serious problems with IT just do not stand any critical scrutiny. A critical assessment of the commercial and economic value being destroyed by the so-called issue will often prove to be minuscule.
- If you discover the problem is the catalyst for serious corporate haemorrhaging, then you may demand funds and resources commensurate with the task of fixing the problem.
- You, as IT manager, establish order and control over what can become the most potent destructive force working against sound long-term management and leadership. You move yourself, the business and your team away from the malignant cancers of reaction and emotional response.
- A sound approach may influence your colleagues in the business and IT to assess technology-related issues in a structured and objective manner. This can help create a climate for a more rationale and objective approach to deploying IT resources on future projects.
- You might even lead them to deal with their own business problems in a structured and objective fashion.

If you would like some further background on rational thinking in problem solving you may find Kepner and Tregoe's[29] *The New Rational Manager* useful. It sets out four key steps: "Situation Appraisal" that deals with the question "what is going on?", "Problem Analysis" which asks "why did this happen?", "Decision Analysis" which determines "which course of action should we take?", and "Potential Problem and Opportunity Analysis" which forces the question "what lies ahead?"

Categorizing hot spots

First, a caution: If you are an internal appointee to the role of IT manager, you may think you know what the hot spots are, but beware of Moltke's words:

> It happens only too easily that one will attach a greater significance to what one sees directly in front of oneself, where perhaps one has taken part, than to the often vastly more important matter which is communicated from afar.[30]

Moltke was writing of the dangers of battle commanders being overly influenced by events in their immediate environment and ignoring reports from other sections of the battlefield. However, the same risk of over-reacting to the obvious lies with all managers, including those in IT.

You will need to place the burning issues into one of the following categories:

- Those which you can and should do something about immediately—hot spots.
- Long-term problems that need to be dealt with in the context of structure, process and SLA improvements—these are not hot spots.
- Issues where both the root cause and the solution lie outside IT.
- Hyperbolical issues—issues which are not issues at all.

The challenge that you may face is how do you distinguish between these types? The answer is to work with three contrivances:

- The set of principles that should have been agreed with your business peers.
- A set of criteria for defining hot spot criticality and scale which you should agree with your peers.
- Rigorous questioning as to why this is an issue.

The first tool can include a principle for judging on issues, but more probably you will find among your well-crafted principles some key business rules and implications that help to point towards a path of resolution. You may even wish to define a principle along the lines of the example in Figure 11.1.

You will need to agree on the criteria for defining which items are really hot spots and which are merely noise. Criteria for defining hot spots could include:

- Causing financial loss of greater than X per day.
- Can be resolved with less than X person-days effort.
- Can be resolved with available skills, tools, and equipment.
- Causes serious public embarrassment that may lead to financial loss.

Principle #8

Issue
How will we determine if a project is a hot spot and warrants immediate redeployment of IT staff from current tasks?

Options
1. The problem meets defined criteria as listed below.
2. IT will make a judgement as to the importance and priority of the problem.
3. Individual managers will determine what constitutes a hot spot on the basis of their experience.

Principle adopted:
(1) The problem must meet the criteria defined below.

Rationale:
It is necessary to differentiate between significant irritations and small but serious problems. Personal judgements by IT of business units may lack objectivity. A published set of criteria ensures all share a common measure and resources are not deployed on small irritating issues.

Implications:
+ Only deserving cases will receive priority attention.
+ We will reduce the misuse of scarce and expensive resources on emotive problems.
+ Some problems will not receive immediate attention despite their capacity to create incessant low level irritation.
− Defining measures against criteria will require cost, effort and accuracy.

Approval: (signature)

For the Executive Committee 07 Oct 2000

Proposed criteria
- The problem relates to a failure or shortcoming in an existing system.
- The direct financial loss exceeds $3000 per day.
- The indirect internal loss exceeds $5000 per day.
- Remedy is expected to take less than 20 man-days work.
- No additional business, organization, people or process change is required.
- IT have or can rapidly acquire the appropriate skills to deal with the issue.

Figure 11.1—Principle for hot spot management

The key is to produce a set of criteria suited to your circumstances that puts small problems with loud voices where they belong and ensures that your IT group focuses on fixing those things that really matter. In the process you may also educate some of the exhibitionists and dramatists in the company's ranks.

The most important tool that you possess, and which you can bring to bear are Rudyard Kipling's[31] servants: ". . . What, and Where and When and How and Why and Who?" Ask the following questions, relentlessly:

- What is the issue?
- Why is this an issue?
- What effects does it have on whom?
- What will happen if it is not corrected?
- Why has it not been fixed before?
- How did this become an issue?
- Who in the business owns the issue?
- What is he or she doing about it?
- What work around exists?
- Can we change the process/remove the issue?
- What would happen if we ceased the process affected by the issue?

Kepner and Tregoe[32] suggest a critical question may also be "Can the effect of this problem *as we have described it* in the problem statement be explained now?"

Ten minutes of tough questioning may very well put the issue to death for all time to come. Do not, whatever you do, suggest solutions or make rash commitments until you have a thorough appreciation of the issue.

Cross-check with your staff and ask them the same questions. Do not be surprised if their answers are at complete variance with the story from the business owner.

Remember, that even several days of investigation and analysis will often pay dividends and spare you the task of fixing, sometimes at enormous expense, something that "ain't broke." At worst, you will show the business you care and that you are professional and thorough in your work.

Outcomes

Out of this process you will, almost definitely find that a significant number of the hot spots have their genesis and their solution outside IT. In the main these will revolve around user training in the use of applications. I can never fathom the mindset that thinks analyst-programmers should train accountants in the use of financial software, or word processing. They lack the business knowledge, application knowledge, training skills and support tools. These issues can usually be addressed by a sound form of service level agreement that clearly spells out the accountability and responsibility of other groups such as Human Resource Management and Training.

A good number of issues are not hot spots at all. The process of questioning will demonstrate that some people's pet peeves are just that. In the big picture they are trifling inconveniences. Don't ignore them—barnacles grate. Do, however, put them in perspective, if necessary publicly.

Some hot spots are not only trifling but can be fixed with minimal cost and effort. It is amazing to see managers spending thousands of dollars of their time and the IT unit's time to-ing and fro-ing over some recalcitrant printer that could be replaced with the equivalent of the salary costs eaten up in an hour-long meeting. One strong recommendation is that you obtain budgetary approval to spend, without further questioning, a reasonable sum on unilaterally fixing these types of problems. The process should have reduced the number of hot spots to a small manageable number.

In considering how to remedy the problem, scrutinize the issue from five dimensions:

- What are the business changes that will arise in fixing this issue?
- What technology challenges do we face in fixing the issue?
- What organization changes will be required?
- What skills and training will have to be hired or delivered?
- How will processes change in the business and IT?

You must also define the criteria that are to be used for judging that the problem has been resolved. (Beware—users have a way of giving hot spots a form of eternal life. There is always one more change . . .)

You must extend the criteria to cover all the five dimensions above. IT may only be responsible for fixing one tiny part of the issue. Don't allow yourself to be hamstrung by users failing to make resources available for analysis, design, testing or training. The IT department cannot alone correct problems such as inadequate training or system abuse.[n]

Once you have considered these factors, consider creating a service level agreement to cover the resolution of the issue. Bear in mind that you may require approval for capital expenditure, staff training, unique expertise or additional staff. Make sure you know who will be responsible for obtaining the funding and resources. Finally, make sure you call out, preferably in the SLA, any projects that will be put "on hold" while this issue is being resolved.

---

[n] For example, user manipulation of operating system parameters conflicts with personal software and games or poor desktop maintenance habits.

Issue-resolution agreement

A possible "Hot Spot Agreement" is shown in Figure 11.2. Note the inclusion of the following:

- Business owner of the issue.
- IT owner of the issue.
- Trigger for the issue.
- Symptoms.
- Monetary/business loss.
- Cost to repair (estimate).
- Timetable to repair.
- BTOPP implications.
- Accountabilities and responsibilities.
- Acceptance criteria.

The template is not perfect and your circumstances may require that you add more to it. It will take time to complete, at least a few hours. The time to complete is nearly always trifling in comparison to the effort required to fix the problem. However, without a sound agreement on what is to be fixed, when, how and by whom, you leave yourself open to a malignancy termed "unresolved issue".

The process you go through to identify and control small burning issues will set you up well for the next step in the journey, introducing or refining service level agreements.

Checklist

1. Have you agreed criteria for judging hot spots?
2. Have you defined principles to govern hot spot management?
3. Have you gathered appropriate data on each hot spot, including:
   3.1 Causes by asking "why is this happening?"
   3.2 Effects, including commercial and economic effects.
4. Has each hot spot been assessed from the five dimensions
   4.1 Business?
   4.2 Technology?
   4.3 Organization?
   4.4 Process?
   4.5 People?
5. Have you considered alternatives to fixing the problem, including work-arounds?

Business Owner: Kim Buchanan   **IT Owner:** Simon Perez

Nature of the problem

The home contents policy maintenance programme has failed to update a recent major insurance valuation increase by a policy holder. The old home contents valuation was $850 000. The new policy is for $1 250 000. This was triggered by a recent re-valuation of the local currency. Approximately 10 000 similar policy re-valuations of a similar scale are expected within the next six months.

Trigger

The update of the valuation over $1 000 000.

Symptoms

The programme accepts the valuation amount at data entry but produces an incorrect premium. This only applies to amounts greater than $1 000 000.

Monetary/Business Loss

The immediate effect is the inability to bill the client for a $5000 premium. The second-order effect is the potential loss of this and up to 10 000 other high-nett worth clients over the next six months with a financial loss equivalent to $400 000.

Cost to repair

Six days re-programming and testing the suite	**$4200**
Three days test pack preparation and testing	**$2400**
One day of quality assurance and verification	**$1000**

Timetable to repair

See attached schedule:

BTOPP Implications

No BTOPP changes required, process remains as it was previously.

Accountability and Reponsibilities:

Business owner:
- prepare test packs by 31st Jan
- assign and manage test team results by 4th Feb
- note and verify test results by 4th Feb
- inform staff and supervise day #1 input—5th Feb
- quality check data daily for first full week after implementation 6–13 Feb
- contact customers and explain delay in processing and offer 5 percent discount for inconvenience caused 28th Jan

IT Owner
- verify cause by 27th Jan
- examine options to repair by 29th Jan
- specify repair and obtain business owner approval by 30th Jan
- verify no BTOPP changes required by 1st Feb
- make good and unit and system test in test environment by 3rd Feb
- advise and coach user test team on sound testing techniques 3–5th Feb
- control release into production on 6th Feb

Acceptance criteria

The application should accept and process six live applications for sums greater than $1 000 000 and produce:
- Accurate premiums for these amounts
- Accurate policy statements for these renewals
- Accurate summarised monthly reports for these renewals
- Accurate agent commission fees for these six renewals

Figure 11.2—Hot spot resolution agreement

6. Do you have adequate resources to fix the important hot spots?
7. Have you considered possible downstream effects that may be problems or opportunities?
8. If not should the resolution of the problem be "outsourced"?
9. Have you set limits on the time and effort *you* will spend on these matters?
10. Should you group and delegate further management of some or all of the significant hot spots to a specific unit in IT?
11. Have you explained the rationale and benefits of your approach to your business colleagues?
12. Have you committed them to the approach, preferably by working in conjunction with them in establishing criteria, principles, assessment and triage?[o]

---

[o] A medical term used by army field hospitals where the wounded are divided into one of three categories depending on the severity of their wounds. It is also used in some hospital emergency departments.

12 Tips for quick-wins

With a single success the stigma of dozens of lost engagements and mismanaged wars had been wiped away. (John Ralston Saul in *Voltaire's Bastards*)

Quick-wins are small projects that have a payback well out of proportion to the investment. This is not so much an issue area as an opportunity area. It is included in this section because it is an area that is usually the focus of high expectations and poor results.

What follows in the normal format of these chapters are the issues, implications, benefits and approaches to managing quick-wins.

Issue

The issue with quick-wins is that they too often fail to deliver the expected benefits in time. Some of the causes of the failures are listed below.

Causes

Two of the most common causes are:

- Quick-wins growing out of scope and becoming major projects.
- The business arm failing to exploit the quick-win.

Benefits

Key among the benefits of well-managed quick-wins are:

- Business perception of IT as a value-adding entity increases.
- Quick-wins are delivered on time and to budget.

- The requisite business processes and people are in place to exploit the quick-win.
- Improved IT staff morale as the hit list of success grows visibly throughout the year.

Approach

The approach proposed is not cut and dried. At the outset of this book we make the observation that most managers are capable intelligent human beings who will adapt suggestions and ideas to their own circumstances.

Discovering quick-wins

The new IT manager is presented with a glorious opportunity to achieve quick-wins by virtue of his or her discovery work. Discovering and mapping your domain will normally reveal a number of irritations and inefficiencies both in IT and in the business that can be readily exploited. Another rich area is the initial modelling of business and IT processes that should form part of the determination of the domain. Again IT itself is usually full of such opportunities, especially in the non-technical and administrative areas described in an earlier chapter.

Study the major user-driven computer processes as part of your induction and understanding of the business. Often, users will live with inadequate systems that can be improved without significant time or cost. One example was a simple decision to make the customer telephone number a customer record key. Customers always knew their phone number when they called in—rarely did they have their account number to hand. This quick-win made for a significant improvement in customer satisfaction and call-centre efficiency.

Another opportunity is to motivate your IT staff to identify quick-wins and reward them on completion in proportion to the value added. A quick-win that generates a million-dollar annual return is deserving of a reward commensurate with the saving.

Scan all major project proposals looking for the golden nugget. That is often the small part of the programme that offers benefits well out of proportion to the remainder of the project. Promote these to quick-wins if it is feasible.

Don't overlook non-technical quick-wins. The opportunities to cull redundant reports, eliminate worthless processes, terminate poor contracts and countless other things may work towards establishing the view of IT as a value-adding entity.

It will often prove difficult to swing your staff to this view—for them a piece of code is the answer every time. However, once the incentives start getting paid for introducing simple non-technical quick-wins, the attitude will usually change rapidly.

How do I do it?

- Define what constitutes a quick-win. This should include the investment and time-span limitations. For example, one organization defined a quick-win any *improvement* programme that could be completed in less than forty working days and at a cost of less than $25 000. The expense had to be balanced by singular returns.
- Ensure that the terms of reference for the programme are as tight as possible, including the warning that if the project is not completed to time or budget it will be killed. There must be no room for incremental growth or further good ideas unless you wish to hatch poorly structured projects that run out of control.
- Manage effectively. Make sure the time and moneybox rules are adhered to, difficult as that will be when the project team asks for "just one more week" or "just another $5000".
- Don't overlook the requirement to ensure business, organization, people and process alignment is in place for quick-wins just as they are for any other project. This is so often the cause of the failure. The wonderful new change is never implemented because of lethargy, laziness or plain stupidity.
- Consider establishing a quick-wins team with the requisite process engineering and technical skills and set their objectives and remuneration on the contribution they make through quick-win management. Frequently the skills required for this team are innovation, lateral thinking, perception and a deep understanding of business processes.

Quick-wins are often the lifeblood of morale and perceived IT success. They can rapidly change attitudes and deliver benefits while the lengthy large-scale programmes rumble along in the background.

Checklist

1. Have you defined criteria for classifying quick-wins?
2. Have you got a rigorous process[p] for examining quick-win opportunities?

---

[p] Quick-wins are often problem-based, so follow the Kepner and Tregoe methods outlined in Chapter 13.

3. Does the business initiative proposal for the quick-win include organizational, process and people changes required?
4. Have you established time and money box limits for quick-win programmes?
5. Do you have a risk management process to control risks with quick-wins?
6. Does your governance system control the potential growth of quick-wins?
7. Does your process allow you to identify non-technical quick-win opportunities?
8. Do your solutions include non-technical solutions?
9. Is the number of extant quick-wins limited to a small, manageable number?
10. Is it worth setting up a quick-wins task force or semi-permanent project team?

13   Living with legacy systems

That which was old is now new and
that which was new is now old again (Wickstead in *Four Lectures on Ibsen*, 1892)

It is a sobering thought that the technology of today, the wireless LANs, DVDs, interactive voice-on-demand and web-based technologies will be legacy systems within your lifetime. Our concern in this chapter is largely with transitioning older application systems. The circumstances in each company differ and it is only possible to give some broad direction to managers faced with the challenges of living with legacy systems.

The first problem

The first problem with legacy systems is dealing with the *irrational* urge to replace them. We have been brainwashed as consumers into believing we need newer, faster, more user-friendly systems. We replace PCs with faster and faster systems which most people use for word processing and e-mail for which there is no appreciable difference for the money spent. This mentality is well and truly entrenched with users who complain about "legacy" systems.

Too frequently the legacy system is replaced with a system that costs millions and provides no significant additional benefit. The reasons for these anomalies are numerous and include:

- A failure to determine *how* user-friendliness will be translated into business benefit.
- A failure to use process engineering to maximize the benefits of the new system.
- A failure to make appropriate organizational changes to exploit the improvements.
- A failure to recognize that the "new technology" system may only execute the same processes as the old technology system.
- A failure to recognize the problems with the old system (often described as its inflexibility) will be replaced with problems of a new order, for example:

- Desktop management issues in client–server environments.
- Limited IT competency with new software development and maintenance tools.
- Lack of in-depth application knowledge that is usually gained through years of application maintenance.
- Lack of experience in configuring and tuning new operating systems and database management systems.
- Unfamiliar back-up and recovery routines.
- Second-order effects like overloaded LAN infrastructure.

The upshot of all this is the new system fails to live up to expectations, and in many cases is significantly more expensive to own and operate than the legacy system it replaced. For this reason you must clearly understand the issues and problems with the legacy system before any replacement or re-engineering of the system is undertaken. Too often a half-understood issue is met with an immediate replacement project proposal from IT.

The first task

The first task when faced with demands to replace a legacy system is to ask:

- What is the problem?
- Why is it a problem?
- What solutions and alternatives have been considered?
- Did considered solutions include such things as process engineering, outsourcing the process, or developing a new process?
- Why have they been rejected?
- What are the resources and changes required to deliver the solution (remember BTOPP)?
- What risks will the replacement bring?

I suggest the problem(s) with the legacy system be analysed using a structured approach similar to that promoted by Kepner and Tregoe[33], which appeared earlier in this book.

State the problem

State the problem precisely. Motherhood phrases such as "low productivity" or "inflexibility" are not good enough. The problem must be stated in qualified and quantified terms. Do not mix problems. If the problem is stated as "poor productivity and inflexibility" change it to two separate problem statements. Deal with each separately.

Specify the problem

Specify the problem, Kepner and Tregoe suggest you need to define the identity of the problem (what), the location of the problem (where), the timing of the problem (when) and the extent or magnitude of the problem.

Develop possible causes from knowledge and experience or distinctions and changes

One useful technique is to develop an IT – COULD BE – IS NOT BE three-column matrix in which the possible causes are categorized. You may find several causes for the problem and any fix will need to consider all. You may find it useful to ensure that all BTOPP facets are checked off in this analysis by setting up the BTOPP items as rows. This approach helps to prevent you jumping to conclusions and maintains objectivity. Kepner and Tregoe[34] also observe: "[It] reduces the incidence of conflict and disagreement in the explanation of the problem."

Test possible causes against the specification

Kepner and Tregoe suggest that this step be driven by the question. "*If* this is the true cause of the problem, then how does it explain each dimension in the [problem] specification?" Check possible causes against the what, where, when and extent facets in the specification.

Determine the most probable cause

You will find it rare that a single possible cause explains all dimensions perfectly and to the exclusion of all other causes, particularly if you take BTOPP issues into consideration. Make sure you spend time and effort verifying what you believe to be the most probable cause.

Verify assumptions, observe, experiment, or try to fix and monitor

In this step you aim to show the cause–effect relationship of the problem. This is the confirmation process. It will require tightly monitored implementation and monitoring.

This is the first and recurring step in living with legacy systems—making sure you rigorously define the problems, causes and effects *before* you define solutions.

Pathways to replacement

There is a wide mix of possible solutions to improving legacy systems. Many can be used as "mix-and-match", that is, selecting a number of them for any one programme. You should at least consider the following.

Surround technologies

In this approach you overlay user friendly interfaces and improved data-capture facilities, such as scanners and OCR technologies, on top of the traditional user interface. This can be done selectively; focusing on the few most heavily trafficked input paths or screens. This is a good approach when the underlying file system and code is robust and efficient.

Database replace

If the code is sound and the user interface efficient but the underlying file structures the cause of the problem, then it is possible to do a total or partial replace of the file system or existing database. Approach this solution with caution. It is often possible to isolate a sub-set of the file system and replace it with an improved database management system with feeds to and from the legacy file system.

Nip and tuck

Most systems can be broken down into very loosely coupled component parts. For example, analysis will sometimes show it is possible to isolate one or two modules from the legacy system. If the cause of the problems is a loosely coupled module then it may be possible to build a replacement module with new technology and use it to feed the legacy system with those few data attributes that the legacy system requires.

Process outsourcing

An increasingly common solution is to outsource part or all of a problem business process to organizations better able to run it. If the company requires some data to be fed back into a legacy system this can be fed in from the external system. For example, underwriting or claims processing for insurance companies can be out-sourced to specialists and, if required, the underwriting data fed back into the host legacy system.

Gradual replace

This is a variant on "nip and tuck". The essential difference is the scale of the task. In this approach large functional areas are replaced by new technology systems. For example, if you plan to replace a legacy financial management system with a new package, one approach is to schedule the replacement so that only one major function is replaced at any time, for example, billing.

Benefits

The benefits of these incremental approaches are:

- The proving process for the most probable cause as defined in the problem analysis is measured and reversible.
- The business and IT gain experience with the new technology over time and with reduced risk.
- The replacement process is targeted and the limited benefits more easily monitored and measured.
- The gradual investment reduces the risk of a cataclysmic big bang.
- Programme scope is more manageable which is critical as sound project management skills are often in short supply.
- The benefits of overcoming the cause of the problem are realized more quickly.

Migrating from legacy systems

Perhaps the biggest challenge facing CIOs when migrating from legacy systems is who holds the baby. Modern IT systems offer IT staff an ideal opportunity to embellish their résumés. Skills in new development languages, architectures and software solutions are highly prized in the IT marketplace. Conversely, there is usually a declining demand for the skill sets that supported the legacy environment.

As such, it is perhaps only natural that the CIO embarking on a major revamp of the business systems will have a flood of volunteers wanting to be assigned to the new implementation while those consigned to maintaining the legacy environment will feel their careers are being by-passed.

The obvious response would be to outsource the task of maintaining the legacy systems. However, this can be easier said than done. The intricacies of the older applications will not be immediately apparent. Some considerable hand-holding will be required before external contractors familiarize themselves with how these function. Moreover, until the new solutions have proved themselves, the business will be dependent on the smooth operation of the legacy environment.

On the other hand, the CIO should also be reluctant to entrust the roll-out of the new system just to contractors. In time the organization will rely on some in-house knowledge being available. If there has been no skill transfer at the outset the business will soon find itself captive to the original contractors as unforeseen problems raise their ugly heads.

This dilemma confronted Dave Kohn when in the 1990s he ran IT at the Australian Industry Development Corporation (AIDC), the former Australian government venture finance company. Dave elected to give all his staff responsibility for both the old and new systems. He saw that this offered a gradual rather than pressured migration and allowed for more emphasis on the skills transfer between the in-house staff and the external contractors. In the end Dave believed this approach offered the best of both worlds. It gave greater protection for the legacy environment and a clear career progression to the new technology for all existing IT staff.

Note that no "benefits" arise from new technology unless that new technology overcomes a known business problem. Benefits must be measurable. For example, even "user-friendliness" must be measured by reduced training costs, time-to-learn, reduced errors and improved skill retention.

Lifespan

A recurrent mistake made by many who replace legacy systems is a failure to consider when the "new technology" will itself become outdated and what will replace it. (All those in banking who focused on teller systems while ATM, web-enabled and telephone banking were emerging will relate to this.) Make sure that you talk to the research companies about the projected lifespan of the replacement technologies. Typically, it takes at least three to five years before the new system can replace the old. What technologies will reign supreme then? Will your new system become technically outdated long before the application reaches the end of its commercial lifespan 15 or 20 years from now?

Risk management

Large-scale new system development has a high failure rate. Researchers in this field suggest as many as 80% of large-scale new systems developments fail. Later in this book, Peter Hind's essay, "Be responsible. Call 'Halt' ", recounts one of many. These failures have cost several IT managers not only their jobs, but have acted as a death trap for future careers. Most large-scale IT projects in recent years have been generated by the desire to replace legacy systems. If you are going to play this risky game, then do what you can to control the risks. The checklist that follows should point to some areas for consideration:

Checklist

1. Have you tested the rationale for transitioning legacy systems as suggested in this chapter?
2. Did the testing follow a sound, rational and repeatable structure?
3. Have you considered incremental replacement options as an alternative?
4. Has outsourcing business processes been considered as an alternative?
5. Is the programme documented in a proper business initiative proposal that treats the project as a programme by including all the business, process, people and organizational changes required?
6. Are sound governance practices and gateway management processes in place to control the programme?
7. Have you developed a risk management strategy?
8. Have you appointed the best possible project managers?
9. Has anyone projected possible business changes that might negate the need to transition the system?
10. Has anyone projected the lifespan of the replacement technologies?

14   Managing vendors

. . . no man is an island, entire of itself;
every man is a piece of the continent, a part of the main. (John Donne, 1572–1631)

The above is true of companies. Relationships with vendors and suppliers are often complex and frequently reflect misunderstandings and failed commitments over a long period of time. Poorly managed vendors can also waste extraordinary amounts of management time. Many years ago an IT manager kept a time and value diary of vendor contacts: who called, how long the visit or phone call lasted and the value obtained. The results showed 20% of the IT manager's time was spent in useless chatter. Less than one in twenty vendor contacts was of any use.

The trouble with vendors

Badly managed vendors are bad news! You have probably discovered vendors:

- fostering feral IT projects directly with business units in an attempt to gain a foot in the door;
- indulging in gouge-pricing strategies that are based on a short-term view of the relationship;
- failing to inform you of impending technology breakthroughs;
- making unplanned sales calls that waste time and are not focused on *your* needs;
- failing to adequately manage their maintenance responsibilities.

Well-managed vendors

The benefits of managing vendors effectively include:

- They have a clear appreciation of your expectations of *their* role and they work to meet it.

- Defined performance agreements that lead to improved service and supply.
- Controlled and productive use of face-to-face other forms of contact.
- Leads to a professional, harmonious relationship built around common long-term understanding.
- It may also rid you of a large number of besiegers.[q]

How do I do it?

The approach suggested here is built around four primary ingredients.

- Setting business-wide principles for vendor selection and management.
- Following an objective and sound process when selecting vendors.
- Limiting the number of vendors to a small manageable number.
- Agreeing service level agreements with vendors.

Set some principles for vendors

The idea of linking principles and vendors may sound incongruous but it can work. The process for setting principles is covered in Chapter 8. Make sure you include vendor management in this process. Some examples of topics that should generate principles are:

- How will we rank price, quality, service capability and product range in vendor selection?
- Will we adopt a preferred vendor strategy and if so what criteria will we use?
- Shall vendors be directed to a single point of contact in the business or will we encourage widespread contact across all departments and levels?
- What criteria will be used to remove a vendor from the preferred supplier list?

Each situation will generate its own issues and principles. What sits above is intended to stimulate thought. It is not an exhaustive list.

---

q Vendors that you don't wish to see because they offer nothing useful and do not understand the word "No".

> ## How many vendors do you have?
>
> Brendan Trezise, when he was Architecture and Planning Manager at Colonial Services, before its acquisition by the Commonwealth Bank, spent a considerable amount of time drawing up a framework for vendor management. The impetus behind this activity was two-fold. Firstly, as a large IT customer in the Australian marketplace, its staff were being subject to aggressive canvassing by suppliers anxious to promote their wares. Colonial saw that these circumstances were needlessly distracting many in IT and could result in different staff unknowingly wasting their time on similar projects. In addition, the company had no mechanism in place to leverage the buying power advantages presented by a diverse and large financial services group that had grown aggressively through acquisition. As such, there was a feeling that it was not realizing potential cost savings in IT.
>
> As a result of these concerns, Brendan began to investigate if there were common processes for IT supplier and contract management. He started by assessing each supplier in terms of the nature of the relationship it had with Colonial. He saw four styles of suppliers. Firstly, there were some suppliers whom Colonial dealt with on a transaction basis, typically supplying commodity items. The objective of this relationship from Colonial's perspective was solely looking for the best price. In others it had a project management association where effective project management was the key to success. As an extension of this Colonial also saw there was a growing group of suppliers who it dealt with as outsourcing suppliers. Finally, it recognized that some organizations had an ongoing and strategic relationship with the company.
>
> Colonial saw that understanding the nature of the relationship was the key to determining the resources it should invest in managing the relationship. As such, when it started the exercise it uncovered 500 IT suppliers in its contract database. However, when it analysed the relationship with these suppliers it found there were only 20 organizations that it would regard as key and 6 that could be regarded as strategic.

However, whatever you come up with will create a framework for vendor management which should serve you well. Two hints:

- *Make sure you involve your fellow executives in these principles as with any other.* If you fail to do so the vendors will find and exploit this weakness quickly—by approaching them directly.
- *Make sure that you let the vendors know the adopted principles.* You may need to rework the words and presentation so you can use the weasel word "company policy" to the recalcitrant.

Pick 'em carefully

Select your vendors carefully and objectively. Not only is this good practice but it also makes it simple for you to explain to your colleagues and besieging vendors why you made the choices you made.

The IT Outsourcing Guide[35] devotes three chapters to outsourcing vendor selection. This chapter has much less detail but the key recommendations are:

- Define the selection criteria in quantitative terms.
- Agree the selection criteria with your business peers.
- Rank the criteria using a numerical scale between 1 and 6 as shown in Table 14.1.

Table 14.1—Six levels of criteria

Criteria	Risk if absent	Pre-selection action
6. Essential	Unacceptable	Any RFP not meeting these criteria will be rejected.
5. Critical	Very high	Absence will put the company through serious inconvenience and will count heavily against candidates.
4. Important	High	Absence will put the company through inconvenience and cost and will be regarded as a serious shortcoming.
3. Preferred	Medium	Absence will create some cost and inconvenience. Absence may be counterbalanced by other criteria.
2. Marginal	Marginal	Absence may result in moderate inconvenience or cost. They will have a marginal effect on the selection process.
1. Low	Low	Absence will not result in any significant inconvenience or cost. The presence of these criteria may sway decisions if all else is equal.

- Include criteria in the following three areas: technology, commercial and organizational.
- Define the measures of fit for each criterion. For example, if you permit a fit between 1 and 6 then define what constitutes a "1", what constitutes a "2" and so on as shown in Table 14.1.
- Rate each candidate vendor against the criteria. This may be done in response to an RFI or RFP or by other forms of objective analysis (Figure 14.1).
- Perform the quantitative, financial and risk reviews of the selected candidates.

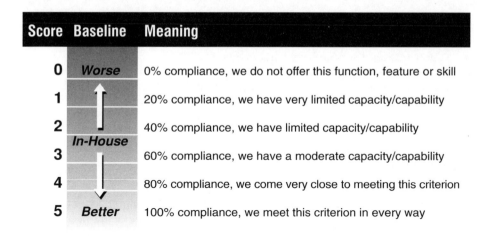

Score	Baseline	Meaning
0	*Worse*	0% compliance, we do not offer this function, feature or skill
1		20% compliance, we have very limited capacity/capability
2		40% compliance, we have limited capacity/capability
3	*In-House*	60% compliance, we have a moderate capacity/capability
4		80% compliance, we come very close to meeting this criterion
5	*Better*	100% compliance, we meet this criterion in every way

Figure 14.1—Scaled response form

- Allow time for reflection—the ranked scores are indicators, not decisions. Decisions require reflection and subjective judgement as well.

There is one difficulty with this approach. You are likely to select some vendors whose representatives are less than charming and vice versa. However, unless you rank charming sales representatives highly, this is a necessary outcome of proper work.

Limit the numbers

If you agreed sound principles and you also followed a sound selection process this should be a natural outcome. If it is not, then you may need to revisit your approach. Bear in mind:

- A large number of vendors will demand a considerable amount of your time to manage them.
- You may face difficulties integrating their offerings regardless of what they say about adherence to industry standards.
- It is also likely to drive up your resource numbers because of the wide range of differing skills which are required to manage their products. For example, if you deal with several database vendors you need expertise in each, regardless of the level of technical standardization promised.
- They will drive you up the wall—eventually.

Limiting the vendors allows you to:

- Negotiate sound service level agreements.
- Properly oversee performance.
- Spend quality time with their technical and sales professionals.
- Use your time effectively in monitoring the wider market.

Agree vendor SLAs

Your vendors will not like this suggestion. Even those consulting companies that have promulgated SLAs as a sound management practice suddenly become coy when you suggest the concept can be applied to them. This is perhaps the most critical action you can take in regard to vendor management. Chapter 10 tells you how to do it. SLAs offer a sound approach to managing vendors' outputs and performance. The nice thing about preparing them for vendors is that you are now customer-focused on outputs you want without having to worry about the challenge of wondering how they can be delivered.

The vendor SLA should also include some *additional*[r] items described below:

- Sales contact schedule and objectives.
- Technology briefings and objectives.
- Staff stability—you don't want a new rep every six months!
- Callback and response times on administrative and product inquiries as well as support and maintenance.
- Pricing agreements and notice of changes.
- Rewards and penalties based on performance.

Vendor service level agreements are *not* product maintenance agreements. Don't confuse the two. You may wish to incorporate product maintenance agreements within the scope of the vendor SLA but they are not the same thing.

Conclusion

Follow the above guidelines, and you will make the vendor's life and your own more stable and productive. Doing otherwise will leave you open to incessant

---

[r] Many of these could be included in internal service level agreements as well!

hammering at the door as vendors nervously seek your attention, which is not a good way to conduct business.

The vendors will baulk! The larger they are, the more they will scream about SLAs. Stick to your guns. Make accepting SLAs a condition of doing business with you.

A good IT manager will also share the future business and IT strategies with your key vendors. If they don't know where you are heading, they cannot help and contribute their resources and skills to your future programmes.

Checklist

1. Have you set principles to govern vendor management?
2. Have your fellow executives accepted those principles?
3. Have you informed your staff and others about the principles and their implications?
4. Have you informed the vendors?
5. Have you set up an organized and defensible method of selection?
6. Have you included criteria covering commercial and organizational criteria as well as technology?
7. Have you told the unsuccessful they are unsuccessful and why?
8. Have you developed SLAs for vendors?
9. Do they include required customer contact agreements as well as the more obvious output related measures?
10. Have you put some simple processes in place to implement and monitor performance?

15   Using consultants

The light that a man receiveth in counsel from another is drier and purer than that which cometh from his own understanding and judgement, which is ever infused and drenched by his affections and customs. (Francis Bacon)

Most IT managers have long recognized the truth of this fifteenth-century philosopher's statement. So much so that GartnerGroup estimate approximately 20% of staff in the "average" IT department today are externally sourced workers (ESW)[36] or consultants in one form or another. However, they need as much if not more management than your staff, and you may need to do it without the help of a Human Resources Department. You may also be less fearsome to consultants than employees.

In this chapter we deal with using consultants on small to medium-sized projects. David Pietsch provided much of the stimulus for the ideas promoted here.

Why is managing consultants an issue?

Frequently this is an issue because of poor selection followed by the failure of the employing company to ensure the consultants are given appropriate induction and adequate task specifications. Common complaints that result from poor management of consultants include:

- Consultants being assigned to projects who lack the appropriate experience and skill level.
- Consultants reusing previous consulting material and generating "standard" solutions to unique problems.
- Consultants charging for time spent, not results delivered.
- Consultants failing to understand their cost to the company.
- Consultants listening too closely to the squeaky wheel rather than objectively analysing the problem.
- Consultants working in isolation from the business and generating unusable proposals.

Poor results from consulting, whether measured in staff resentment, failed projects, useless reports and wasted money harms the business.

If you want to manage them right you will need to make sure some robust processes are adhered to. Doing it right may take time, but it will take less time than correcting the wrongs.

Understanding consulting fees

How do consultants set their rates? David Pietsch formerly ran his own software and consultancy company before he was enticed to run IT at the Melbourne distribution company Associate Retailers. As such, he recognized he could be viewed as something of a poacher turned gamekeeper. At an IDC InTEP meeting in 1997 on the topic of minimizing consultants he showed how most consultants set their hourly rates.

Firstly, they start with an aspired annual base salary plus an allowance for employment costs and taxes. At an entry point this would usually equate to a base salary of $70 000 plus $30 000 ancillary costs. This is doubled to cover costs such as overheads and non-chargeable items like training and marketing. This new figure is then divided by 1650, the number of chargeable hours in a year (37½ hours per week by 44 weeks). At an entry level this is $125 per hour. However, these fees go up depending on the firm's reputation, the nature of the assignment, the prevailing rates in the market and the perceptions of the expected benefits. It may pay to work backwards to see what your consultant suppliers are setting as their annual salary. You may have a good opportunity for negotiation!

Benefits

Well-managed consultants can:

- Offer great leverage to the IT department instead of undermining it.
- Contribute expertise well beyond the range of the internal unit.
- Bring an objective, arm's-length perspective to issues.
- Move more freely within the business, as they are often free of political taint.

Approach

The following steps can lead to more successful outcomes when using consultants on small to medium-sized projects.

Select carefully

Define the criteria for selection in advance—don't pick the first name out of the phone book! Ensure you agree on who precisely will work on the project, who in their company will mentor and monitor them and who will act as the contract agreement manager. Check the CVs of all three. If the consultant lacks a mentor or monitor ask how the vendor intends to undertake quality control. Check references and ask bold questions—and check the individual consultant's record with previous customers.

Define task specification

Ensure the task specification or work-contract specifies:

- Who will do the work and what your rights are in regard to termination for any reason, but most importantly failure to perform. Ensure you don't pay the consultant to rework the sub-standard deliverables!
- Define the inputs to the project, the expected processes and the outputs. Include the content, form and scale of the output.
- Demand a schedule that includes milestones and project reviews.
- Define the external participants (business or vendor) and specify their roles in the project.
- Determine and document how knowledge transfer will take place and how success will be measured in this arena. Never forget the consultant may walk away with a significant amount of undocumented knowledge in his or her head that may be lost to you for all time.
- Make sure each individual has their role in the project clearly defined and agreed. Don't overlook the BTOPP model. Ensure that the business, organization, people and process changes and accountability for managing all these aspects are defined and assigned.
- Be clear where the consultant's role starts and finishes. More so than with internal IT projects, your fellow workers are often too ready to be bystanders and watch a project crumble and crash when it's the consultant's head that will roll.
- Finally, make sure that overrun or *underrun* pricing is agreed. Motivate performance if necessary. There is nothing like remuneration at risk to stimulate clear focus, but beware it doesn't lead to short-cut answers.

Induct the consultant

Ensure that you give the consultant a proper induction. If your company runs regular induction programmes for new staff, include the consultant. If not, ensure that you brief them on the company, its history, goals, culture, key staff and expectations.

You can't do your job unless you know your "customer"—your company—and nor can the consultant. Make time to introduce them to the company, its history, its people and its practices. You are going to pay the consultant well. Ensure you improve the probability of their being successful on *your* project.

Introduce the consultant to those he or she may need to interview or consult. Ensure that each of these people is handed a summary of the task specification and understands their role in regard to it.

Provide resources

Provide the consultant with adequate resources. It is astounding how many companies will pay a consultant $2500 a day and then sit this expensive resource in a noisy corridor, without a phone or clerical support. Don't set up the consultant to waste time and effort undertaking clerical tasks in a sub-standard environment.

Ensure that you assign a "buddy" to the consultant to guide them on company protocols, introduce them to key people and assist them with general housekeeping. If this can be the same person as is the object of knowledge transfer, so much the better.

Monitor progress

This is a perennial problem with smaller projects that can quickly blow out to extraordinary levels. Make sure the project Task Specification and schedule makes it clear *when* reviews will take place and *what* will be reviewed at each meeting. Require the consultant to submit outlines of all proposed reports before they are written so that you can see if they are on the right track—or worth while—or even required.

Check other project participants' views of project progress. You do not need to hear any of your colleagues make the comment "It was evident from the first day that the consultant was off the rails" at the *end* of the project.

Compare progress to the schedule. This seemingly obvious task is often given cursory attention. Remember Rudyard Kipling's[37] servants when checking progress: ". . . What, and Where and When and How and Why and Who?". Question the consultant!

Educate the consultant

This may seem a surprising recommendation. Consultants often fail to appreciate their cost to the company. Take the example of a consultant employed to review a business opportunity and provide a 20-page feasibility report. If the consultant takes twenty days to complete the task at a day rate of $1000/day that distils down to $1000 a page or $2.50 per word! Point that out to the consultant and make them appreciate you want more than $1000 in value-added per page.

David Pietsch made two additional recommendations that have considerable value:

- Invest in long-term relationships.
- Remind them they are there to make you look good.

Unfortunately, consultants often feel they have to justify their existence by making what are often simplistic criticisms and derogatory remarks about the IT department. They forget how hard it is to implement change and often have an unwarranted view of their own superiority. Remind them that you hire them—and you are in charge—and that they are contract "employees".

Checklist

1. Have you got a clear definition of the tasks the consultant is expected to undertake?
2. Do the selection criteria for the consultant reflect the skills and competencies required?
3. Does the selection process adequately probe for and measure those criteria?
4. Have you developed task or assignment brief for the consultant and clearly specified the expected outputs?
5. Does it cover all the things required of the consultant, for example planning, reporting, monitoring, educating users, knowledge transfer and the like?
6. Have you got a packaged induction for consultants or can you insert them into the company induction programme?
7. Do the people who will be working with the consultant know their roles and responsibilities?
8. Have you made it clear that failure will benefit no one and that you will judge everyone involved by the consultant's success or failure?
9. Have the BTOPP considerations been included in the consultant's brief and role assignments?
10. Have you established your own monitoring schedule for the consultant?
11. Have you given the consultant an employee handbook if you have one, so they are aware of *your* company's standards and policies?
12. Have you ensured the consultant is introduced to all the people he may have to work with?

Business process re-engineering

The only things that evolve by themselves in an organization are disorder, friction and malperformance. (Peter Drucker in *Forbes Business Quotations*)

Some might argue that their engineering process is not within your domain as IT manager. It does not matter whether it is or not. You will need to factor it into your planning and your programmes. If you accept the BTOPP model then you will see it is fundamental to programme success.

The literature on business process re-engineering (BPR) is vast. A quick check of any major bookstore or on-line reference site will confirm this. This short chapter cannot replace thorough study in this arena.

IT involves everything

One common issue with BPR is failing to recognize the interplay of BTOP (Business, Technology, Organization and People) on process. Computer systems, forms, stationery, training, people, supervision, working hours—you name it: if you change process, you usually affect many of these. It evens spills into the areas of consultant management and vendor management because BPR frequently involves both.

You as IT manager are often better placed to understand this and guide your fellows than those whose jobs do not involve the regular management of change.

Some common weaknesses in BPR

One common weakness is failing to ask the important question: "Why do we do this at all?" rather than: "How do we improve this process?" A second problem is making the mistake of asking people to BPR themselves. This is tantamount to asking them to make a recommendation for their own redundancy. Equally common and problematical seems to be the assignment of untrained people to undertake BPR analysis and design.

The other side of this issue is the common one of hiring consultants and excluding company staff from the process. This can lead to savage resentment and the company winds up trying to push the solution onto an unwilling workforce.

Another mistake is to concentrate BPR on clerical tasks rather than the overarching company processes. Last but not least is the failure to bench-test the new or changed process and make a proper risk assessment of its BTOPP implications. The common effects of these failings include:

- Proposals that cannot be implemented because Business, Organization, Technology and People change were not adequately considered.
- Improvements in redundant processes—which is more common than imagined.
- Low-level low payback BPR projects that undermine the value of the BPR concept.
- Major disruptions resulting from attempting to bring in untested BPR processes.
- Changing the process without considering and managing the people, technology, organization or business implications of the change.

BPR is easy to mismanage. The reported failures are myriad. The probable reason is that too often it became a *project* focused on *process* rather than a *programme* focused on *change*.

Doing it the right way

Doing it the right way, in addition to correcting the above, the business should enjoy the following benefits:

- BPR projects that are aligned to corporate strategy and direction.
- Proper governance of BPR projects using the same techniques outlined in Chapter 9.
- Successful programmes that incorporate all BTOPP facets within the proposal.
- High-level BPR change that sweeps myriad low-level processes out of the door.

There are others but they are largely self-evident from the issues described in the opening to this chapter.

Some tips

This is *not* a formal approach to doing BPR! What is proposed here is a set of considerations that the IT manager needs to ensure are covered in any BPR project.

- Read about current BPR thinking and methods including process modelling and evolving BPR analysis techniques. This will give you a strong hand when discussing BPR with the consultants.
- Ensure the task is properly understood. Foremost you must define *why* the BPR project is being undertaken. Cover the issue, the outcome expected, the deliverables or outputs, the project schedule, participants, timetable, resources and other issues.
- Make sure the proposal to undertake BPR is well defined and documented. Use the business initiative proposal in Appendix B as a guide. All aspects of the programme need to be called out and approved by the Investment Committee.
- Ensure the BPR programme is managed through stage gates under the corporate governance regime described in Chapter 9. Make sure investment is careful, progressive and results based.
- Ensure that the team clearly understands the BTOPP programme concept. You cannot re-engineer process without consideration and change in these areas as well.
- Follow a sensible life cycle, similar to that for an IT project. Analyse, design, build, test, implement—but do so in an incremental manner.
- Select carefully, whether using consultants, internal staff or a combination of both. Follow the recommendations in Chapter 15, and apply them where it is appropriate to internal staff as well.
- Don't expect people to BPR themselves out of a job. That is one of the weaknesses of the warm and fuzzy team approach of asking people to BPR themselves. Involve them but be realistic.
- Select and commence work on the highest-level processes you can. Work from the top down. If the high-level process is invalid, then you can sweep a lot of low-level processes away with limited effort.
- Ensure the current and proposed process are properly documented and the gap analysis complete.
- Ignore exceptions until you have dealt with the standard. Do not allow the process engineering project to fail because 0.0001% of the time an exception occurs that seems at odds with the re-engineered process.
- If vendors or suppliers are likely to be affected in any way, include them in the project as early as possible.

BPR is a subject that has created a sizeable literature that reports on the successes and failures. It has also evolved from the simple "time and motion" studies of the

1950s to the full-scale revamping of business and electronic process modelling using sophisticated mathematical theories.

However, these reports generally paint a dismal view of BPR implementation. Armchair analysis suggests that in many cases insufficient thought may have been given to the BTOPP facets of the project.

A common excuse made for BPR projects is "lack of executive support". This excuse is also common in excusing IT project failures. This is not a satisfactory explanation. If the executives of the business failed to support the project, then ask what was wrong with the project. Don't blame the executives for not enforcing an unworkable or unrealistic programme of change.

Finally, remember that BPR opportunities are great but resistance to BPR is greater! Hammer and Champey[38] made a statement to the effect that BPR projects started and failed in the executive suite. They were right. What they might have added is that the executive suite should perhaps be the first focus of BPR.

Checklist

1. Has the programme been proposed in a satisfactory manner, preferably using a template similar to the business initiative proposal?
2. Have all the BTOPP implications been spelt out and assigned?
3. Has the Investment Committee set a suitable set of investment gates?
4. Have the people assigned to the programme been given clear definitions of their roles, deliverables and responsibilities?
5. Have the staff who will be affected by the programme been informed about the goals and aims?
6. Have the legal and employment law issues been considered?
7. Have you bench-tested the proposed new process?
8. Do you have to do the research? Is there a competitor or supplier whose process you can copy?
9. Have all the small items, like stationery, forms, etc. been considered?
10. Has anyone told the customer . . .?

17 Benchmarking

Take heed of computation!
How woefully and wretchedly we have been misled by it! (John Owen, Chancellor of
Oxford University, 1690)

The issue you face with benchmarking and performance measurement is that it is
often done poorly, if at all. Further, those performance targets that are set are often
arbitrary and fail to consider infrastructure limitations or other constraints. Rarely
do they make a distinction between business measures (outputs) and technology
or IT measures (inputs). None of this is good news for an IT manager who may
experience the following unpleasant side-effects:

- Business units complaining that your IT people fail to understand what is
  critical to the business.
- Both business and IT expending effort and money on low-value but highly
  emotive targets.
- A failure to link the services demanded and the cost to provide those services.
- Your staff complaining they are faced with ever-moving goalposts.

The benefits of good benchmarking

Among the many benefits of good benchmarks and associated service level agreements are:

- Clarity on what the business values as outputs from IT.
- Sound budget models based on service demands.
- Proper projection of the effects of growth and change on constraining
  resources.
- Clear distinction between those measures that IT should focus on and those
  that belong outside of IT.
- Shared cost and effort in measuring. In many cases this will be incurred by
  paying an external benchmarking consultant.

- Sound change management processes that allow measures to be reset in an atmosphere of cooperation and understanding rather than confrontation and conflict.

Colgate Palmolive[39] found the following additional benefits:

- Benchmarks provided feedback to IT staff on their performance.
- Benchmarks allowed management to assess IT performance. Tony Talbot[40] pointed out that "as these managers are the final arbitrators on the allocation of funding it is essential to provide them with objective yardsticks by which they can determine the value of IT to the organization".
- Colgate Palmolive also experienced quantum leaps in performance, as there seemed to be a natural desire to beat established key performance indicators.

Obtaining and setting benchmarks

The task is complex and unless you have staff experienced in this work you may find it cheaper and faster to use an appropriately skilled consulting group to undertake this task as was done by the Commonwealth Bank of Australia:[41] "CBA assigned a dedicated project manager to oversee the due diligence. Gartner consulting provided financial and resource consumption templates. Gartner Measurement provided benchmarking studies to compare CBA against representative peer groups."

The consultant will normally have access to a variety of:

- Templates and tools for measurement.
- Benchmarks from peer organizations.
- Specialist expertise.

The expert should:

- Identify all things that are to be measured both as inputs and outputs.
- Establish the current measures for these things.
- Document the environment in which those measures are achieved.
- Note any infrastructure or other impediments to measure improvement.
- Compare the measures against best practice where possible.
- Ensure that recommendations for any improvements consider all the BTOPP implications.

The current measure of things

Do not make the mistake of ignoring the need to establish current benchmarks just because the task is lengthy, tedious and prone to significant error. You must ensure that the process of measurement ensures that constraints on improved performance are identified.

If you do this, then you can properly consider whether demands from business units to achieve improvements are achievable or whether there are infrastructure or resource constraints. Don't be tempted to skip this step. If constraints exist in LAN bandwidth or CPU throughput, then these may define the upper limits to performance under the service level agreements. Therefore the expert may also need to measure response times, packet collisions or function points delivered per programmer day *if* they are in some way germane to the delivery of the business objectives.

If you are new to the company you may find you've just inherited a unit performing at its optimal level or a legacy of poor performance because of poor process, outdated documentation, sub-optimal skills and poor management structure.

Measuring business outputs

The business will normally be interested in outputs; licences, policies, metres of fibreboard, tonnes of steel or bottles of beer. You as IT manager will also be interested in technical measures because you expect to measure, manage and control your unit's *technical* activities.

PA Consulting Group stated the difference in the following way: "In general terms, the IT unit's interests lie in specifying low level parameters, whereas the business user's interests lie in specifying and managing high level outcomes."[42] The IT manager's low-level technical measures are of no interest to the business executive if the resultant *business* activity is disrupted. For example, disk usage, transaction response, and bandwidth usage may be entirely satisfactory while an important business output has failed abjectly because of an operational error screwing up the end-of-month processing.

The bad news is that measures of business outputs are frequently difficult to define and are often affected by external variables. Success will, however, come from doing the hard and difficult work of identifying and agreeing sensible outputs. This is a good reason for using an honest broker in the form of a third-party organization to establish current measures of business outputs and what is reasonable to expect IT to achieve as future goals.

We suggest the adoption of a balanced scorecard. GartnerGroup's newsletter (*Inside GartnerGroup This Week*, **XV**, No. 36, 9 September 1999) provides an excellent article on the subject. It suggests that the manager uses a family of scorecards, including The Strategic IT Balanced Scorecard which applies to the whole IT organization and an Operational IT Balanced Scorecard that, in the main applies to the set of activities within the IT organization.

Rose-coloured spectacles

Ensure that current business levels of performance and the IT contribution are recorded. There is no doubt that a number of people will in the future retain rosy memories of a wonderful past, which are based on splendid but imaginary levels of performance.

Collecting the data

The measurers also have to ensure that if it becomes necessary to delegate data collection to internal staff that they have a vested interest in ensuring it is both accurate and complete. ICI's (now Orica) Ian Mackay[43] warned against using staff without any vested interest. He also suggested that it is important that the people collecting the data "understood it and could do a quick sanity check on it [for accuracy and completeness]."

Selecting measures

Frequently challenge *what* is proposed to be measured and exhaustively question *why, why, why*. Challenge every proposed measure until there is no doubt they are valuable and acceptable to the business and IT. Some possible questions include:

- Why is this measure important?
- What does it tell us?

- What can affect it?
- What can IT do to control this performance measure?
- Who else or what else can control it?
- What will happen if IT exceeds the measure?
- What will happen if IT fails the measure?

Types of measures

Business outputs

These are difficult to define in advance but will typically be things the business produces such as:

- Creditor statements
- Cheque or payment transactions
- Invoices
- Reports
- Product (e.g. tonnes steel, insurance policies, freight manifests)
- Services (e.g. call-centre responses, banking transactions).

Clearly all are or may be influenced by any number of elements. However, they form the basis of legitimate measures and IT has a significant role in meeting them.

IT operations measures

Don't forget to cover the often-overlooked area of operational efficiency and effectiveness. Do take measures and do not be afraid to set benchmarks for the following areas of concern to IT and the business:

- Back-up and recovery
- Periodic processes such as month-end and year-end
- Disk farm management
- Maintenance management
- Batch management
- Security management
- Change management

While these things may seem skewed to IT input measurement they often lie at the heart of performance disputes as the inevitable growth in file sizes extend things like backup and recovery time. Your business colleagues need to comprehend that speed and duration of these processes is limited by hardware and utility throughput. Now is the time to establish the understanding that reducing duration or improving speed may only be possible with the purchase of additional hardware or upgraded software.

These measurements can also support investment proposals to overcome the frequent reluctance to purchase systems management tools required to deliver improvements in operations management. These include network management, systems management, change control and security management products.

Take cognizance of these factors from the outset. Some improvement in operations quality and efficiency may take place without substantial investment. However, both parties need to understand the investment necessary to move beyond that point.

Infrastructure measures

Infrastructure measures normally include:

- Response times.
- Network error rates.
- MTBF (Mean Time Between Failures) on critical hardware.

Do not overlook the fact that infrastructure performance control may lie outside of IT. The IT department cannot directly influence MTBF; it is a manufacturing quality decision. Do also consider potential contributors to overall success such as poor-quality cable plant that can seriously affect actual and perceived response times and network stability.

Make sure that the business understands that there are limits to what IT can control. Many units can relate stories of irate colleagues who blame power failures, flood damage and hardware failure on the IT unit staff. The business and IT must be clear about what is to be regarded as a performance failure and what is to be regarded as an "act of God" or outside agency failure.

The operating units and IT also need to agree in advance on the limitations of the current infrastructure, for example, the user ceiling for the current network, processor or data storage device that may limit the achievement of preferred measures.

Project measures

These are often generic in content with a few key parameters tuned to the specific project. Nevertheless, the prudent manager will enter into a service level agreement and associated measures with the business owner covering expected output during the project and from the "deliverable".[s]

Never overlook the need to agree the accountabilities and responsibilities on *both* sides of the fence as part of the process.

Common contributors to failings with project measures include:

- The failure of business staff to meet deadlines for sign-off and tasks such as user testing. Consider what penalties IT may impose on the business unit, for example charging them for idle staff time.
- Inadequate user testing which allows specification faults to carry into production. Consider the penalties that might be levied on the business unit for this, for example penalty rates for remedial programming.

The keys to introducing satisfactory project measures include:

- Clearly defining the responsibilities and accountabilities of each party.
- Ensuring that accountabilities and responsibilities incorporate the BTOPP facets.
- Defining the standard method or steps that will be followed for each project.
- Sound change management process to ensure project deviation is properly approved.

Agree these issues before any programme is undertaken. Ensure all staff involved in the project are aware of them.

Help desk measures

The help desk merits a section of its own. In many businesses it is the focal point of criticism. Typical help desk measures include:

- Time to fulfil procurement requests.
- Wait-time for training.
- Wait-time for loading new software acquired by the business.
- Wait-time for requested hardware upgrades and new peripherals.
- Time to assign a member of staff to the problem.
- Duration from assignment to observable action on the problem.
- Time to remedy the problem.
- Number of problems fixed on first contact (call).
- Satisfaction rating measuring courtesy, completeness, recalls and satisfactory job closure.

[s] Deliverable is the output from the project. This may be a package implementation, in-house software, hardware upgrade or other.

There are others and the field is open to more as the desktop becomes an increasingly sophisticated tool supporting additional peripherals such as digital cameras and PDAs.

The chapter following on desk-top management includes a useful table of help desk call types. This may prove useful in categorizing help desk measures.

Not the help desk

Two of the above measures do not properly belong to the help desk and you should see that they are passed on to the appropriate people.

First is procurement, which is the business of purchasing officers. It should be delegated to procurement. It makes no sense to treat personal computers as an exception to standard procurement processes. Many purchasing officers acquire much more sophisticated equipment than PCs from a wider range of suppliers.

Second is training, which is the business of trainers. It should be delegated to training that is commonly under the stewardship of the Human Resources department. It is a nonsense to include it within IT.

This latter point is significant. Many of the problems relate to the use of packaged desktop software. Analysis suggests that a significant proportion of calls to help desks is to inquire how to carry out simple processes that are related to application function. IT staff may often have less reason to use word processing, presentation software or spreadsheets than business people may. They therefore lack familiarity with the software. Often the request for support will require them to study manuals or call the vendors for help.

Issues with help desk measures

Some of the other issues that surround help desk measures commonly include a reluctance to enforce sound management disciplines on the desktop. For example:

- The business may be reluctant to implement a standard desktop operating environment (SOE). This leaves users free to alter configurations and settings and so trigger unpredictable and untraceable failures.

- A second common problem is staff requesting the resetting of user passwords. This may account for as much as 25% of help desk calls. A problem like this suggests that something is wrong in the management of passwords rather than the technology.

The other measures seem to suffer from the difficulty of a large number of staff needing to maintain accurate records about when problems were passed to them and what they did about it. Their problems are exacerbated by continually changing priorities that divert them from their daily work plan. It would seem that the focus of help desk measures should be on eliminating the issues that give rise to many of the calls.

Companies seeking to control this area have followed a number of steps. These include:

- Implementing a standard desktop environment.
- Removal of diskette drives and CD drives to inhibit loading of unauthorized software.
- Constraints on downloading software from Internet or bulletin boards.
- Formal training as a prerequisite for software access.
- User self-help units including "expert user" support in the business units.
- Improved password management regimes.

You may wish to consider these. Whatever steps you take, you will need to make sure that your colleagues in the business understand the limitations that apply to help desk management, and agree in advance what steps can and cannot be taken to control the user environment.

Statistics, statistics and damn lies

When measuring levels of performance, consider using statistical method to obtain sensible measures. Ideally, you should make sure that the consultant measures ranges, modes and medians to gain a complete picture of the pattern of current achievement. This is generally superior to a single number, which can be very misleading. (For example, in a set of five closely spaced measures with one outlier, the average can be a very misleading number.)

Consider the pattern of numbers in Table 17.1. The risk here is that a performance level of 96% may be set which is 2% better than "average". However, this would allow delivery of a much poorer level of performance than has been

Table 17.1—Averaging benchmarks

Measure	Achieved percentage
January	98.0
February	98.5
March	72.7
April	98.0
May	98.5
June	98.0
Average	**94.0**

achieved in five of the six previous months. In this example, the mode or *most frequent measure* of 98% is a far sounder choice.

What about the environment

Make sure that that the consultant or staff member properly documents the context or environment in which these measures were taken. The environment should define, where appropriate:

- The current numbers of users, preferably broken down into categories of light, medium and power users.
- Details of the hardware platforms, both servers and desktops.
- The current application scope preferably listing all modules.
- The version of the operating systems (server and desktop), and network operating system in use.
- Other infrastructure details, such as cable and hub-router configuration.

Any change in any of these environmental factors may affect the performance positively or negatively. The most pernicious change usually occurs in application software where incremental modifications add up to significant change over time. This is important as you must "Guard against the danger that people will develop a rosy view of past performance and past allegiances."[44]

Considerations with future benchmarks

The single most awkward issue in defining target measures is that substantial and unpredictable change may take place, or need to take place, in the environment in which the future measures are to be delivered:

- Substantial changes may occur in the environment that might militate against the achievement of desired levels of performance. Business population growth, modified applications, changed hardware, infrastructure or business operations may drive these.
- Target measures may require substantial change in the environment or business processes if they are to be achieved. At one end of the scale, the changes may demand business users conform to new disciplines. At the other end, it may require considerable expenditure on new equipment or tools. Make some allowance for the implications of such changes.
- As mentioned, there will be inherent limitations in infrastructure capacity. IT units resound with stories of organizations that demand transaction speed improvements with the same hardware or for operating windows to be extended without providing tools to reduce backup time.

There is at least one other facet of the current benchmarks and target measures that can lead to considerable angst if not trapped at this stage. This is the existence of shadow IT staff that currently participate in delivering those outputs. These may be sub-contractors, business experts or suppliers who may not be under the control of the IT unit and their costs may be hidden. Beware!

Give yourself time

The task of measurement is large. Ian Mackay,[45] IT manager at ICI (now Orica), found: "that data collection was a major and laborious task . . . ICI found that the only way to go was to collect a representative sample of around 10 per cent." He went on to say that it took approximately two months to prepare for collection, a week to gather the data and two months to validate the results. We suggest that both data collected to establish measures and to measure performance can be based on statistical samples rather than entire populations.

Summary

Hire measurement experts, make sure they are properly briefed and managed. Refer to Chapter 15 if you need further guidance.

Measure the present performance of IT and business benchmarks alike and document the current state of the environment and capacity and capability of all resources involved in the process.

Relentlessly challenge all new performance measures until you are convinced they are worth while and that by achieving them you improve your company's performance.

Also define the hardware, software, skill improvements or staffing changes required to bring about the change and maintain it.

Do not allow yourself to be led into making unreasonable commitments. If it is physically impossible to deliver the improvements on the current infrastructure or with the current staff composition, then it stands to reason that improvements cannot be delivered unless these are changed.

And finally make sure that measures and performance targets are based on formal statistical method, selecting the best measure (range, mean, mode and acceptable deviations). Do not fall into the trap of accepting simplistic averages as either current measures or future targets.

Checklist

1. Have you measured the present?
2. Did the measurer include an assessment and description of the environment and people achieving the measures?
3. Have you identified any limitations to improving measures?
4. Are the new benchmarks business output oriented?
5. Do you know which factors are inside your control with these measures?
6. Have you drawn attention to the factors outside your control and ensured they will be managed?
7. Do the people collecting data have a vested interest in its completeness and accuracy?
8. Has sound statistical method been applied to old and new benchmarks?
9. Have you defined what will be needed to achieve the new benchmarks?
10. Does the business manager agree—and can the funds or resources necessary to achieve them be provided?
11. Have the BTOPP requirements of the new measures been fully identified and assigned to appropriate people?

18 Help desk management

When a person responds to the joys and sorrows of others as if they were his own, he has attained the highest state of spiritual union. (The Bhagavad Gita (6:32))

The choice of quotation is neither cynical nor blasphemous. Help desk management frequently demands exceptional consideration for the needs of others.

If you've just finished the previous chapter on "Benchmarking" you might wonder what else could be said about the desktop. The reason it is given such a high profile is simply because dealing with desktop issues is often the most visible, contentious, frustrating and demoralizing part of your job. We have reached a stage in the evolution of IT where a mainframe shutdown affecting the whole company dwarfs by comparison with the angst created by a glitch in an executive's laptop five minutes before a presentation. (The manufacturers have designed them so that they only ever break down five minutes before a presentation.)

Many of the suggestions in this chapter derived from a presentation made at an InTEP forum in Sydney by Dean Wilkinson, then of the Commonwealth Bank. If you didn't read the previous chapter then it will help to look over the section on help desk benchmarking.

Issues

Help desk management is probably the single most contentious area facing IT management today. The problems experienced by users are often trifling in comparison with the other operational problems faced by the department. However, an office worker having problems with word processing is likely to demand more help, more quickly than a runaway process that is in danger of crashing a mission-critical system. Part of the blame does lie with IT who have consistently placed low-level junior staff on the help desk and given the overall help desk management area little proper *analytical* management attention.

The boxed text from a 1998 GartnerGroup report categorizes calls into two groups. Request Calls and Help Calls. This form of analysis can prove invaluable in developing strategies to deal with the demands on help desk personnel and developing the appropriate mix of help desk skills.

Help desk call types

Request Calls

- *Service Requests.* IT and non-IT-related service calls (or status checks on requests) regarding a range of support-specific service offerings.
- *Changes.* User-placed calls resulting in changes to the IT infrastructure that are not a result of an IT infrastructure failure.
- *Moves.* A sub-set of change calls, moves are end-user calls regarding the physical or virtual movement of IT resources or physical assets. (In another document Gartner identified the cost of a single PC move at US$320).
- *Adds.* A subset of change calls, adds are specific—end-user-placed calls requesting guidance on how to install or upgrade end-user IT resources.

Help calls

- *How To.* End-user-placed calls regarding how to accomplish, access or operate IT resources.
- *Break/Fix.* End-user calls placed as a result of a problem with accomplishing, accessing or operating IT resources.
- *Password Reset.* A specialized end-user call regarding establishing or regaining access to privileged IT resources.
- *Outage.* A specialized case of end-user break/fix call regarding a substantial group of end-users (flood calls); calls are placed to the help desk to inform, inquire or complain about accomplishing, accessing or operating IT resources.

Reproduced by permission of the GartnerGroup.

User attitudes to help desk management are akin to airline passengers' attitudes to aircraft. The engineering and airline crew understand that it is critical that avionics, airframe, engines, rudders, and navigation systems operate perfectly as mass incineration results from the failure in these components. Technical IT people likewise concentrate their efforts on the technology infrastructure that lies behind the help desk service.

The average passenger, on the other hand, probably does not give these things more than a momentary consideration and judges the airline on the quality of the meal tray. Likewise, the average user often judges the help desk, and by inference the IT department, on aspects that technical professionals consider trivial.

Effects

The effects of poor help desk management tend to be:

- Users measuring the whole of IT performance on this single area.
- Excessive consumption of IT management time smoothing ruffled feathers.

- Escalating costs as we add more and more PC and network staff in an effort to reach an unattainable goal.
- The IT manager and his department become the scapegoat for poor staff training in using what are now basic business tools.

Benefits

A well-managed help desk can:

- Eliminate some of the prime triggers for help desk calls.
- Place accountability for business tool usage with the right people who can address any shortcoming. (There is no point in just buck passing the problem. Seek to have it addressed.)
- Educate users about costs and so control them.
- Reduce incidents that destabilize the LAN and operating infrastructure.
- Develop self-sufficiency in the right areas of user desktop management.

Approach

It was tempting to make an exception of this chapter and write a lengthy text on help desk management! The guidance that follows is by necessity brief but it should be sufficient to point the able manager towards some potential solutions. This chapter focuses on internal help desk management but many of the lessons can be applied to external (customer, agent, supplier) help desk support.

- *Put your best people on the help desk.* These people need to have sound communication, self-management and technical skills. They are the front line to the business. The help desk is not the entry point for IT staff. Let there be no argument about this. One major financial institution put its MBA graduates on its customer help desk. Why? The customers were serious investors. When they phoned in they wanted to talk to knowledgeable financial experts about their investments, not to unsophisticated junior staff who had never bought stock in their lives. The same lesson applies to the IT help desk. Overall a well managed help desk can cost a fraction of a poorly managed help desk.

  Gartner later observed that the difference between the worst and the best labour cost for help desk management ranged from $745 (worst) to $88 best.[46]

Gartner also noted that "How to" (27%) and "Password reset" (25%) accounted for more than half (i.e. 52%) of help desk calls!

- *Reward your help desk staff*—make the help desk a place to aspire to, not a place to avoid. That will happen if you put the best people there. You will pay much more per head but probably less overall as you may need fewer but more competent staff.
- *Install a help desk system that enables you to monitor service and measure trends and identify causes.* These may be recurrent hardware faults or training issues (most common). If the problem is hardware based then evaluate the cost of replacing the lemons. It is maddening to see hours and hours of desktop support put into a faulty printer that could be replaced for less than $500.
- Establish SLAs for help desk support that includes:
  - Criteria for ranking the criticality of calls and therefore the "to fix" targets.
  - Response time measured as the time between the call being made and the problem being attended to, not fixed. This should differ according to criticality.
  - User obligations including training, call protocols, self-help, and work-arounds. The Commonwealth Bank of Australia issues each user with a credit card-sized card that reminds users of these requirements.
- Establish and *enforce* policy on games, meddling with configuration parameters and using illegal or personal software. Use an auditor to carry out a quarterly inspection and take action against offenders. This can range from a simple "lock down" of diskette drives and removal of Internet access software to dismissal.
- Analyse the trigger for help desk calls. If the problem is a lack of user skill, talk to the HR unit about running appropriate applications training sessions and also raising the barrier to entry for staff. Do not volunteer the IT department as the *de-facto* trainer in desktop applications. Don't fool yourself. IT staff have no special skill as educators or with desktop application areas. The business should use professional trainers who are expert both in teaching and in the appropriate applications.
- Set user expectations. A memorable comment made by Dean Wilkinson of the Commonwealth Bank at a conference some years ago was: "The only requirement most users have is for their problem to be fixed as quickly as possible." Refer to Gartner, IDC, Norton Nolan and similar research material and data to educate the users about the cost of help desk calls. Include this type of information in the Help Desk Newsletter.
- Tie the service to budget. Research points to a ratio of about 1:50 help desk analysts to users if you wish to provide an effective level of service. Most companies are not prepared to pay for this level of support. Strive to strongly convey the message that *you get what you pay for.*
- Circulate—by e-mail is fine—a monthly one-page newsletter on trends, tips, issues and future plans from the help desk.

- Maintain proper asset details. Too many help desk problems are triggered by IT staff making inventory changes that are in conflict with part of the existing configuration. You may find Chapter 25 worth visiting on this subject.
- Each month seek out the top 20% or so of help desk callers and establish why *they* make more calls than anyone else does. Typically you will find the Pareto principle or 80:20 rule applies. Twenty per cent of the staff make 80% of the calls. Fix them and you reduce the burden considerably.
- Join your local help desk institute or association if there is one. They can provide invaluable information including benchmark measures and ongoing advice.

None of the above tasks is difficult to undertake. The single most challenging is overcoming the common habit of putting the least experienced and often immature staff in charge of this key process.

Checklist

1. Have you clearly defined the role of the help desk in your organization?
2. Have you made sure that the business understands what the help desk is there to do, and *not* there to do?
3. Have you arranged with others to provide those services traditionally associated with the help desk that belong elsewhere?
4. Have you developed service level agreements to cover help desk support?
5. Do the service level agreements include the users' responsibilities?
6. Have you got the vendors of desktop products and services bound by SLAs that further your interests?
7. Have you taken measurements of current performance and set measures for improved performance on the help desk?
8. Have you considered and actioned the BTOPP initiatives required to support these improvements?
9. Have you installed a decent help desk management and reporting system that enables you to focus on the critical?
10. Have you got the nerves to put your best people on the help desk?

19 Disaster recovery planning

. . . caught in a tide of death from which there is no escaping, death in the fruitful flowering of the soil, death in the pastures . . . and pestilence, a fiery demon gripping the city . . . to fatten hell. (Priest in *Oedipus Rex*)

It will never happen to me

Jon William Toigo wrote an excellent book[47] on disaster recovery planning. He quotes the following statistics for the loss of the computer centre.

1. The average company will lose 2–3% of its gross sales within 8 days of a sustained outage.
2. The average company that experiences a computer outage lasting longer than 10 days will never fully recover. 50% will be out of business within 5 years.
3. The chances of surviving a disaster affecting the corporate data processing centre are less than 7 in 100. The chances of experiencing a disaster are 1 in 100.

More frightening are the statistics by industry type that shows a two-day maximum downtime allowance for the financial sector, and three days for the distribution sector.

None of this will surprise staff from those small to medium-sized companies that closed down after the floods in the UK, the fierce winter storms in the USA or the earthquakes in Turkey and South America during 2000. Larger companies tend to be distributed and more resilient. The damage to them is local not global.

Toigo makes no mention of what happens to IT managers who preside over these disasters without a recovery plan. It may be that the violence meted out to them is X-rated.

The crux of the matter

The crux of the problem is simple—few small to medium-sized companies bother with any form of disaster recovery plan[t] (DRP). If they do it is often an IT backup recovery plan which is of limited use when faced with fire, flood or earthquake. One suspects the reason that larger companies are more conscientious is because banks, insurance companies, chemical manufacturers, petroleum distillers and the like face regulatory demands to have disaster recovery plans.

This chapter does not tell you how to carry out a DRP planning exercise. It seeks instead to highlight some things you should consider in managing the development of such a plan.

Without a DRP

Lack of a DRP may have the following outcomes:

- Serious financial loss including business closure.
- Consequent litigation for damages by shareholders and others.
- Escalation of minor incidents into major disasters as a result of inappropriate response.

With a DRP

The typical benefits include:

- Structured and rationale response to incidents and disasters.
- Consideration of all the BTOPP components in the response.
- Tested and assured procedures that work.
- Lower insurance premiums—maybe.

One second-order effect of good DRP is that it often acts as a *de-facto* form of business process re-engineering (BPR). DRP requires proper analysis of key

---

[t] The pedantic might argue that disaster recovery plans and business continuity plans are not synonymous. This text treats them as similar, meaning they are close enough in shape and texture to be interchangeable for our purposes.

processes in order to design protective measures. This study often turns up a number of opportunities for re-engineering and cost reduction.

Next steps

Often the first task facing the IT manager is convincing business colleagues that the risks are real and the investment necessary! Some cues are:

- Investigate whether legislation requires DRP for your business type. Both federal and state legislation exists in some countries.
- Gather statistics—use external research groups to gather data on the issue.
- Use your auditors—many of those which offer DRP services to clients will have useful support data.
- Cost-justify the plan based on risk and probability. Include potential cost of lost sales, customer dissatisfaction, legal fees and fines. Calculate the effect of downtime based on average wages for employees.
- Include the potential for BPR savings based on a small percentage of the wage costs of the key processes to be analysed and projected.

The second major task is to convince the organization that DRP must cover the BTOPP model. There is no point in recovering the technology component of the business model if the organizational, people and process aspects are not equally organized to support the recovery. This means consideration must be given to such things as:

- Office equipment and stationery—fax, telephone, forms and other paraphernalia of the common office.
- Facilities including offices, desks, chairs, benches and the like.
- Reference materials including price books, catalogues etc.
- Logistics—how will people be notified and if necessary how will they go to their new workplace?
- Press and publicity management—how will the disaster be communicated to suppliers, customers, shareholders and others?

The third task is to select a planner and planning system that is competent. This requires that they show proof they have the following:

- Appropriate experience demonstrated by other projects. You must contact their customers and obtain a view of their satisfaction.
- Appropriate tools to diagnose potential disasters and model, document and test appropriate responses.

- Ensuring the DRP focuses on the critical procedures required for business continuity. That makes the plan manageable in action, as well as keeping the costs under control.
- Plan maintenance tools. Maintaining a DRP can be a time-consuming job. It needs to be made as easy as possible. There is software available. Use it if appropriate.

The fourth task is to enter the agreement with the DRP consultant. This should follow the guidelines in Chapter 10 on SLAs and Chapter 15 on managing consultants. Some tips:

- Make absolutely sure that the risks and probabilities are determined so you plan for the probable, not the improbable.
- Make sure the plan is reflective of the (high) probability of appropriate disaster types.
- Make sure the processes selected for DRP are critical, not ancillary.
- Make sure the plan, agreement and terms of reference include all parties under the BTOPP model.
- Keep the plan at a reasonably high level. Now is the time to remember Von Moltke's[48] words: "In general, one does well to order no more than is absolutely necessary and to avoid planning beyond the situations one can foresee." When disaster does strike you will find "In war, as in art, we find no universal forms; in neither can a rule take the place of talent."
- These words are a timely reminder that help keep the depth and scope of the plan at an appropriate level. The circumstances of disaster are such that sound guiding principles and direction are required, not detailed procedures that may be totally at odds with the actual circumstances.
- Make sure the plan's development follows the "gate" principle described in Chapter 9. It must follow a series of incremental approved steps to completion. The first milestone should be completion of the initial analysis and risk assessment.

A DRP at some level is an absolute necessity in any business. Regardless of its quality and depth it will help to prevent the management of the disaster lapsing into blind arbitrary action. Read Toigo's book and other related material, talk to DRP specialists and then arrange for a plan to be developed that is practical and prudent. Above all, keep it simple and remember BTOPP.

Checklist

1. Can anyone find the current DRP if it exists?
2. Are copies stored offsite so they can be accessed outside the disaster zone?

3. Does the DRP process include stocks of basic items such as stationery, chequebooks, company forms (i.e. investment prospectuses, invoices, insurance policy application forms, etc.)?
4. Does the DRP consider transport requirements to any recovery site?
5. Does the DRP include a communication plan to deal with media, customers, staff and suppliers?
6. Does the DRP consider the BTOPP issues of recovery, not just IT?
7. Has the cost of a disaster recovery programme been modelled?[u]
8. Has anyone modelled the cost of *not* having a DRP?
9. Have the benefits of the DRP process been exploited in the form of new or remodelled business processes?
10. Do the current (accurate) asset and human resources records form part of the DRP appendices?

---

[u] The modelling would cover *all* possible costs. If the figure is not frightening, then review it.

20 Managing change

Observe always that everything is the result of a change, and get used to thinking that there is nothing Nature loves so well as to change existing forms and to make new ones like them. (Marcus Aurelius (121–180), *Meditations. iv*)

The issue with change management in information systems environments is that it is too often technically focused. It is not "change management" but software promotion.[v] It frequently ignores the BTOPP model and associated hardware and network impacts.

As with many of the other issues there exists a comprehensive body of knowledge on change covering every aspect from human behaviour to technical management. This chapter provides guidance on what seems to be *lacking* in many of the texts that concentrate on the psychology or technical management of change. Major bookshops stock a comprehensive range of texts on these skills. These aspects are not covered in this chapter.

Narrowly focused change management

Some effects of narrowly focused change management include:

- Failure to include the organization, people and process changes related to the (customarily) software or hardware change.
- Failure to consider second order or downstream effects of the change.
- A failure to assess all the risks in both the technical and organizational sphere and a failure therefore to mitigate these risks.
- Overlooking the need to inform and perhaps involve external parties such as suppliers, customers and agents.
- Overlooking cultural obstacles to change or trying to introduce methods, beliefs and processes alien to the receiving national or business culture.

---

[v] Software promotion is a term used to describe the progression of software from the development environment, to a testing environment and finally to a production environment.

Paul Kennedy[49] in his fine book *Preparing for the 21st Century*, stated "Cultural obstacles to change are common to all societies, for the obvious reason that an impending transformation threatens existing habits, ways of life, beliefs and social prejudices." Cultural obstacles to change will stand in the way of business change as well. Indeed, Kennedy went on to paint a picture of the complicated and deep-rooted obstacles to changing the nature of Western businesses to cope with the (now toothless) Asian tigers. One might expect similar cultural resistance to introducing a regime of dark suits, white shirts and dark ties to Apple Computer.

Eat the elephant

Eat the elephant one bite at a time goes the old saying. Too often people try to swallow it whole. Have you ever worked for an organization that has undergone so much change its staff don't know whether they are Arthur or Martha. Tony Marxsen, the CIO at the Transport Accident Commission in Melbourne, believes this is because organizations fail to appreciate the importance of "hull speed".

Hull speed is a yachting term. It refers to the ability of a boat to harness the full potential speed of a new wave. Tony sees analogies with the ability of an organization to absorb change and progress. Too often organizations create change *en-masse* and then see staff thrashing around madly trying to keep up. Such change creates so much turmoil that customers can get neglected and key staff can feel overwhelmed. Thus, instead of progressing forward it seems everyone is spending twice as much effort to stay in the same spot. The same happens to yachtsmen who overlook the hull speed of their boat.

Tony believes business needs to identify how much change the organization is able to absorb and harness. Why invest in a $10 million project if at the end of the day nothing of value is generated out of the investment? Instead, why not invest $5 million in one year? Make changes that can be successfully harnessed by the staff and then spend $5 million the next year to complete the work. Change is relentless in the modern world. However, if an organization is to progress from this change it would do well to appreciate the "hull speed" of the business.

Well-managed change

Well-managed change will ensure that the process flows smoothly and does not generate mayhem. Change is a constant in IT and it must be properly managed. A well-managed change will consider all BTOPP elements and be protected by sound risk evaluation and recovery procedures. It is important to remember it is not the size and cost of the change that should dictate the depth and rigour of the change control procedures, it is the potential dangers *if the change fails*. The Apollo 13 mission is a tragic example of how a failure in a small, unsophisticated, low-cost component—the rubber seal—led to a billion-dollar disaster and the loss of the astronauts' lives. Analysis of how this was allowed to happen shows a mass of people, process and cultural issues that stood in the way of revealing the problem and stopping the lift-off.

Software changes of a minor nature may likewise corrupt an entire database and bring a company to its knees for days. They too are often surrounded by a complex web of change issues beyond the limits of the product.

Approach

Van der Heijden[50] believes change moves through a four-step process:

- Specification of the present situation.
- Specification of the desired future.[w]
- Clarification of the gap to be bridged.
- Development of the plan to make the transition.

These seem sensible and necessary steps. In specifying the present situation and the desired future, include *all* the things encompassed by the change. These may include organizational restructure, business relationships, human resources, training, documentation, processes and others.

Making change happen is not a trivial matter. Some essential elements in change management are:

- Ensure that you consider *every* change from all five perspectives of Business, Organization, Technology, People and Process.
- Specify processes that must be followed for every change. Do not rely on change control software as the sole means of managing change.
- Define, where appropriate, one or more principles governing change management in your organization.
- Ensure that change request forms include the following elements:
  - Business, Organization, Technical, People and Process impact and the steps planned to manage these.
  - Titles of all parties involved or affected by the change and their obligations and responsibilities.
  - Immediate risks of the change and mitigation plans.
  - Second-order or downstream effects and how they will be managed.

---

[w] Van der Heijden adds: ". . . which needs to be clearly stated as one choice among many within an environment which becomes more and more uncertain the further we look out."

- Involve HR people in all change that affects people's work processes or responsibilities.
- If necessary—and it may be if the change is substantial—seek the help of an industrial psychologist to assist in change conditioning.
- If appropriate, modify or develop service level agreements that are impacted by the change.
- Manage all these things and make sure they are done. Less than 10% of the effort in information systems changes relate to the technical aspect. Make sure the other 90% are properly covered.
- Ensure that the project manager for the change is properly trained in change management, not just software promotion.
- Communicate the change honestly.

On the last point it is easy to be as cynical as Scott Adams when describing what he calls "Content Free Communication". Scott's cynicism is well founded when he observes much change communication is based on the idea:

> You can fool the ungifted . . . by having plenty of meetings, e-mail messages, newsletters and voice mail broadcasts that speak of good things ahead without addressing specific people . . . the goal of change management is to dupe slow-witted employees into thinking change is good for them by appealing to their sense of adventure and love of challenge . . . this is like convincing a trout to leap out of a stream to experience the adventure of getting deboned.[51]

Conditions for change

Pettigrew and Whipp[52] identified five conditions required for any planned change. These were:

- Exercise leadership to put the "change project" on the agenda and keep it there.
- Active recognition that people are the asset through which change is created.
- Awareness in the organization of the business imperatives of change.
- Expression of the strategy in operational and actionable terms.
- Coherence of action among all members of management.

Ensure that these are well appreciated by all those involved in your change programme.

Leading the charge

You might also like to consider the most appropriate person in your organization to manage the change. Roger Collins[53] said that a certain type of leader, the *transformational leader*, was most required to manage change as they had to overcome apathy, resistance to change, and tensions among employees from a large number of sources. He states "According to Tichy the characteristics[x] of transformational leaders are:

- They identify themselves as change agents . . . They are skilled 'professional' managers who have grown to transformational leaders.
- They are courageous individuals . . . Prudent risk takers . . . able to take a stand, being able to take risks, and stand against the status quo in the larger interests of the organization . . . need healthy egos and need to be emotionally robust.
- They believe in people . . . They have a set of principles for dealing with motivation, emotion, pain, trust and loyalty . . . act as coach, cheerleader and counsellor. They empower others to make things happen.
- They are value driven. Transformational leaders have a set of core values, which they freely articulate. More importantly their behaviour supports their values . . .
- They are lifelong learners. Transformational leaders never stop learning. They learn from their mistakes . . . [and one hopes the mistakes of others].
- They have an ability to deal with complex ambiguity and uncertainty. They . . . build models or theory, develop principles, examine assumptions and 'what if?' scenarios.
- They are visionaries. Such leaders can dream and translate their dreams into images so that others can share them . . ."

From the above it should be clear that you shouldn't hand the job of managing significant change to one of our reclusive technocrats hidden in the bowels of the IT unit. And a simple caution—don't fall into the trap of seeing yourself in the above terms unless you truly are a transformational leader. Remember—good managers make things happen through others, it's fine not to be a transformer as long as you manage them—from above and below.

A fable

A seemingly minor software change by a large financial institution points to the importance of thinking through all aspects of the change. The organization (which

---

[x] These quotes summarize the material in Collin's text. The full text expounds the attributes further.

will remain nameless) modified its system to capture a single additional character to improve its customer relationship management. The idea was conceived by marketing. No-one modified the form on which the data was captured. No-one told the front-office staff the data was mandatory. No-one told the data entry people that the field required one of four codes to be entered. No-one considered the privacy law implications of the change. The results:

- The data entry people had a huge number of customer application forms that the system rejected (in a batch run of all things).
- The task of collecting the data after the event proved hugely expensive and difficult.
- Some customers who had completed the applications were never processed, and indeed were lost to the bank.
- Front-line and data-entry staff were understandably annoyed and worse. They called in the union over management's "heavy handedness".
- The institution was sued for breach of privacy legislation.

Pretty impressive result for a ten-minute software change to a single screen and database table!

The literature on change management is vast. It covers a wide range of views but is sometimes surprisingly narrow in focus. (I may have read the wrong books, of course.) However, if you read further and use both the business initiative proposal—which incorporates change definitions—and the checklist, you have some chance of getting it right.

Checklist

1. Why is the change being proposed? Has this been well justified?
2. Does the proposal include a picture of the current environment and the future scenario?
3. Are those pictures complete in every respect?
4. Does the change programme allocate accountability and responsibility to every aspect of the change?
5. Have milestones or check-gates been included in the change programme?
6. If it is a significant change, does the investment committee have a review schedule for the change programme based around those gates?
7. Have you recruited the right resources into the change programme, including unions, human resources, legal, corporate communications and even an industrial psychologist if necessary?

8. If the change is significant, do the attributes of the person driving the change match those of a transformational leader?
9. Have you got a recovery plan to cover the risk that the change may go off the rails?
10. If the change might affect external parties, has someone told them?

21   Outsourcing

A highly complex, often fraught management practice that can be occasionally, spectacularly successful. (Emma Connors in *Boss Magazine*)

Of course, you know it is also often spectacularly unsuccessful as well! If you have managed an outsourcing project you will know there is little published or available on a proper process for outsourcing. The bulk of the literature to date has concentrated on the benefits and drawbacks of outsourcing.

This short chapter doesn't tell you how to outsource. It doesn't even argue all the pros and cons of outsourcing. It aims solely to highlight those things that need to be done, and explain why you should do them.

When it is bad . . .

The effects of poorly structured outsourcing agreements often include:

- Serious misalignment between the word of the contract and the motives of the company.
- Micro-management of the outsourcer with all its costs and implications.
- Lack of clarity about what the business expects and the mutual obligations and responsibilities of the parties to deliver these outcomes.
- Major cost escalation as forgotten and shadow IT systems, projects and people emerge after the contract is signed.

Journalists and auditors have neatly reduced the sanitized statements above to more direct and simple terms like "a bloody disaster". Tales abound of extraordinary problems that now exist between organizations and their service provider. To exacerbate the painful situation that these people find themselves in there is little experience to draw on about the task of disengagement.

Some time soon now someone will write a handbook entitled *Disengaging from an Outsourced Relationship*. It should sell well!

When it is good

A well-managed outsourcing process will deliver an outsourcing relationship that:

- Is directed to achieving well-understood business goals and objectives.
- Accounts for the whole domain to be outsourced so there are no surprises.
- Allows the company to focus on its goals while the outsourcer manages inputs and performance.
- Ensures the relationship is well managed throughout its life and at termination.

How do I do it?

A number of authors have written extensively on IT outsourcing including Halvey and Melby, Gay and Essinger, Klepper and Jones, Greaver, Wilcox and the doyenne of outsourcing, Mary Lacity. The works of these authors are listed in the section entitled "Further reading" at the end of this book.

Some key elements in outsourcing successfully include:

- Knowing your motives. Define precisely *why* you are outsourcing. Ensure that the *why* is consistent with your corporate goals and is supported by your senior executive. You must know the service providers' motives as well. Why are they happy to run what you aren't happy to run? Are the operations managers in the outsourcer aware what the sales people are promising you?
- Know *what* you are outsourcing. Make every effort to discover and document the assets, processes and people that will be covered in the agreement. Tales abound of serious misjudgement in this area, including significant undercounting of computers and people.
- Select carefully. This topic is referred to earlier in this book. It is covered at length in *The IT Outsourcing Guide*.[54] To select carefully you must develop sound criteria on which to base your selection. You need to investigate, analyse and test responses. You need to look at organizational, commercial and technical considerations. You need to use subjective as well as objective criteria.
- Put real effort into ensuring the contract reflects what you want. Too often companies treat the contract as an aside to the real business. Do not fall into this trap! Make sure it reflects your motives, goals, management processes, rewards, punishments and termination options. To do this effectively you will need to have the right people, tools, aids, experience and control over the whole contract process.

- Define service level agreements that cover *outputs* and focus on obligations, responsibilities and performance. You will need to ensure that these are representative of what the business needs, that they are stretching but achievable. You will need to monitor performance and deal with resultant issues.
- Manage the transition. This is change management on a grand scale and the BTOPP model will stand you in good stead. The scale of the change is huge and you will need transformational management skills coupled to rigorous programme management.
- Manage the relationship. This may require you to hire and position contract managers, project secretariats and governance procedures. This is where so many outsourcing projects go wrong.

The *IT Outsourcing Guide* provides a comprehensive reference on *how* to go about outsourcing. Outsourcing is difficult and dangerous. Mistakes are easily made but are difficult and expensive to rectify. If you are considering outsourcing read about it, speak to those who have done it and seek the advice of experts in the field. Most major consultancy companies offer high-quality advice in this area.

Whatever you do, don't mistake it as an easy way to off-load a pernicious problem. It is not!

Given the importance and risks attached to outsourcing, you are encouraged to read further on this subject. Potentially useful texts are listed in "Further reading" at the end of this book. If you must outsource, do it properly!

Checklist

1. Does the company know its real motives for outsourcing? Really?
2. Do the senior executives agree with these motives and support them?
3. How is outsourcing going to meet the objectives set for it?
4. Why can't those objectives be met more effectively and efficiently another way?
5. What criteria must the service provider meet to achieve these objectives?
6. Do the criteria cover organizational and commercial attributes as well as technical attributes?
7. Have you tested the veracity of the outsourcer's claims?
8. Have you interviewed the outsourcer's staff, in particular the people who will be doing the ongoing work—not just the sales suits?
9. Have you got a sound management process in place to cover every aspect of contract negotiation?
10. Have you got the appropriate skills on your team? These may include mediators, financial modellers, auditors and technical consultants as well as lawyers.

11. Do you know what[y] exactly you are outsourcing?
12. Have you developed a sound change management programme?
13. Does the programme contain checkpoints and gates to ensure it advances under control?
14. Has anyone developed a risk mitigation plan in case the project goes sour during the outsourcing process?
15. Has the termination process been worked through in every aspect? Is it workable?

---

[y] GartnerGroup[55] reported: "Companies who abdicate a proper discovery process, go to the negotiating table without being able to accurately describe the dimensions of the deal within a desirable 5 per cent margin of error . . . some clients have miscalculated distributed computing assets by more than 50 per cent while their business cases assumed a 20 per cent worst case variance."

22 Give the business intelligence

Will there be time for him to learn what he ought to know when the occasion for its use arises? That I do not know. What I do know is that it is impossible for him to learn it sooner. (Jean-Jacques Rousseau in *Emile*)

Why is it so hard?

"Why is it so hard to just give me a report on the top ten customers this month?" "Why don't these two reports show the same figures?" Questions like these are the despair of IT management. Our responses tend to cover the standard ground of data being duplicated over multiple systems, lack of integrity and timeliness and the many other weaknesses that make for low-quality business intelligence.

Frequently, the business manager goes off in a huff and the issue dies down only to arise in another forum a few days later. The ire of business managers is understandable. GartnerGroup[56] point out that:

> business people are required to make more and increasingly critical decisions . . . [knowing] huge volumes of internal and external data exist that, if distilled, would provide valuable guidance in the decision making process . . . [while] skilled analytical resources have become scarce and are dramatically overloaded . . . Hence users and managers make decisions in a virtual vacuum using outdated information.

Many executives and managers outside IT have not been properly informed about the legacy of early information management practices and they are frustrated by what they perceive as a lack of cooperation from their IT colleagues. The challenge facing today's IT manager is to help them understand the constraints and what needs to be done to prevent the problem from becoming worse.

Do yourself a favour

You can deal with this debilitating issue before it eats away at your credibility. The process can begin immediately and with little direct investment. That is not to say the total journey will be inexpensive or easy. Nevertheless the first steps in the process are quite simple and manageable. They are the foundation for all that follows so start on them now!

The steps to improving business intelligence

All steps are not required in all instances; however, it is a rare organization that does not need to implement the majority. The steps include:

- Making people aware of the nature of the obstacles to deriving good business intelligence.
- Educating the business on the cost and benefits of creating and maintaining high-quality data.
- Developing business principles to govern data management and quality.
- Rationalizing table files and other data sinks where appropriate.
- Replacing and/or cleansing or scrubbing of databases to improve integrity.
- Defining organizational responsibilities for the future management and maintenance of data.
- Extending the principles to govern the creation and management of any data warehouse.
- Establishing a data warehouse system with an appropriate management and support team.

Each of these steps is explained in more detail in the remainder of this chapter. Don't be tempted to jump straight to the technology solution—implement a data warehouse.

Making people aware of the obstacles

Whatever you do don't brush off those that come to you seeking help with BI (Business Intelligence) because data is "inconsistent", "duplicated", "split over different systems", "incompatible" and so on. And don't even dream of mentioning concepts such as normalization, keys and foreign keys, SQL or database indexing systems, or replication. Instead, obtain help from a graphic illustrator to prepare a simple educational package that illustrates these problems. Remember what sounds intelligible and simple to people involved in IT sounds like a foreign language to outsiders. Prepare illustrations that show what inconsistent means. An example is shown in Figure 22.1.

Do the same for duplicated data. Identify how an entity may be held many times over in different systems. For example, a financial services company may hold the same person entity in different roles, such as policyholder, investor and pension-contributor!

A graphical representation will be far more convincing than a list of file names and systems. This business "picture book" will help to rally the business around your possible solutions.

Circulate the picture book alone or by attaching it to the help desk or IT newsletter. If your company has a corporate newsletter discuss the concept of an IT expertise and tips section with the editor.

Explain *why* and how much!

People won't be interested in learning anything unless you tell them *why* they need to know it! The "why of improving BI" is to create an environment in which business people can better manage their business by having faster access to accurate information both for analysis and managing day-to-day business transactions.

Develop some approximations of the cost of mismanaged data. You may find this encourages the CEO to support your ambitions. The cost of past mismanagement may be high. A recent evaluation in the situation in a medium-sized organization showed the following opportunities for cost savings:

- An average of five instances of approximately 100 000 legal entities[z] with each instance taking $2.00 a year in staff, hardware, software to maintain represented unnecessary expenditure of $400 000.
- Seven per cent of customers that year had expressed serious dissatisfaction over issues related to incompatible data records. Further analysis showed it cost on average $53.00 each to console these customers. The dollar value of a clean database was approximately $371 000.

This was a small organization with high market volume of a relatively low-cost and marginal product. A clean database was the difference between significant profit and limping along!

Show your CEO that good practice in managing information can pay large dividends.

---

[z] Legal entity is a concept that recognizes customers, suppliers, employees, people and companies can be held in a single table. It further recognizes that any one legal entity may appear in more than one of the above roles.

Life Insurance System Name & Address Record

Size	Name	Contents
10	Title	Professor
30	Name	Richard F Somerville
20	Street	10 Entwhistle Road
15	Suburb	Wolloomooloo
15	State	New South Wales

Pension System Name and Address Record

Size	Name	Contents
3	Title	Pro
20	Name	Rick
1	Initial	F
20	Surname	Somerville
20	Street	10 Entwhistle Road
15	City	Wolloomooloo
3	State	NSW
2	Code	02
8	Phone	7611-891
8	Fax	7611-892

These simple diagrams may convey three messages:

1. Only one part of the records is the same size, contains the same information and has the same label.

2. Inconsistencies exist with regard to naming conventions, eg Pro, Rick, NSW versus Professor, Richard, New South Wales.

3. One record contains more information than the other does, which is Phone and Facsimile.

This can be used to explain the issues that will arise in trying to:

- Match records—are they the same people? How do we know?

- Search and index with different standards for names and such like.

- Consolidating where data is not available or inconsistent.

Figure 22.1—Illustration of information inconsistency

Introduce principles governing data

Once people understand the cost and possibly the chaos that surrounds BI data, then introduce them to solutions. The first step in this process will be to *agree* what needs to be done to correct the problems.

Develop business principles to govern data capture and integrity. Some topics to cover include:

- Is data to be treated as a corporate or a departmental resource?
- What rules will apply to archiving and deletion of data?
- Who will be responsible for correcting identified anomalies in data?
- Will the company maintain a single logical[aa] database for mission-critical subjects?
- If attributes can be defined in advance, will a pick-list be provided? For example city, day, date, colour, model, etc.

These may seem simple questions but if we explore some of the options, we have a flavour of the possible range of answers to these questions and some of the implications. If data is a corporate resource, then who is responsible for it at a corporate level? Who will determine business standards for data entry and accuracy? Who will measure the integrity of data and who will be responsible for laundering dirty databases? What rules will apply to data entering the organization? Will it be entered at point of entry, which may require company units with no interest in some of the data having to staff for and manage that input? What restraints will be placed on departments or divisions creating databases?

Don't overlook spelling out the implications. For example, if the company introduces a principle to support a belief that the person most familiar with the data should create it, this may have significant impact on future system design and reach. (For example, if a customer is the best person to enter and maintain their address and personal details, then future systems must be accessible to customers.)

An example of an information management principle is shown in Figure 22.2.

Rationalize the physical infrastructure

Do what you can to reduce the physical complexity and number and variety of data sinks. It is rarely possible to rapidly rationalize a portfolio of systems.

[aa] The proliferation of packages often makes it impossible for a business to maintain a single physical database for entities such as customer–supplier. A logical database recognizes the existence of the physical but directs all maintenance and management through a front-end system, which in effect updates all the physical databases as one.

Principle #6
Issue: *When will data be captured and by whom?*

Options:
    1. We will capture data at its first point of entry into the organization.
    2. We will capture data in the department that has most use for it.
    3. We adopt a *laissez-faire* approach and will capture data 'wherever it falls'.

Principle: **(2) We will capture data at its first point of entry into the organization**
Rationale: *Data is a valuable resource. Hands off of forms between departments and differing business processes often mean that critical data is not caught in a timely fashion, or not caught at all.*

Implications:
    + *The business will have timely accurate information to manage critical production and service.*
    + *Removes uncertainty about what data should be captured by whom.*
    + *Integrates the business processes and data closely over time.*
    - *Business units may incur cost capturing data they have no use for.*
    - *Applications may have to enable capture of data that is not required by the application.*
    - *Significant effort will be required to modify systems and behaviours to implement this change.*

Approval: (signature) For the Executive Committee   07 Oct 2000

Figure 22.2—Information management principle

Sometimes it is easier to develop strategies to rationalize the portfolio of files or tables and provide common access and usage. For example, it may be possible to direct a number of applications to read and update a single centralized table/file and replace many localized tables. Beware the technical guru who frets at the potential for slight response time delays, while ignoring the cost of creating transaction anomalies!

Scrub it clean

The hygiene can commence at any time. The main consideration is to determine the most cost-effective and simple approach for your business. This may be "as is", post-rationalization or pre- or post-data warehousing. The prerequisite is that a corporate data standard exists so that the scrubbing is to an exacting, predefined regime. The scrubbing of data can be done in many ways. Some considerations that you should consider are:

- Can clean versions of this data be bought from outside sources for example post office or telecommunications carrier?
- Can automated scrubbing tools be employed to clean data?
- Would it be better to avoid a clean-up and create the data afresh?
- Can transactors (customers, suppliers, and staff) be given incentives to clean the data themselves?
- Can data scrubbing be integrated into normal transaction processing by highlighting data that is not consistent with corporate guidelines and standards?

There is no point in treating data scrubbing as a one-off exercise and then allowing the database to deteriorate again. The business must consider how best to manage the ongoing maintenance of data. Some organizations have removed critical data entry from front-line operators and handed it over to specialist data entry staff working with both on- and off-line reference material and edit-checking tools to ensure that data is of the highest quality. The approach adopted by one company is described in the box on the next page.

The data warehouse

If building a data warehouse is justified, then make sure it does not become a rubbish tip! Don't build one unless you can be sure you can fill it with data that is both *relevant* and clean. Relevant means that 80% of the company's data does *not* belong in the data warehouse!

Work with your business colleagues to define the attributes (not tables) that are relevant to the business. Design the data warehouse so that it can be populated with these attributes properly indexed and linked to reflect extraction (business intelligence) linkages. Make sure that you question, challenge and argue every candidate. The best single question for proposed candidate items for the data warehouse is: "How will knowledge about this item be used to make the business more profitable?" Expect some strange answers!

How one company cleaned their data

One sound model adopted by one company was to do with the following:

- Appoint a corporate data management team that was responsible for maintaining critical logical databases. Key subject-types like customer were "entered" by a field staff but flagged to the data management team for quality control. They had bonuses and remuneration at risk that was dependent on the overall quality of the company's data.
- Extend the data management team responsibilities to include database scrubbing, error correction and reporting. These staff were also provided with tools, training and tips for maintaining database hygiene.
- Set a principle that data was to be entered once at its point of entry into the organization, even when this was not to the direct benefit of the business unit receiving. The data management team monitored departmental performance and reported to the CEO on quality.
- Established corporate standards for data at the technical data dictionary level. This company used ISO, EDI or similar objective standards to govern column (field) size, type and edit controls where possible.
- Established corporate conventions for data entry, governing salutations (e.g. Doctor, Professor, and Colonel), names including initials, surnames, suffixes such as junior, profession and occupation, street addresses, and many more. To the extent possible these were made available through drop-down lists.
- Established clear accountability and responsibility within the business for various other aspects of data entry and maintenance.
- Adopted a logical model of key entities. For example, an individual working with a financial institution could concurrently hold the roles of agent, policyholder, investor and shareholder. It made sense to have one table with flags and profiles appropriate to role type.
- Created a suite of data maintenance systems that provided a single point-of-entry for critical data that then populated a number of physical databases. This recognized the reality that a single physical database was an unrealistic dream in an environment littered with packaged software solutions.
- Created small data warehouses that served as extract-sinks for consolidating data from diverse systems for analysis and reporting.
- Acquired laundered databases from public utilities and vendors to rapidly create sterile accurate databases of a critical nature.

Don't be misled by cheap disk space. The game here is to capture, analyse, manipulate and exploit business intelligence, not to provide somewhere to dump corporate data. Then you can ensure that the proper effort and design goes into the extraction *filters* to ensure that properly controlled high-quality information moves into this space.

If you haven't done so already, ensure that you define the roles, competencies, obligations and responsibilities of the data warehouse management team—those responsible for managing the *data*, not the technology, and their business colleagues.

Summary

The lack of access to business intelligence is one of the most frustrating aspects of your business colleagues' lives. They are driven to make large, risky decisions on limited, inaccurate, incomplete or plainly unavailable data. They know it is "there". They do not understand why you can't obtain it for them. Show them the way to the future. They have to take the first steps now! There is no miracle on its way. This is an arduous, lengthy but hugely worthwhile thing to do—properly!

A last word: GartnerGroup believe a common data platform, data scrubbing, method and decision-support system integration are the weakest links in business intelligence systems. In the same paper[56] they note that the four criteria of information quality are relevance, timeliness, completeness and consistency. Importantly, they also point to the web as playing a more important role in business intelligence. Be prepared.

Checklist

1. Have you developed principles to govern information management?
2. Have they been promulgated throughout the business?
3. Does the enterprise have standards governing appropriate types of data such as titles and abbreviations?
4. Have the number of entry points for data been rationalized where appropriate?
5. Can the number of files and systems be rationalized in the interest of data integrity?
6. Can clean static public data such as name and address be purchased from a vendor?
7. Do the people entering data have a vested interest in its accuracy and completeness and do they have the greatest incentive to ensure it is correct?
8. Can you introduce a programme of disincentives towards those who enter data carelessly or inaccurately?
9. Can improvements in data collection instruments and tools improve the quality of data capture?
10. Can you improve data capture edits and introduce selection rather than entry when suitable?
11. Can you establish a data maintenance group tasked with maintenance of high-quality data?
12. Have you ensured that data maintenance responsibilities are spelt out to relevant department line managers?

23 Planning the future

Time present and time past are both perhaps present in time future and time future is contained in time past. (T.S. Eliot in *Four Quartets*)

The future

The future will arrive so you might as well be prepared for it. As IT manager you have more reason than most managers to be concerned about the uncertain future. Your programme timeframes tend to be measured in years. Investment demands are large, usually stretching into tens of millions of dollars. Change may be driven by factors outside your control, for example legislators, customers, suppliers or competitors.

The IT manager of any medium or large company must look well ahead. In many ways your job is analogous to steering a supertanker. If you think you can navigate by taking the occasional quick glance from the bridge, you will fail. Even if you see the rocks ahead you will not be able to turn the massive vessel quickly enough to avoid going aground.

To manage well, you must manage for the future as well as the present.

I'll take one day at a time

If taking one day at a time is your motto then you probably already know that you:

- Make poor investment decisions on projects that can never reap the projected benefits because of future change.
- Select inferior technology components that are inappropriate for the future business direction.
- Fail to grasp significant opportunities, which can be driven by technology components.

- Fail to appreciate market forces that demand a new approach to technology management.
- Manage demoralized staff who do not enjoy working in a rudderless ship.
- Will collect your redundancy cheque in the near future!

Do keep IT strategic planning in perspective. There is limited value in a ten-volume, 2000-page IT strategic plan that is impossible to keep up to date and never read. It may convince the gullible you know where IT is going, but that is all. The future is not that certain that it warrants such a level of detail. You are better off with fifty pages that are read and understood by all and can be rapidly changed to reflect emerging scenarios. Beware though—the research to write those fifty pages might take as much effort as the biblical version.

Planning for the future

Mary Sharp, the CIO at Standards Australia, had a bone to pick with Peter Hind. Just after he had written a column chastising CIOs for not participating in market surveys she questioned whether he had any idea of the number of requests she got each day from research companies. She believed she could spend her life answering questionnaires. As an analyst, dependent on CIOs to provide him with data to monitor the local IT marketplace, Peter was sensitive to Mary's complaints.

Mary though recognized that she too needed market data to help support her own business cases. As such, she advised her two major terms for doing surveys. Firstly, they should not be conducted in working hours. If researchers wanted her to complete phone surveys they must ring after 5:30 pm each night. Better still, they should forward the questions in advance and ask her to nominate an accept-able time for calling back. Next, the survey must seek data of interest to her. Then she expected a summary of the responses to provide her with some reference data to help support her business cases.

Peter also advises CIOs to exploit research companies better. If you are con-sidering a future implementation you know that when you come to present the business case you will be asked at least one stock standard business question. What are our other companies doing? Why not get the research company to gather the data for you? Ask them to include the question on their next survey. Then you can trade a survey response with the overall data you will need to support your business case.

How does forecasting the future help me?

The first part of the future will arrive later today, the remainder shortly after. Being prepared for it with a documented IT strategy offers you:

- A framework for considering investment proposals.
- A basis for reviewing the value of existing commitments.
- A model for considering your future resource requirements, human, technical and intellectual.
- A means of conveying and checking that the business and IT share a common view of the future.
- It also fills a critical part of a manager's role namely the future facing aspect.

The IT management strategy must show how you will meet future demand with appropriate resources, including:

- Staff skills, competencies and numbers which may include skills outside the mainstream, such as multimedia, digital photography, voice recognition.
- Structure of organization to accommodate new technical and organizational skills, including process designers, performance measurers, contract managers and others.
- New forms of hardware, for example improvements in digital photography, effective voice recognition, wireless, adaptive mobile devices and others, yet unknown.
- New forms of software including intelligent extended mark-up languages, intelligent image management and the like.

The list of potential changes and their implications is infinite. What is important is to map out the key business initiatives over the next major planning period, typically five years, and determine what demands this will place on IT:

- Technology
- Organization
- Process
- People.

Semantics

First, a word is needed on semantics. The terms goals, objectives, initiatives and outcomes are used in the following pages. The words have different meanings to different people. Below are the definitions used in this text. I am grateful to Paul A Strassman[58] for his definitions and paraphrase them as follows:

Goals are hopes and aspirations for a distant future, which are not necessarily attainable. Goals are expectations, prospects, possibilities and ambitions. Goals are lofty ideals . . . one should not trifle with goals; they are the bonds that bring together all the constituencies in organizations.

Objectives must be explicitly measurable performance commitments. Objectives are reality, schedules, benchmarks, and cost-targets. Objectives must be measured to determine how near you are to where you want to be. They should be the products of well-considered arguments concerning the balance between ambition and reality.

I am equally in debt to John Thorpe for his definition of initiatives and outcomes. These terms are used by Thorpe in his book, *The Information Paradox*.[59] Some techniques from this book are discussed later in this chapter.

Initiative: an action that contributes to one or more outcomes. It always refers to an element that can be acted upon directly.

Outcome: change in or maintenance of the state of an element that cannot be acted upon directly. An outcome can be intermediate (contribute to another outcome) or be ultimate (the final desired state).

How do I do it?

The following challenges may face you:

The absence of a documented corporate strategy. This is the rule, rather than the exception. Most companies muddle along from year to year without a clearly articulated road map for the future. If the company does not have a documented strategy you will need to take the following steps:

- Interview the chief executive and other key executives. Probe to see if they have unspoken goals and objectives. You may find it necessary to give them a definition of these terms.
- Ask how they think the company will evolve with products, markets, service offerings and direction.
- Ask if they have any planned or future projects or initiatives to support these changes whether or not they have an IT component.
- If they do not articulate any, then see if they are hidden in a variety of marketing plans, five-year plans or annual reports.
- Read marketing plans, future production schedules, financial forecasts— anything that must in part be future based. Here you will often discover the company's assumptions about future earnings, where they will come from, and what will need to be done to achieve them.

- Analyse every future-based document, seeking any IT implication. They may be well hidden! Don't be surprised to find that the planners blithely assume new systems will magically be in place to accommodate new lines of business, changed volumes or high-profile customer relationship management schemes.
- Read and analyse the company's past to gain a picture of how it is likely to behave in the future. Pay particular attention to the demands made on IT in the past. Question what involvement IT had in these changes, how well planned were the changes, what are the lessons for the future.
- Document or map these findings and test them with your colleagues. Some tips on documentation techniques are covered later.
- Ask, and keep asking "What do you see as the IT implications of this change?" I suggest you go further and press for details of the BTOPP (Business, Technology, Organization, Process and People) implications. Don't be surprised if they have not been thought through.

Do *all* these things and document the results. Do not rely on any single one to provide a satisfactory prognosis of the company's future demands on IT.

Alternatively, if the situation is such that the company lacks any plans and seems to blunder from point to point, then agitate for a combined business and IT strategy, however shallow, to provide a basis for future navigation and resource planning.

If all these avenues fail and you have to manage without a considered view of the future, you will need to be reactive, but nimble, in adapting your IT department to meet emerging needs.

Even if you do find a formal strategic plan exists, beware of hazards such as contradictions *in stated goals and objectives*. This is a surprisingly common occurrence. This seems to occur for two reasons:

- Large organizations with many lines of business collate the strategies of individual divisions, but fail to review and rationalize conflicting or contradictory aims.
- Organizations speak to many constituencies, employees, shareholders, legislators, and competitors. They may each be given quite different messages.

Your challenge will be to identify which aspects of the proposed strategies are most likely to occur, that is, which are most probable.

Techniques

Strategic planning specialists use a number of techniques to identify and document a company's long-term strategy. Value added planning, brainstorming, issue diagrams, ResultsChain™ (see following section) and others. The literature on strategic planning is vast, with titles ranging from James Martin's seminal treatise, *Strategic Information Planning Methodologies,*[60] to Mintzberg's properly caustic overview on *The Rise and Fall of Strategic Planning.*[61] It is also critical to know what architecture-based planning can offer. Texts on architecture planning are listed in "Further reading" at the end of this book.

There is considerable merit in all these approaches. A good planner might well select a number of techniques from the potpourri. This book is not a strategic planning handbook. If you need to undertake strategic planning, select a few suitable titles from the list of recommended readings at the end of this book. Then hire a management consultant who has a sound record and use the consultant to drive the process and document the outcome.

ResultsChain™

One reference that is worth studying for those interested in sound techniques for modelling the future is *The Information Paradox.* This book promotes a method known as the ResultsChain™ which "enables you to prepare 'road maps' that support understanding and proactive management of the four dimensions of complexity (linkage, reach, people, and time)." A simple ResultsChain™ and an Example ResultsChain are shown in Figure 23.1.

The ResultsChain™ is an excellent tool for mapping out business initiatives, contributions, outcomes and assumptions.

PERT chart (network dependency diagram)

Whether you use the ResultsChain™ or some other technique for documenting your set of initiatives, you may also benefit from dependency mapping using a network dependency diagram. The steps are as follows:

- Gather all explicit *and implicit* initiatives described in the strategic plan or as part of the undocumented corporate strategy.
- Include the full range of business, technology, organization, people and process related implications for each initiative.
- Test your findings with your business colleagues. You may find they will whittle the planned initiatives when they see the scale, cost and demands they will make on the organization.

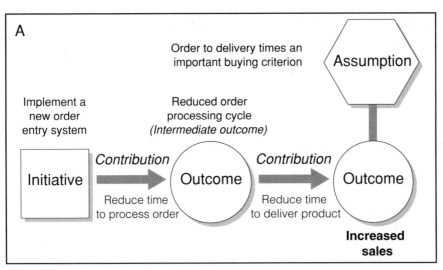

Outcomes: the results sought, including intermediate outcomes in the chain; those outcomes that are necessary but not sufficient to achieve the end benefit, or ultimate outcomes; the end benefits to be harvested.

Initiatives: actions that contribute to one or more outcomes.

Contributions: the roles played by elements of the ResultsChain, either initiatives or intermediate outcomes, in contributing to other initiatives or outcomes.

Assumptions: hypotheses regarding conditions necessary for the realization of outcomes or initiatives but over which the organization has little or no control. Assumptions represent risks you may not achieve desired outcomes. Any change to an assumption during the course of the benefits realization process should force revision of your map.

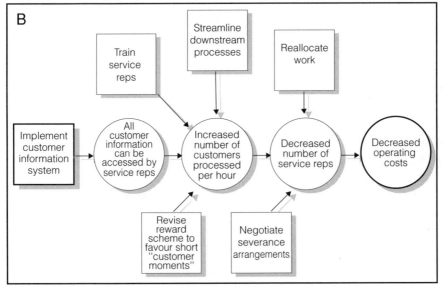

Figure 23.1—Simple ResultsChain (A) and Example ResultsChain (B).

Thorpe JM, *The Information Paradox*, copyright © 1998 McGraw-Hill, Toronto. Reproduced with permission of McGraw-Hill Ryerson Ltd.

- Establish if there are any dependencies between the initiatives. This is done by drawing a PERT[bb] chart or network diagram of the dependencies.

A network diagram will provide the framework for documenting future demand in a comprehensive, visible and accessible manner. The questions that need to be asked in developing the network are:

- What initiative immediately precedes this initiative?
- What initiative immediately follows this initiative?
- Which initiatives can run concurrently?

If you have documented the initiatives in detail using the business initiative proposal in Appendix B you will find this relatively straightforward. Those not familiar with network diagramming can refer to any number of texts including Kerzner's superior reference work *Project Management*[62] or Lockyer's *Critical Path Analysis*[63] which are in their fifth and fourth editions respectively.

Enterprise architectures

Enterprise architectures are described in Chapter 24. They are the most excellent way of documenting the future business and target environment for IT. They can be readily understood by the business.

Tabling your findings

Test your findings with your business colleagues. This may take courage. Peter Hind made the following succinct observation in a personal communication:

> A common thread through all these activities is that at some stage IT will find itself in battle with the business . . . This requires a thick skin and is not for the faint-hearted.

Courage and communication are critical components for good management. IT people tend be intuitive, thinking, judging, introverts with a distinct disinclination to indulge in face-to-face communication.

[bb] PERT charts and the disciplines for constructing them will be documented in any good book on project management.

However, you must discuss and review your strategic analysis with your peers and the leading executives in the company. The process may be illuminating for them, and if you have done your homework well, you will establish your credibility by demonstrating your clear thinking, perception and making a notable contribution to the company's understanding of its strategic direction.

Not all will be delighted with your findings. Expect the full gamut of emotions, denial and even anger from your fellow executives. Your analysis may show the full extent of work required and programme costs for the first time. Thorpe observed:

> Indeed, in the case of enterprise application packages, our experience suggests that of the work involved in delivering benefits [approximate to projects], 80 to 95 per cent lies in the areas of organization, processes and people—on the business side. Like an iceberg, the real work lies out of sight, with only the IT group's work visible.

Once the full extent of the initiative is properly defined, the dependencies and a lack of money, people, technology, time and capacity for change will kill a few golden calves. Expect to listen patiently while the self-interested accuse IT of "killing a worthwhile project". People will weasel and wriggle around every issue in an effort to keep cherished projects alive. Be brave—you haven't killed the project. It was stillborn. You are protecting the company against a black-hole investment.

You may also find some in this world do not understand the concept of dependencies. They tend to congregate in marketing. Expect to spend time in chicken and egg arguments.

If the company refuses to accept and reflect on your analysis and fails to modify its goals and objectives, then remember Peter Hind's closing words in discussing the need to confront the business:

> Perhaps more IT managers should ask what they have to lose. Success establishes your career and if the business does not want to co-operate there are plenty of other organizations out there looking for IT executives willing to help them make better use of their information resource.

Readings on strategy

It was earlier made clear that this is not a "how to book" on IT strategic planning. The texts listed under "Strategy" in the "Further reading" section at the end of this book are some that I have found useful.

There are countless others, some good, some bad. If your company lacks any documented strategy, then you may find these useful. I would also propose that it might be worth reading a few texts on military strategy, which deal with classical strategic thought.

Checklist

1. Have you identified all the planned future initiatives?
2. Have you checked whether there exist any undocumented or implicit future initiatives?
3. Have you defined each one, and covered all the business, technology, organization, people and process demands that the initiative will make on the company?
4. Have you costed all the demands to a reasonable degree of accuracy?
5. Have you modelled the initiatives and dependencies, preferably using a network chart?
6. Have you entered estimated start/finish dates for the initiatives to establish potential demand curves on resources and change?
7. Have you discussed the initiatives and network model with the key executives and sought their confirmation to your interpretation?
8. Do you think you know the planned future well enough to project the evolution of your IT organization and management framework?
9. Have you set a calendar for initiating and reviewing each of the initiatives through the Investment Committee and programme gates?
10. Is the plan for the future "doable" from your perspective?

24 Understanding architecture

Architecture is the learned game, correct and magnificent, of forms assembled in the light. (Le Corbusier)

Architecture? I don't do hardware

Enterprise architectures are not hardware architectures. Enterprise IT architectures are probably the most misunderstood aspect of IT management. No-one misunderstands them more than IT staff—including IT managers!

Zachman[64] wrote: "The architecture process begins with an understanding of the enterprise and the data that constitute its information infrastructure." Spewak and Hill, who enlarged on Zachman's work, explained it thus:

> Enterprise Architecture Planning is a process for defining the top two layers of the Zachman Information Systems Architecture Framework. EAP results in a high level blueprint of data, applications and technology that is a cost-effective, long-term solution; not a quick fix. Management participation provides a business perspective, credibility and demystifies the systems planning process . . .[65]

Times have moved on and today a full and proper IT architecture will cover at least four views: work processes, application, information and technology (WAIT), and possibly a fifth—organization.

If you don't know what this topic is all about, then immediately turn to the works of Zachman[66], Spewak and Hill[67], Martin[68] and others. This chapter is no substitute for those fine texts.

How do we use architectures?

The issue with IT architectures is straightforward. Few seem to know what they are or how to use them. However, as Zachman[69] observed: "To be most useful, information systems must be derived from this base of knowledge [architectural] about the enterprise". He went on to say in discussing the evident failures of many organizations to translate strategy into systems that: "Over the years, the [business] strategy and the implementation [of systems] have remained separated by a cavernous, conceptual 'black hole.' . . . during the 1980s, I became convinced that *architecture* whatever that was, was the thing that bridged the strategy and its implementation."

Can I live without architectures?

Spewak and Hill[70] answer this question with a delightful story about Winchester House in California. The house was owned by Sarah Winchester who inherited a fortune from her husband's rifle company. Spewak and Hill relate how Mrs Winchester was haunted by the ghosts of people killed by her husband's rifles. Her spiritual advisers told her that as long as she kept building she would remain alive. Without any blueprint or long-term plan, Mrs Winchester commissioned builders to work 24 hours a day, seven days a week, for 38 years. Rooms were added randomly, stairs built that went nowhere, windows blocked by walls, a chimney added that falls short of the roof. Spewak and Hill observe most systems portfolios resemble Winchester House—there was no set of blueprints and construction charges ahead. A new screen here, a report there, a new data set, another module—the system expanding like a triffid. Architectures are about blueprints—about having a plan.

An IT unit without an architecture is building its IT infrastructure, applications and information stores blindfolded. You would not pour millions of dollars into a building without some drawings that showed what went where and when. People build IT systems that are equally if not more complex and costly without any plan at all!

Working without an architecture is to develop systems that fail to match the evolution of the business, using incompatible technical components, creating information that is fragmented, duplicated and inaccurate and assembling infrastructure that cannot support emerging business models such as B2B, B2C.

Benefits

The benefit of a proper enterprise architecture is that every IT decision on software, hardware, information or staffing is directed to the construction of a *defined* future. Spewak and Hill[71] defined a list of benefits of which a small selection are listed below:

- Focus is on strategic use of technology for managing data as an asset.
- Documentation increases understanding of the business.
- It considers integration of current systems with the new.
- It is easier to assess the benefits of and impacts of new systems and software.
- It allows for easier accommodation of dynamic business changes such as mergers, acquisitions, new products, lines of business, and so on.
- Architecture eliminates complex, costly interfaces between incongruent systems.

This chapter aims to inform the new manager about IT architectures and provide a simple overview of how to use them to manage IT. In that it differs from the other chapters in this section which are more issue focused.

A simple way to understand the interlinking of architectures is to examine the Zachman Framework shown in Figure 24.1. This illustrates the links between what Zachman termed data, function and network and the five views of architecture as he saw it. Later models have been developed by those that followed Zachman but few have the illustrative power of the original.

It is normally the practice to record the "current" architecture at a high level as well as develop a "target architecture". This then permits gap analysis and direction. The architectures are described below.

Work architecture

Current work architecture normally includes a model of the business including current organization, products, customers, suppliers, business units, processes and classes of employee. This will usually throw up a number of anomalies and over-laps between departments. It may also highlight redundant processes and even critical process gaps.

The future model is based on a rational review of what work will be done by the business, where and by whom in the future. The future work architecture will identify new logical work groups. These are logical groupings of processes that have a strong affinity based on process, data and user class. It will include locations at which these logical work groups are expected to function, for example in head office, branch, and mobile or fixed. In essence, the future work architecture is a high-level location, function, process and organizational map of the future.

Information architecture

The current information (or data) architecture will have identified all the major data entities used by the business, usually including the details of the applications that create and maintain this information. The current architecture will usually

	DATA — What	FUNCTION — How	NETWORK — Where	PEOPLE — Who	TIME — When	MOTIVATION — Why	
SCOPE (CONTEXTUAL) / *Planner*	List of Things Important to the Business — ENTITY = Class of Business Thing	List of Processes the Business Performs — Function = Class of Business Process	List of Locations in which the Business Operates — Node = Major Business Location	List of Organizations Important to the Business — People = Major Organizations	List of Events Significant to the Business — Time = Major Business Event	List of Business Goals/Strat — Ends/Means=Major Bus. Goal/Critical Success Factor	SCOPE (CONTEXTUAL) / *Planner*
ENTERPRISE MODEL (CONCEPTUAL) / *Owner*	e.g. Semantic Model — Ent = Business Entity, Reln = Business Relationship	e.g. Business Process Model — Proc. = Business Process, I/O = Business Resources	e.g. Business Logistics System — Node = Business Location, Link = Business Linkage	e.g. Work Flow Model — People = Organization Unit, Work = Work Product	e.g. Master Schedule — Time = Business Event, Cycle = Business Cycle	e.g. Business Plan — End = Business Objective, Means = Business Strategy	ENTERPRISE MODEL (CONCEPTUAL) / *Owner*
SYSTEM MODEL (LOGICAL) / *Designer*	e.g. Logical Data Model — Ent = Data Entity, Reln = Data Relationship	e.g. Application Architecture — Proc. = Application Function, I/O = User Views	e.g. Distributed System Architecture — Node = I/S Function (Processor, Storage, etc), Link = Line Characteristics	e.g. Human Interface Architecture — People = Role, Work = Deliverable	e.g. Processing Structure — Time = System Event, Cycle = Processing Cycle	e.g. Business Rule Model — End = Structural Assertion, Means =Action Assertion	SYSTEM MODEL (LOGICAL) / *Designer*
TECHNOLOGY MODEL (PHYSICAL) / *Builder*	e.g. Physical Data Model — Ent = Segment/Table/etc., Reln = Pointer/Key/etc.	e.g. System Design — Proc. = Computer Function, I/O = Data Elements/Sets	e.g. Technology Architecture — Node = Hardware/System Software, Link = Line Specifications	e.g. Presentation Architecture — People = User, Work = Screen Format	e.g. Control Structure — Time = Execute, Cycle = Component Cycle	e.g. Rule Design — End = Condition, Means = Action	TECHNOLOGY MODEL (PHYSICAL) / *Builder*
DETAILED REPRESENTATIONS (OUT-OF-CONTEXT) / *Sub-Contractor*	e.g. Data Definition — Ent = Field, Reln = Address	e.g. Program — Proc. = Language Stmt, I/O = Control Block	e.g. Network Architecture — Node = Addresses, Link = Protocols	e.g. Security Architecture — People = Identity, Work = Job	e.g. Timing Definition — Time = Interrupt, Cycle = Machine Cycle	e.g. Rule Specification — End = Sub-condition, Means = Step	DETAILED REPRESENTATIONS (OUT-OF-CONTEXT) / *Sub-Contractor*
FUNCTIONING ENTERPRISE	e.g. DATA	e.g. FUNCTION	e.g. NETWORK	e.g. ORGANIZATION	e.g. SCHEDULE	e.g. STRATEGY	FUNCTIONING ENTERPRISE

Figure 24.1—The Zachman Framework (updated, 2000).
Copyright © 1987 International Business Machines Corporation. Reprinted with permission from *IBM Systems Journal*, **26**, No. 3.

highlight duplication, inconsistency, overlap and other serious shortcomings in information management.

The future information architecture seeks to provide a high-level logical view of a rationalized information base. It will show the major data entities, subjects, major attributes and relationships. The future information architecture serves to provide the model for the rationalization and refinement of the existing data model over time.

Application architecture

The current application architecture will seek to list all current applications, the key processes they support and the major subjects maintained by those applications. It should, where appropriate, also illustrate interactions between the applications.

The future applications architecture will usually define *logical* applications based on a rational grouping of functions and data subjects. These logical applications may provide existing functionality or new functionality. The model will also show the links between the applications, for example interfaces to word processing or spreadsheets, as well as shared data management between distinct applications. It is recognized that in many cases the practicalities of life will dictate that the logical applications are made up of a number of less than perfect marriages between packages and in-house applications.

Technical architecture

In some ways, this is the most changeable and most misunderstood member of the architecture family. The current technical architecture will normally describe the current infrastructure and standards.

The future technical architecture will normally seek to identify appropriate software structures (client server models and so on), infrastructure covering mainframe, mid-range and server roles and relationships, operating system standards, data access and network service considerations and systems management products and technologies.

This model will be derived from analysing what work is required to be done where, by whom, using what information and function (application). The purpose of the technical architecture is to deliver the information and application function to the user at the right place at the right time.

From this it should be obvious that the four architectures are linked and interdependent. If one changes, all change.

Spewak and Hill developed a model (Figure 24.2) to show the interlinks between the various architectures. It focused on data, applications and technology.

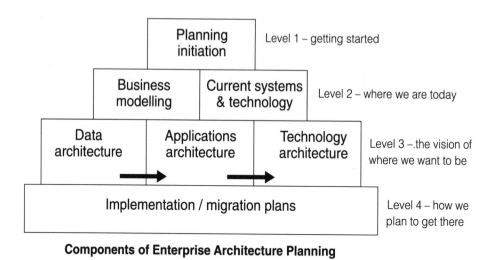

Components of Enterprise Architecture Planning

Figure 24.2—The Enterprise Architecture Model.

Adapted from Spewak S and Hill SC, *Enterprise Architecture Planning*, John Wiley & Sons Inc., New York, 1992. Reproduced with permission.

Spewak and Hill's model did not include the concept of a "work architecture" as such. I believe, however, it was implied in the business modelling or "owner's view" as Zachman termed it.

Using the architectures

The previous descriptions should make it clear that the four architectures paint a picture of *where we are today* and *where we want to be in the future*. The architectures should therefore be used to:

- Verify that all business cases for new or enhanced systems are consistent with the expected future.
- Verify that all IT investment in hardware, software, or networks is consistent with future directions.
- Inform the rationalization of data subjects and databases throughout the organization.
- Eliminate troublesome overlaps of functionality between applications, for example customer name and address maintenance.

- Educate and inform vendors about the company's future IT-centred directions.
- Educate and inform staff and new recruits both in the *business* and IT about future directions and ambitions.
- Form a basis for budgeting and planning over extended periods, particularly in relation to BPR and other re-engineering projects.

The preferred method is to create an architecture-audit checklist that is completed for all business cases, investment proposals or change requests that ensures they are compatible with future goals.

Bear in mind, however, that business changes, the environment changes, technology evolves, new products appear and the unforeseen can happen. The architectures, too, must change and evolve. They should not be a straitjacket that constrains the business; they must serve as a robust checkpoint that ensures the "builder" does not do the equivalent of placing the toilet in the middle of the boardroom! The architectures are above all a management tool and should form part of the business strategy and investment management governance process.

Checklist

1. Do you, the IT manager, really understand what enterprise architectures are?
2. Have you got an enterprise architect (full or part-time) and are they keeping the EA up to date?
3. Do you have a sound process for ensuring EAP governance?[cc]
4. Are senior people who are new to the company in both IT and the business introduced to the architecture?
5. Have you informed and educated your suppliers and vendors about your enterprise architecture and its effect on them?
6. Do you have a programme to bring those things that are out of line with the long-term EA into line?
7. Have the BTOPP implications of all the required changes been considered?
8. Has the business model[dd] changed and if so has anyone tested the EA for continuing relevance?

[cc] Part of every business initiative proposal review should be a check that the new systems comply with the enterprise architecture.

[dd] The growth of the virtual company is leading to drastic remodelling of traditional businesses.

25 Taking stock of your assets

God is in the details. (Ludwig Mies van der Rohe)

In a paper covering outsourcing GartnerGroup[72] reported:

> Companies who abdicate a proper discovery process go to the negotiating table
> without being able to accurately describe the dimensions of the deal within a desir-
> able 5 per cent margin of error . . . some clients have miscalculated distributed
> computing assets by more than 50 per cent while their business cases assumed a 20
> per cent worst case variance.

Personal experience as a management consultant reinforces the truth. Most IT
managers don't know how many systems, people or places they are responsible
for!

Death in the boardroom

You will find out what you don't know sooner or later. Either you find it out for
yourself or one of your colleagues who loves you least will drop the grenade on
you during a board meeting. Of the two options finding out for yourself seems less
painful.

The bad news

The bad news is that finding out for yourself often requires considerable effort and
some cost, even in a medium-sized enterprise. You can take three things for
granted:

- The hardware and infrastructure inventory is hopelessly inaccurate.

- No-one knows where to find all the licences and maintenance agreements signed over the last ten years.
- There are ferals[ee] working on your information systems.

The process of finding, recording and maintaining the records may take months. But you must carry out the process. Simply put, if you don't know what you are responsible for, then you cannot hope to manage it.

How much work do I have to do?

The scope of the work you have to do extends to every nook and cranny of the business. There is nowhere you should not look. Many years ago I discovered a feral IT unit masquerading as a logistics group installing an illicit computer system in a company's warehouse. No-one in the business, other than the warehouse manager, was aware of it.

Don't just concentrate on recording the existence of hardware and applications. You must make sure the team records the age, condition, performance limits and capacity of each asset.

> An effective IT asset management system should, at a minimum, track acquisition details, for example, amount paid, when they were purchased and book value; financial management, for example lease tracking and depreciation calculations; general ledger reconciliation; electronic ordering; software contract profiles; moves, adds and changes; and retirement history.[72]

Probe for the existence of staff, equipment, contractors and consultants hidden outside the IT budget. The task is often colossal and you should expect to face a certain amount of resistance.

Whatever you do, make sure the body of information that is gathered is stored in a well-indexed and readily accessible information recording system. After all it is the map of your domain and you need to know what is in it. Don't forget that information will change as you gather it and afterwards, so make sure you have the appropriate processes and support staff to maintain it.

A set of templates for recording assets is included in Appendices E1 and E2.

[ee] Employees and consultants building, implementing and maintaining information systems without the knowledge of the information systems department. Strassman commented: "According to a survey by the Diebold Group user spending on information systems outside IT budgets was equivalent to another 64 per cent of the IT department spending in manufacturing and 27 per cent in service firms."

The scope

The scope of the task is as follows:

- All employment contracts with independent IT contractors, whether entered into with IT or directly with other business units.
- Inventory of any shadow IT staff employed in business units, including, to the extent possible, their skills and competencies, service records, performance appraisal summaries.
- Inventory of *all* applications, technical details, maintenance records, capacity details, user numbers, classes and hours of work and the nominated business "owner" of each application.
- Inventory of *all* hardware big and little, owned by IT and owned outside IT. This may prove illuminating!
- Inventory of *all* communications equipment and software used by the organization, which may include equipment or software that currently appears to lie outside the scope of IT.
- Telecommunication contracts which are typically let outside IT.
- Licences and maintenance agreements on databases, utilities, development tools, systems and network management software as well as applications, large and small.
- Disaster recovery agreements or business continuity programmes, internal or external.
- Outsourcing contracts that may have been entered into by IT or outside IT. These may be more common than thought, particularly for outsourced business processing.
- Available furnishings, and fittings including whiteboards, fax machines, desks, office space and the like. This will often throw up anomalies that need to be resolved about the resources available to you.

It is also important that the inventory extends to *your* human resources and delivers you a clear and reliable profile on skills, competencies, and work history. This issue is covered in Chapter 4.

Discovery issues

The research is also likely to uncover a number of unpleasant things that have remained hidden for many years, for example maintenance and service contracts that should have been cancelled many years ago. You may discover a substantial amount of unlicensed software running on desktop PCs. The cost to remedy the latter by purchasing appropriate licences always seems to dwarf the savings made by cancelling the former!

You are also likely to run into considerable disagreement about the role of the IT unit in the management of a number of information technology assets. The issue of what lies within your domain and what lies outside may lead to the odd border clash.

Typically, these will be over "departmental applications" usually built with spreadsheets or small-scale (PC) databases by enthusiastic amateurs. These are principally found in engineering, accounting, marketing and actuarial departments. IT don't own these until they fail or deliver some disastrous result at which you are frequently awarded backdated ownership!

A new area tends to be those applications that sit on the boundary of traditional information technology, including telecommunications and related products such as facsimile software, telephony management systems, web-site management and electronic customer links. You will need to determine the IT manager's role in managing these.

Discovery will raise sensitive issues of ownership and accountability for technology-related assets. You will strike pockets of resistance from fellow executives who don't want IT playing in their sandpit. But you must map every inch of what you are responsible for if you want to avoid serious embarrassment in your often short life as an IT manager.

Mapping your domain and SLAs

Service level agreements (SLAs) are covered in Chapter 10. They are mentioned here because one critical benefit of discovery is that it enables you to ensure that later SLAs are formed on a sound base of knowledge. If you base the SLAs and the complex network of people, tools and structure required to support them on incorrect technology and business information, you will fail. It is as elementary as that.

For example, if an SLA commits you to support 500 desktops and you later discover the number is closer to 700, *you* have a serious problem. Anecdotal evidence suggests that effective help desk support demands a ratio of about 1:50 IT help desk staff to desktops. An under-count by 200 PCs leaves IT in danger of being four people short in establishing the resources required to properly support the service level agreement.

In *The IT Outsourcing Guide* we quoted the following example of a discovery process in a modestly sized company.

Equipment	Asset Register	Discovery
Mid Range	1 HP K series	1 HP K series and 1 HP 8000
PCs	245	325
Laptops	4	15

Don't be surprised to find the same gaps in your own asset recording system. Mapping your domain is a pre-requisite to developing serviceable SLAs.

Feral IT

An issue mentioned earlier is the potential discovery of feral IT projects or units within a business. These groups may masquerade on the payroll as "business analysts" or "maintenance engineers" or in one company as "warehousing specialists" (they were building a logistics management system). These units often work outside the disciplines and processes that are expected to surround corporate IT. The software they build reflects this lack of sound software engineering discipline. You must clarify who will provide ongoing support for these applications, manage their performance issues and carry the can if they are subsequently found to be faulty and have failed to process information correctly. It doesn't have to be IT. Don't be greedy, but ensure you are not the fall guy later.

The discovery team

Discovery of the domain is no trite task and you may need to assemble a small multi-disciplined team to undertake the task. The team proposed below may seem extraordinarily large and complex if you haven't done this before.

To make the discovery process effective at least five specialist skills must be assigned to your discovery team, along with other IT and business skills as required. The specialist skills are:

- Project management for planning and oversight of the task.
- Audit skills and experience in identification and tracking of business assets and information.

- Record management for creation of the repository and index for the discovered material.
- IT infrastructure sizing skills so that the current infrastructure and its limitations are properly documented.
- Financial analysis skills to ensure that the current and projected costs of delivering the outputs in the future are properly framed and robust.

If you are expecting to introduce SLAs into the mix in the future, then it may prove worth while to include performance measurement skills as well. Use a consultant if you want an independent assessment of the current measures of performance.

The above skills may be distributed among few or many people. No one person is likely to possess all. The size of the team will be dependent on the size of the environment. We have read of discovery teams ranging from as few as three and as many as three hundred!

Issue the team with project role descriptions that define their accountabilities and responsibilities. Below are some suggested accountabilities and responsibilities of each of the roles.

Project manager

- Define the scope of the discovery process.
- Prepare the schedule of work required to carry out the process.
- Organize resources to execute the process.
- Manage the process.

The project manager may require support to organize travel, security access, procurement and recruitment of other members of the team.

Auditor

- Identify and record the location and condition of all assets.
- Resolve issues with missing licences and assets.

Auditors may require application software to support their role. Again, the role is not trite and may well require additional support staff if asset management has not been disciplined in the past. The effort required in identifying and documenting many hundred desktop software licences and identifying, tagging, valuing and registering thousands of PCs and peripherals may be very large.

Auditors may well identify other issues in the discovery process and their professional training will be useful in a number of areas.

Records manager (librarian)

Surprised? You shouldn't be. A common observation in the old days was that you built two new computer rooms when IBM delivered a system, one for the computer and the other for the manuals. IT need to make sure they record, index, maintain and update a vast number of records pertaining to IT, including manuals, specifications, operating instructions, correspondence, licences and others. You must ensure you have available:

- Staffing records (which may be confidential)
- Licences
- Maintenance agreements
- Purchase orders and invoices
- Service agreements and performance standards
- Contracts and variations
- Project statements
- Project reports
- Budgets
- Plans
- Design documentation
- User documentation
- Assets and inventory.

A qualified librarian should be asked to set up the form and index methods and assist in establishing archive and destruction rules. Acquire a software package to index and manage records.

Infrastructure expert

The infrastructure expert is required to investigate the state of the current infrastructure. The infrastructure expert is responsible for:

- Defining the level of maturity of key components, ranging from state-of-the-art to obsolescence.
- Documenting the limitations of the current infrastructure, for example, disk space constraints, bandwidth utilization, and CPU usage.
- Making a prognosis of the effects on planned projects of all types on the current infrastructure.

The infrastructure expert will have to work closely with the performance measurement expert, either now or later, to ensure that current measures are understood within the context of any infrastructure limitations, and that future performance goals include an appreciation of changes that may be required to the infrastructure.

The infrastructure assessment appears to be a common blind spot in discovery. You will usually be told your new employer has "state-of-the-art" technology. Many years of promoting this myth to potential customers and staff has often led to this almost religious belief. Often you will find they delude themselves.

Benchmarks and performance measurement

It may be premature to try to establish factual well-documented performance measures or benchmarks in the first stages of discovery. This restraint may apply because of the scale, depth, duration and demands of the benchmarking activity. If you are fortunate enough to have the staff and resources to measure existing technical and business output performance, then do so now.

Financial analysis

Beware of relying on last year's budget for a picture of the costs and revenues related to IT. They may not cover what we earlier described as hidden IT. They may be poorly structured or based on a weak appreciation of financial principles for treatment of assets, costs or revenue. Modelling the real costs of the IT department may be a difficult business. Obtain a proper financial analysis of the IT unit and establish a sound basis and accounting guidelines for budgeting and reporting in the future.

Technology domain issues

Mapping your domain may bring to the surface a number of administrative issues that need to be dealt with. Among these are:

- Licence and maintenance agreements may have lapsed and need to be renegotiated.
- Corporate assets may need to be revalued, either up or down, depending on number and condition of undiscovered assets.

- Surplus assets may need to be disposed of. They may be large in number. (Just where did all those old PCs and printers go? To the basement storage area!)
- You may discover a lot of unlicensed software that needs to be "legitimized". This may incur considerable expense.
- Some assets may be difficult to identify properly. This is often true of software, where the original supplier cannot be traced.
- The process may generate large second-order tasks such as updating or rationalizing subsidiary registers, for example help desk asset records.
- The company may also discover that the cost and effort of establishing current performance measures is beyond its reach.

Needless to remark, the legal counsel and financial units of the business may find themselves involved in sorting out the issues that arise from the discovery process.

The task of discovery is time-consuming and tedious, but it must be done. If not, personal and financial embarrassment will follow as surely as night follows day. If you do not discover the state of your sphere of operations when you take accountability for managing it, you will do so, painfully, at a later time. Your business colleagues will see to that.

Summary

Learn everything you can about the business, organization, processes, people and your IT technology domain. Failure to do so will lead to failure in the role. Much of the work can take place in parallel with setting management principles and establishing SLAs. What should be self-evident is that these other pillars of sound IT management depend in part on knowing your domain.

The extent and detail might appear overkill at first sight. A sound test of what you can do without is to review the chapter and give a cogent reason why you should not know this information if challenged by your chief executive or governing board.

Checklist

Assets and measures[ff]
- Mainframe computers
- Mid-range such as UNIX, OS/400 and other
- Intel servers
- PCs
- LAN hardware (e.g. routers, switches, hubs)
- LAN cabling
- Other telecommunications (e.g. modems)
- Printers
- Scanners

Software assets
- Operating systems
- Mainframe
- Mid-range
- Intel server
- Desktop
- Laptops

Applications
- Mainframe
- Mid-range
- Intel servers
- PCs
- Laptops

Utility assets
- Mainframe
- Mid-range
- Intel servers
- PCs
- Laptops

Tools
- Systems design
- Systems development
- Change management
- Systems management

Telecommunications
- Equipment (e.g. modems)
- Lines (e.g. data/phone, cable, X.25)

[ff] Performance measures should be noted for all relevant assets. Very few assets escape this requirement as most have some performance limitations.

Library/reference materials
- User manuals
- Technical manuals
- Vendor correspondence

Furnishings, fittings and office equipment
- Computer room (environment)
- Workstations
- Desks
- Telephones
- Mobile phones
- Facsimiles
- Photocopiers
- Shredders

Management processes
- Budget preparation
- Planning preparation
- Existing strategic, tactical and operational plans

Moribund assets
- Hardware
- Software
- Utilities
- Tools

Non-IT assets
- Human resources
- HR files complete and up to date
- Contractor agreements
- Skills register
- Benefits (pensions, bonuses, stock options)
- Turnover rates
- Training commitments
- Equipment provision (such as phones, home PCs)
- Sub-contractors' profiles

Other items
- Operations management agreements
- Application maintenance agreements
- Systems development projects reports
- Procurement agreements
- Inventory management status
- Strategy and architecture status and documentation
- Security management status and documentation
- Disaster recovery agreements
- Current performance records

- Back-up/recovery timetables
- Database management arrangements
- Upgrade management procedures
- Fault-reporting procedures
- Problem-resolution procedures
- Software distribution procedures
- Transaction-monitoring procedures
- Customer satisfaction measurement

New performance measures[gg]
- Key outputs
- Agreed baseline
- Target improvements
- Measurement
- Milestones
- Benchmarks
- Adjustments

Intellectual property agreements
- Contracted development
- Purchased software and tools
- Vendor-supplied manuals

Payments status
- Outstanding
- Disputes
- Payment cycles
- Purchase commitments
- Hardware
- Software
- Contractor staff
- Services

Audits
- Audit letters

Current compliance status
- Confidentiality agreements
  - Staff
  - Contractors
- Insurances
- Hardware
- Disaster recovery
- Public liability

[gg] The details can be contained in schedules that attach to the contract. This method can also be used for inventory, environment, human resource and other key details.

Structuring the IT organization

As Freud put it, work and sex are the two most important human activities. The time is long overdue for attending to the former in as great depth as we have attended to the latter. (Elliott Jacques in *Requisite Organization*)

This chapter deals with a topic rarely considered by IT managers: the theory and rationale of structuring the IT department. The topic is demanding and the design and implementation of proper organization structure may require you obtain specialist support. What this chapter aims to do is ensure that the structure and organization of the IT unit is built on a logic that can be explained to IT staff and other business units.

The problem

The problems are twofold. The first is that a large number of managers in IT and elsewhere are unaware that sound principles exist on which to organize a business unit. The typical approach is to structure the IT organization either around application-centric groupings, for example looking after the "life insurance application", or technical skills clustering, for example LAN and PC staff. This approach is then distorted by contortions to meet staff reward and retention needs.

IT has a further and somewhat unique complication. IT management is a comparatively new field, a field that has evolved rapidly from the tiny coterie of uniquely skilled individuals with sandals and beards to the grim, grey army of roles, ranks and specialities that bewilders the average CEO . . . and IT manager. Any large IT unit now includes network specialists, web-masters, architects—data, process and technical, strategic planners, help desks, MCSE, CICs specialists, project managers, technical writers (software), disaster recovery specialists and even the odd analyst/programmer.

There is no tradition borne of long experience to guide the IT manager like there is in bureaucracies, the Church and the military. In addition, HR specialists[hh]

[hh] My HR adviser annotated this item as follows. "If they cannot do this they are not HR specialists." Enough said.

sometimes lack the knowledge and insight to propose a method under which an IT unit can be formed.

This chapter provides a rational and step-wise approach to designing the IT organizational structure to deliver its products and services.

Guessworked structures

If the organization chart is a creative drawing that seeks to meet a myriad personal, business and service needs you may experience the following outcomes:

- Instability as the structure is constantly reworked in reaction to poor performance. The organization of IT is reactive, not proactive.
- Technical people being promoted to lead when they have no competence or skill as leaders or managers.
- A serious mismatch between the unit's organization and its outputs.
- Diffused accountability and responsibility because the structure leaves too much of the ownership of deliverables in limbo.
- Problems with pay, promotion and motivation that may be poorly linked to outputs.
- Misuse of rare technical skills which are directed to such things as purchasing, contract management, project administration, tedious periodic reports and indifferent customer relationship management.
- A lack of accountability and customer frustration because the buck never stops here!

If there is no *rationale* for organizing the IT unit then the result lacks any foundation to provide stability and allow explicable justification.

The soundly structured organization

A structured and rational approach to organizing the IT unit will overcome many of the difficulties listed above. It may also:

- Provide a structure that is logical and explicable to business and human resource colleagues as well as members of your department.

- Align IT resources with processes and valued outputs.
- Group IT staff more effectively and minimize demarcation disputes and muddled responsibilities.
- Be more stable as it is based on more concrete foundations and has inbuilt flexibility. You can remodel the structure using the same fundamental principles.
- In the long term, simplify and rationalize pay and conditions.
- Free IT professionals to concentrate on delivering IT outputs rather than being bogged down in work that rightfully belongs with other professionals.
- The expected outcome of a well-structured IT unit is one that is effective, efficient and working in harmony with the rest of the business. It also better serves employees, business colleagues, customers and suppliers.

Theory

Thomas Kuhn[73] correctly observed that any number of theories could be applied to one set of facts. The set of essays at the end of this book reinforces this view. Indeed, some theories stand in direct contravention of each other while considering the same facts. That does not mean we should dismiss theories. They give us a framework for understanding our world.

The work of Elliott Jacques dominates this chapter. Biographical details on Jacques are included in the later essay. His view, expressed in his book, *Requisite Organization*,[74] is:

> What is needed is to come to grips with the fundamental problem of organization of our managerial systems . . . You may think, as is all too commonly believed, that organization, or "too much organization," undermines the innovative adaptability and initiative you like to have. It is bad organization that does that. Good organization has precisely the opposite effect. Creativity and innovation, like freedom and liberty, depend not upon the soft-pedalling organization, but upon the development of institutions with the kinds of constraints and opportunities that can enable us to live and work together harmoniously.

Those seeking to understand the richness of Jacques theory would do well to study his book, *Requisite Organization*, and his later writings. The following précis is not a replacement for the book. The foundations of Jacques' theory are:

- Task complexity and time-span determine organizational strata, for example:
  - An individual whose role encompasses world-wide data accumulation and diagnosis and overseeing complex systems, with a 10–20-year time-span belongs in what Jacques terms "Stratum VI" (stratum six).

- – A person whose role requires them to only overcome obstacles using practical judgement in a time-span that lies from within a single day to up to three months lies in Stratum I (stratum one.)
- There is a natural, measured and observed basis for determining these strata and the behaviours of people interacting between them. Regardless of how the organization chart is drawn, staff seek guidance and advice based on an internal model, not the paper model. For example:
  - – Everyone in a role below 3 months time-span feels the occupant of the first role above 3 months time-span to be the *real* manager.
  - – Between 3 months and 1 year time-span the occupant of the first role above 1 year time-span to be the real manager.
  - – Between 1- and 2-year time-span the occupant of the first role above 2 year time-span is felt to be the real manager.
  - – [and so on.]

Jacques determines stratum from *both* task complexity and time-span measurement. The concepts of task complexity and time-span measurement is shown in Figure 26.1.

This model offers a basis for making the following judgements:

- What are the appropriate levels for each role?
- How deep should the structure be?

Without such a basis for deciding these matters they can only be based on intuition or imitation. Leave the former to clairvoyants and the latter to monkeys. Guidelines for determining complexity and time-span measurement are covered below.

Approach

It is proposed you use Jacques' theory and other instruments to develop a soundly structured IT unit. If your business has a professional HR unit *and* they apply sound theory-based organization structuring method, then seek their help.

- Build an inventory of current human resources and existing competencies as described in Chapter 4.
- Build an inventory of *required* human resources and competencies as described in Chapter 5.

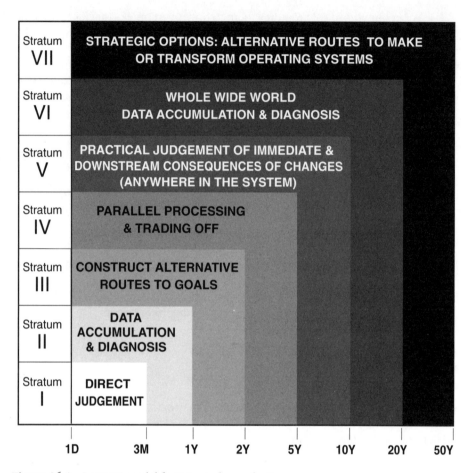

Figure 26.1—Jacques' model for time and complexity.

Time-span and complexity analysis

Now analyse the time-span and complexities demanded in each role and determine which stratum it belongs to. Appendix D1 lists the steps Jacques suggests for determining the time-span measurement. It also provides an additional illustration of a time-stratum continuum. Appendix D2 lists the steps Jacques suggests for determining the level of task complexity and a model of the stratified systems theory.

Update the required competency matrix with the appropriate stratum levels. This will help to determine the level that each role should reside at in the organization hierarchy and give some concept of relativity between roles and appropriate remuneration.

Affinity analysis

The task is now to determine which work groups can be sensibly grouped. This should be determined by process dependencies. Typically help desk, LAN and Office Automation Server Management will form a logical group. Other logical groups are not always so evident (Table 26.1).

Table 26.1—Affinity analysis

	#1 Insurance	#2 Pensions	#3 Agency	#4 Call Centre	#5 Phone M'gmt	#6 General Ledger	#7 Billings
#1 Insurance		High	High	High	High	Med	Low
#2 Pensions			Med	Low	Low	Low	Low
#3 Agency				Low	Low	Low	High
#4 Call Centre					High	None	High
#5 Phone M'gmt						None	None
#6 General Ledger							High
#7 Billings							

Proposed groupings

Team A	Pensions, Insurance
Team B	Call Centre, Phone Management
Team C	Agency, General Ledger, Billings

The purpose in creating logical groups is threefold:

- To facilitate communication and avoid discordant activities where groups have strong upstream or downstream dependencies.
- To determine the optimal management structure required to coordinate sub-groups.
- To recognize that management and supervisory skills are often in short supply and some multi-group management will be required. This is better done by affinity analysis than creating a jumbled mixture of teams with divergent responsibilities.

These logical groups should also become easier to manage as the resulting structure will demand a less developed managerial skill set which is often in short supply in IT units.

Structuring

At this point the process *appears* to become more subjective. This is not so. The difference between the process that follows and the traditional "doodled" structure is the difference between blindly throwing everything in the pantry in a pot and hoping it is edible, and assembling specific ingredients which are blended together according to a recipe.

1. Take a whiteboard and mark it with horizontal lines representing the stratum levels identified by Jacques.
2. Add the roles of the defined affinity groups to the chart, placing each role at an appropriate level.
3. Review this against the known demands of IT processes and service level agreements and ensure there are no obvious gaps.
4. Refine the model into a clean structure, while retaining the groups and levels.

What should emerge is a largely logical organization chart. Realists will recognize that at this stage a number of seemingly illogical issues will need to be factored into the model. Defining the structure demands compromise, intuition and risk taking.

Take care of logistics

Determine the following aspects of the environment for each team:

- Tools required for the task, for example manuals, reference books, authoring software, CASE tools, change control software, systems management, and so on.
- Hardware and office equipment such as facsimiles, photocopiers, binding equipment.
- Fittings, including cupboards, shelving, desks, workbenches and the like.
- Some less obvious but often required extras include security changes, rostering software, clerical support, library support, refreshments and meeting rooms.

There is no surer way to guarantee that the new team will be disaffected and demoralized from the start than to assemble them, commit them to their new roles, and then require them to work in a sub-standard environment without the tools and equipment required for the job.

Finalize role descriptions

You must now:

- Finalize role descriptions[ii] for your direct reports based on the new structure.
- Issue guidelines to your direct reports on forming role descriptions and task assignments for their subordinates.
- Ensure quality control is exercised to ensure that subordinate role descriptions and task specifications align with the underlying IT process model, SLAs and organization chart.

There are some basic rules:

- Describe the role requirements. Do not twist the requirements to meet the current incumbent.
- Define the role competencies.
- Prescribe the accountabilities and outputs of the role.

[ii] The jargon of HR is inconsistent, much as it is with IT. In this text, role description is defined as the document that sets out an individual's role in the company.

- Make sure that reporting lines are based on scalar theory.
- Identify key customers that the role serves.
- Estimate the cost of the new structure. It may go up or down. Enlist the help of your HR unit to define salary and on-costs for each role.

> Do not underestimate compensation increases. High service demands, huge application backlogs, anywhere–anytime computing, integrated information, E-commerce and the fusion of business and IT will continue to challenge compensation traditions.[75]

- Work with HR on succession planning for the new structure both for its immediate population and for the longer term. Some may only require minimal training to advance, others might require more.

Assign people to roles

The final step will be to populate the logical model with real people. This task should not be intuitive. Make sure you have the following material on each employee available to you when you start:

- Competency inventory
- Performance appraisals
- Job history
- The motivations and preferences of each person.

You will need to *talk* to staff to obtain an accurate picture of the latter. They will need to know the type of avenues opening to them. This is not simply a paper-based exercise.

Now start matching the individuals to the roles based on individual competencies, skills and personality to the job requirements.

Obstacles

You will not have the ideal number of resources, all perfectly skilled and docile enough to be herded into their new stables. You will need to trade off a number of factors including:

- The practical need to create sinecures to access special salary and condition scales for scarce technical resources.
- The difficulty of ridding a business of marginal performers and the need to accommodate them, at least temporarily, in the IT structure.
- The existence of conflicting demands from business colleagues on the always-limited resources of people, infrastructure and time.
- The limits to IT authority and power over things outside its jurisdiction.

Be prudent

You must follow sound HR practice on obtaining employee agreement to their new roles. It is important that you document any disagreements and seek to overcome them. Bring your HR specialists into the process to support you and ensure that an "honest broker" oversees the process. Do beware that you may run foul of industrial relations legislation if this is handled badly.

The expected outcome of this step is that you will have:

- Staff assigned to roles and a signature of confirmation on the form.
- Gap analysis by role that will direct your staff development plans.
- A number of unfulfilled roles which will direct your recruiting.
- A number of staff who do not fit any role in your revamped IT department, which will direct your redundancy programme.
- The basis for your staff development plan, which should be directed to closing the gap between requirements and resources.

The above process is likely to be tedious, emotive and frequently disheartening. Fail to do it though, and *your* role will be continually tedious, emotive and disheartening!

Introduce the teams

Do make sure that:

- You brief each team on their overall responsibilities.
- You ensure each team member knows each other's role and accountabilities.

- You introduce teams and explain co-dependencies where they exist.
- You introduce teams to their customers and brief the customer on the team, and the individuals.
- You set out clear lines of communication.

Everyone has a copy of their task specifications and the service level agreement they are part of, including the *customer's* staff.

Fill the gaps

The process described above will show that the current inventory lacks some key competencies and is over-supplied with others. Chapter 7 provides some tips on both overcoming shortages and recruiting.

Implementation issues

The pragmatist within recognizes that the gritty realities of business life will debase the pure vision, as follows:

- The reality that "due process" and "formal service agreements" cannot, and will not foresee all eventualities and the need to be flexible, and bypass agreed rules where it makes commercial sense to do so.
- The need to accommodate the structure within the company's broader relative structure and possible contention over IT compensation levels and relative pay-scales *vis-à-vis the business.*
- Staff not understanding that jobs with the same title may be rewarded differently.
- The problem of allocating a single resource across more than one project.

Traps for the unwary include:

- Assuming every process must have the highest-grade competency in each category. That is an easy trap to fall into.
- Grading the *required* resources based on *available* competency. That is putting the cart before the horse.

- Overlooking non-technical resources required to effectively deliver the outputs.

The good news is that once the underlying rationale is understood and the framework constructed, you as a manager have a robust basis for organizing your IT unit.

Expect trouble

The literature on forming teams suggests that they will go through Tuckman's five-stage sequence:[76]

- Forming is the period of initial anxiety and uncertainty.
- Storming is the emergence of tension and conflict.
- Norming is when the group focuses on what is common rather than the differences.
- Performing is when the team address the job to be done.
- Terminating is coping with the ending.

Don't be afraid of these reactions. Your job is to weather the storm, not wilt before it. Turn to Appendix A for guidelines on managing conflict. Allow some of it to run its course, it is necessary and clears the air. The key strategies for handling this period are:

- Don't hide. Be visible. Keep your eye on things.
- Act if the problems are seriously damaging but beware of becoming a wet nurse on every minor grievance.
- If necessary, obtain advice on team-bonding exercises and other methods of managing people change.
- As each part of the team starts norming and performing, signal the end and give them praise. It is not necessary to wait until every last person is happy—or departed—to do this.

Maintaining the structure

The first rule of maintenance is "if it ain't broke, don't fix it." Don't over-react. The new teams will take time to settle in. New allegiances have to be forged within the teams and with the customer. New things have to be learned, and new ways of working. Give it a chance. Don't rush to rearrange the deckchairs when the first squall hits. It will be particularly important to keep your nerve during the storming phase.

Remember, you have used some sound techniques to settle the structure and composition of your IT unit. If something isn't working first ask "why?"

Tips

Set yourself some criteria that must be met before you trigger change. Try to keep them as objective as possible. Three examples follow:

- Repeated failure to perform critical tasks.
- Personality clashes that lead to sub-standard work and cannot be resolved.
- Intense customer dissatisfaction as measured by customer-satisfaction surveys.

Don't fall into the trap of reallocating staff within roles when some training or education can move them up to the next level of competency.

Involve the HR unit if the problem appears personality based. They should explore both sides of the argument and may suggest another course of action. Do follow sound (and where defined, statutory) staff counselling guidelines in dealing with performance and personality issues.

Give the new organization time to work. This admonition is repeated because too often managers over-react to the initial settling-in pains. They are people and it probably won't work perfectly first time.

Finally—your job is to manage a team to deliver results, not win votes. It may be that you will have to suffer some lack of popularity in attaining those results. So be it, that's management for you. Over time, staff will respect a leader who gets results.

Modifications

If you have to modify your unit, then take the following into consideration:

- Ask yourself *Why?* Do the reasons hold up?
- How will this affect any agreed principles of management?

- How will this affect any extant service level agreement?
- How will this affect immediate, upstream or downstream IT processes?
- Is the issue properly described and something I can fix?
- Is the issue within the business domain and something another must fix?
- How will this change impact the overall organization model?

At the risk of becoming repetitive, do seek the help of HR professionals. They know as much about HR as you know about IT.

Summary

Structuring the IT unit requires that you demonstrate a direct relationship linking the activities of the IT unit with the key technology-based demands of the remainder of the business. You will face limitations imposed by the integrated nature of IT infrastructure, the competing, even conflicting needs of business users. The unit may lack appropriate skills, both technical and management.

Following the guidelines will not guarantee an excellent, effective, flexible department. However, the prospect of hard work for a less than perfect result is not an excuse for doing nothing or structuring your IT unit on the basis of a doodled drawing.

Checklist

1. Have you developed a comprehensive high-level process model of IT?
2. Does that model include processes of contract, procurement and administrative management?
3. Have you defined the competencies required in your IT unit?
4. Have you analysed each process and SLA to determine the work-effort required to support delivery of agreed measures?
5. Have you determined the competency levels and potential resources to fulfil the resource demand?
6. Have you considered tools and equipment required to support the processes and SLAs?
7. Have you carried out affinity analysis to determine dependencies and suitable work groupings?

8. Have you carefully analysed each role to determine its position on the management scale?
9. Have you considered the implications of differing levels for some roles, for example different grades of project manager?
10. Have you considered pay differentials between the grades and established some sound basis for maintaining the differential?
11. Have you conferred with the SLA owners on the resource implications and shortcomings that exist?
12. Have you considered the location of each team?
13. Does that location possess the appropriate furniture and fittings for the team?
14. Have you completed descriptions for each role?
15. Do they map to your competency matrix? Does either require updating?
16. Have you appropriate public spaces such as meeting rooms and workshop areas?
17. Have you considered the communication and management control issues of remote teams? (Remote may be one floor up!)
18. Have you entered into a service level agreement with your recruiter, and/or your HR department on recruiting?
19. Have you introduced each team and explained team accountabilities?
20. Have you made sure each team member knows the role of each other team member and their individual responsibilities?
21. Has the customer been briefed on the team and the individuals within the team?

27 Where to next?

Cheer up! The worst is yet to come. (Philander Johnson in *Forbes Business Quotations*)

As an IT manager you will need to have a firmer view of the future than many of your fellow executives. This chapter does not offer tips and hints. It poses questions and considerations for the IT manager.

Shortages of IT staff

This phenomenon is widely reported in virtually every developed company. GartnerGroup[77] made the observation that: "Through 2003, the effective employment rate for the IT industry globally will be substantially negative; for every 10 full time hires required, only 7.5 IT professionals will be available, albeit with regional variations." This points to the need for IT managers to think outside the box as suggested in the anecdote about Jim Hepburn in Chapter 7.

Changing structure

GartnerGroup pointed out in the same report that "By 2003, the traditional hierarchical IS organization will have virtually disappeared in 80 percent of midsize and large enterprises and will be replaced by a more modular, process based model." This view is linked to the perception held by managers that up to 20% of IT staff will come from within the business. It also complies with the evolving nature of work in areas outside IT. The challenge will be to take cognizance of theories of organization such as that of Elliott Jacques and adapt them to suit the evolving structure of work.

Changing face of work

Issues that you must consider as an IT manager include the changing face of work. The following changes merit consideration.

Telecommuting

You will need to consider how you will manage your staff who telecommute:

- Will you introduce SLAs to govern their work and outputs?
- How will you pay them? Piece-rates? Standard salary? Hourly?
- What equipment and services will be supplied to them?
- What controls can be exerted over maintenance and care of assets in their care?
- How will support be provided for the equipment and software they use, and will you organize software licences which double for home and work?
- Who pays if the system needs fixing (that is, done by a local PC specialist over a weekend)?
- Who pays for insurance coverage, and will this include personal use and use by family members?
- How will they communicate and be communicated to, other than the obvious e-mail and telephone infrastructure?
- How will sound human resource support and evaluation take place?
- How will you know them well enough to mentor, develop and promote appropriate staff?

These few questions should stimulate some ideas and issues that need to be faced. Think about them in regard to your staff. Then you will be partially prepared when a business unit announces they are telecommuting and ask you to support this initiative.

New technology

As IT manager you must be constantly aware of technology life cycles and position yourself for change. Some key considerations you must consider include:

- Will this technology last the life of the application?
- Will this technology be supplanted by a shift in the way business is done?
- Will this technology supplant a current business process? (ATMs supplanting tellers.)
- Will the business evolve in the same direction as this technology? (For example, wireless applications to support a now obsolescent sales force.)

- What are the risks this new technology poses to the business?
- What risks are associated with the provider of the technology—including commercial and financial?

A common issue is the "new technology" being superseded during the construction of a new system or failing to last anywhere near the applications commercial life. There are no easy answers to these issues but you can prepare yourself to meet change.

Business focus

The need to focus on business outcomes permeates the advice in this book. IT is increasingly treated as a critical asset and less as a simple means of process automation and tool to achieve headcount reduction. The change to sound governance models will increase the demand for IT to produce quantified and rapid value add to the business. The model by which business will translate the business impact of IT is illustrated in Figure 27.1.

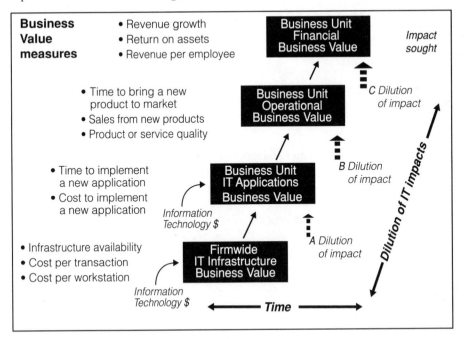

Figure 27.1—Translating the business impact of IT.

GartnerGroup, *IS & IT Management: Using IT for Value Creation and Business Effectiveness*. Report 5601, USA, 1999. Reproduced by permission of the GartnerGroup.

Blueprint the future

If you are managing in a medium or large-scale enterprise then the best way to prepare for the future is to develop a set of work, application, information and technology architectures. This process will *force* you and more importantly *your business colleagues* to think about the future and how they are going to handle it. If you are unfamiliar with the concepts, review Chapter 24 and then read some good reference books. Possible titles are listed at the end of this book in "Further reading".

Consider a strategic plan

Depending on the method followed to develop your architecture you may wish to include or integrate it with an IT strategic plan. Some architecture development methods do not address all the longer-term issues of IT organization, principles, and related issues.

   If you develop a strategic plan, try to avoid the multi-volume behemoth. Keep it short and sweet, focused and pertinent. If you employ a consultant do to this remember the BTOPP and ResultsChain™ mentioned earlier.

Review what you do now

Consider the rationale for some of the services provided by your unit. Does it make sense to have an internal e-mail system when you can use that of an ISP with global as well as local reach? Is your IT unit providing user training or other services that are inappropriate and belong elsewhere? Can you outsource some of your processes to others including administrative processes?

Learn

One question you must ask yourself is: where next for *me*? As a manager who has come from a technical professional background the answer is that you must take the time and effort to study management skills.

What follows is a series of short essays on two topics. The first series of essays explores some views by those outside our profession on what is wrong with IT management. The second series of essays discusses some major management theorists and their work.

Both, we hope, will serve as a stimulus to inquiring minds that IT management is first and foremost about *management*.

PART B
WHAT IS WRONG WITH IT MANAGEMENT?

This part contains a series of essays written by IT managers, management consultants and others. The intent is to illustrate the extent of dissatisfaction with current IT service delivery, management and organization. The contributor's words are unabridged—they vary in writing style and length. However, they all contain some useful messages for IT management professionals.

The IT Manager's Survival Guide does not pretend to address every issue that could be raised. It is doubtful if anyone can, given the complex interplay of corporate cultures, individual behaviours and workplace types, business demands, resources, training and change management required.

What the book does seek to do is provide a path through the morass which will ensure that the organization and management of the unit is based on the sound principle of meeting appropriate business demands where it makes commercial sense to do so.

These essays also show how those outside the arena view the issues in IT management. The views expressed may disappoint those who expect the topics to deal with technical skill shortages—the point so lovingly embraced by politicians, educators and associations keen to further their own views. The weaknesses seen by this group of contributors lie in what is wrong with IT *management* and the absence of management, organization and leadership skills.

That should be a sound indicator of what needs to be done to improve IT management. This book goes some way towards pointing IT professionals in that direction.

Essay 1   Incomplete education

R Aalders
2001

This essay proposes that one of the key causes of dissatisfaction with IT units today is that they are, on the whole, managed by technical professionals who have little, if any, formal management education. This essay traces one reason why this is so, why it persists and the resulting effects.

At the tertiary level, when formal computing skills were first taught, the faculty owner was usually the department of mathematics. Undergraduates who were encouraged to study outside the standard sequence of courses required for a major were generally directed to additional mathematics, electrical or electronic engineering and formal logic.

Few, if any, early information technology graduates were encouraged to study what Hilmer[ii] described as mainstream management skills, namely:

> The **core** disciplines include data analysis—the dreaded math and stats—economics, organizational behaviour, accounting, finance, marketing, law, and possibly political science. **Applied** subjects built on the core include corporate strategy and policy, change management, new product development, information systems, technology management, human resource strategy, operations, international and comparative management, and marketing strategy. Key **skill** areas include—writing, presenting, listening, interviewing—negotiation, numeracy and technical literacy, and interpersonal and leadership skills.

It would be fair to say that very few computer systems professionals can point to any of the core disciplines, let alone the set of applied disciplines that follow. This has changed—a little—with the emergence of "MIS" majors that have sought to build both technology and management skills. However, the average computer systems graduate is very poorly prepared for an appointment to manage a small team, let alone run a substantial organizational unit of many hundreds of people. One suspects that the high turnover of IT staff, the segregation of IT from the "real

---

[ii] The bolding was added to the original quote for emphasis.

business" and much of the antagonism that lies between other business professionals and IT staff stems in part from this weakness.

To exacerbate matters, when computing studies were introduced to schools they tended to focus on elementary programming logic, basic PC operating system commands and physical system structure. The schools saw themselves as equipping students for university and the advice and guidance the educationalists received was to teach them basic programming. In time this changed and, in many countries, schools have shifted the focus to computer-based skills such as word processing and spreadsheets, and using the computer as an information resource tool.

Nevertheless, curriculums are slow to change as education is a highly orthodox, conservative field that finds it difficult to throw off the mantle of Plato and Aristotle, the first educational theorists. Despite the clear evidence that life skills in a white-collar workforce demand at least some basic understanding of human resource management, operations, budgeting, finance, project planning, self-management, organizational behaviour, law and simple economic theory, they simply do not appear in the choices offered to students.

Of course, IT professionals are not alone in these shortcomings. It would appear that this is true of all specialist professions. However, it does seem that students of marketing, human resource management, and finance are exposed and encouraged to study more of the "core management" subjects identified in Hilmer's list.

Many professionals recognize this shortcoming, and the graduate schools are besieged with students seeking the magical MBA, or at least a graduate diploma in management. It might be argued that this is "just in time" teaching, but looking at the average age and position of many MBA students one might conclude it is "just-too-late" teaching.

So, how is the new manager or supervisor trained? Too often, it is by being sent on one-day "motivational courses", or by slow and gradual accumulation of piecemeal knowledge based in part on experience, in part on reading and in part on observation as to how others do it. You then may start to become a good manager just at the terminal point of your career!

The challenge then for the IT manager is to become educated yourself in what the business pays you for—managing!

That does not necessarily mean enrolling in a formal course. While the certificate is useful to have, a formal course may be constrictive, stressful and possibly structured in such a way that does not meet your needs in relation to time available and current issues. This is not to decry formal courses; indeed, they are to be highly recommended. The intention is instead to encourage you to list the areas where you are weakest, rank your need to know something about them, and read a few good books in "study mode" to build your knowledge in the appropriate areas.

In summary, this writer's view is that a significant contributor to poorly managed IT departments is the lack of training and education in management given to intending IT professionals. Remedying this would do much to improve the overall professionalism with which IT units are managed, and indeed bring an end to the "us and them" attitude that prevails among IT and other business professionals.

Essay 2 Leadership skills

Jeremy Tozer
Leadership Initiatives
2001

Many IT departments are not alone in suffering from a lack of leadership; a lack of effective leadership is common in many organizations and enterprises. However, there are some problems particularly prevalent in the technology areas. Before we discuss them, though, we must be clear about what is meant by the terms leadership and leader. I define leadership as: the capacity and desire to rally people to a common purpose by someone with the character that inspires confidence and trust. I define a leader as: a person responsible for achieving objectives through the work of others by creating the conditions for success, and for building and maintaining the team of which he or she is a member.

This essay will raise certain issues but the constraints of space prevent solutions being provided. For enquiries about solutions you should contact us at enquiries@leadinginitiatives.com

The character of IT "leaders"

Let us first look at leadership character in the world of IT. While it is wrong to generalize about individuals, generalizations exist because many people in a category display similar characteristics. Many IT people join the technology world because they like to "interface" with machines which are designed to be predictable, often in preference to "interfacing" with people—who have unique personalities and reactions and who are unpredictable. Much social time is spent surfing the net and sending e-mail rather than in engaging people with face-to-face communication. Consequently, under-developed social confidence and a lack of self-awareness and interpersonal effectiveness abound (a lack of emotional intelligence, if you like new terms for old ideas).

This is exacerbated by the usual approach to promotion in badly organized organizations—take a technical expert and make him or her a leader (this is regularly repeated in the sales function). All too often the result is a demoralized team. Why is this?

First, too many people occupy IT leadership roles because they seek the status and pay that comes with a leadership role, but who fundamentally do not want to be leaders. Where the fundamental "will" to lead is missing or when the value placed on being a leader (and all that that entails) is absent, there can be no behavioural (or emotional intelligence) development. If IT leaders fundamentally do not want to be responsible for people and be leaders of people—guiding them and welding them into a cohesive team—they will not succeed.

Many IT professionals are forced into leadership roles to obtain higher pay. The "system" does not let them be paid more for high-level individual work, because the pay system relates to the number of people working for them rather than the level of work complexity that is managed. This is not a requisite approach to organization.

Second, too many IT leaders are technical experts. Instead of creating the conditions in which others may be successful—by removing obstacles and roadblocks, creating clarity and developing the climate and enhancing individual's competence—the leader who is a technical expert often thinks it quicker that he or she do all the work. Instead of investing the coaching time to develop others, allowing them to learn from mistakes and then grow to lighten the leader's load; many technical experts are prone not to trust others and to interfere in the work of others, thus stifling all initiative. Figure B1 shows the conditions for leadership success.

Clarity of thought

In the work that we have conducted with many IT professionals and groups to develop problem-solving ability (whether the problem is an obstacle, challenge or opportunity), we commonly observe a systematic mode of thinking (systems thinking is to be applauded). However, this systematic approach often includes sequential thought within narrow confines and over-reliance on bending past experience to fit (which is information retrieval rather than genuine problem solving resulting in a unique solution or choice of solutions).

In short, there is little clarification of the higher-level direction purpose behind problem solving in a dynamic and iterative fashion that considers the implications of changing situations. Nor is deductive or inductive thought systematically used to rigorously analyse the factors affecting a problem with the result that few options appear to be open. We have thus seen a wasted expenditure of emotional energy, time and money on projects that fail to deliver.

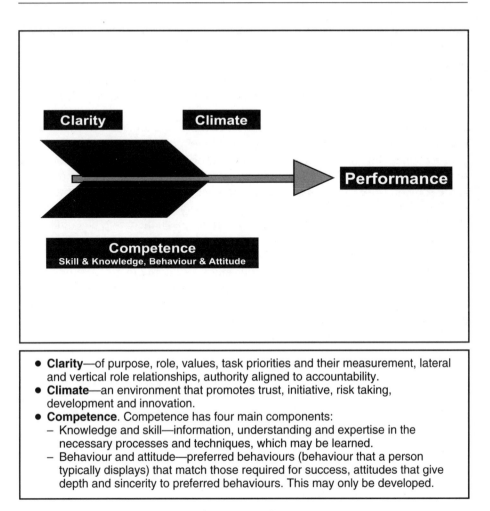

Figure B1—Creating the conditions for success—the 3Cs

Organization

Many IT departments (like their parent organizations) are organized in such a way that no-one is effectively led because organization (or lack of effective organization) prevents it. Ill-defined matrix dotted lines prevail, and people are urged to use influencing skills and to learn to work with ambiguity—both of which are often a "cop-out" for a lack of clear thinking about structure. Clear thinking about structure creates the framework—the defined playing field—within which people can work and cooperate without ambiguity, role overlaps or gaps creating unnecessary conflict.

To whom one reports is irrelevant, the essential point is that only one person can be accountable for your output and thus set priorities for you, and that is your "boss". Therefore your "boss" in a day-to-day sense and in an annual appraisal sense may be a business unit manager; with IT policy, remuneration and IT career development coming from the IT department head.

If accountability is not matched with authority then fundamentally a role is untenable. It is wrong to rely on authority, but at the end of the day if you cannot cause someone else to do what is needed to meet your accountabilities, then your role is set up to fail. If your boss is to be held accountable for your work then he or she needs to have certain authorities, as does their boss if there is to be equilibrium of leadership quality across any three-layer organizational groups. Likewise, if you are to meet your accountabilities to your "boss" you will probably need some authority with regard to other lateral colleagues—authority to advise, audit, initiate, delay and so on. This does not mean your colleagues report to you in the sense that you are their line manager with accountability for their output. Their managers remain accountable for their output, but you have the authority to ask them to stop, start, delay or to consider something.

Essay 3 Speak plain English

Anna M Hinder
Accenture
2001

This essay was sub-titled: *Peter Pan: The IT Director In Never Never Land*. Peter entered Never Never Land as soon as he graduated from university. All the roles Peter has held since university have taught him the culture of this land, the work habits, the codes, how to treat people and the way the people of Never Never Land work with internal clients.

The golden rule is never, never speak in plain English—if you do you might accidentally communicate with the person you are talking to and they might understand what you said! After 10 years in IT, Peter has been granted full citizenship.

Alas, at the time Peter was granted full citizenship he was also promoted to IT director. One detail was missing from his new role description—relocation was required. Planes and luggage were not needed for this trip; it was a mental journey from Never Never Land to Real Land. The hardest part of the journey is that no-one will tell Peter what he needs to take, to pack or what his new home will look like.

Peter needs to make the trip from professional to manager. In many organizations the journey never takes place. Newly appointed IT directors do not change their mindset from being an IT professional in Never Never Land with their defrags, pings and load balancing to the Real Land of business processes, cost cutting and new products.

Peter's colleagues at the management table dream about an IT colleague who can speak without jargon, use a metaphor to illustrate a concept and who can see their point of view. They dream of an IT director who can speak both languages and translate. The sad result is a group of people dreaming about how wonderful it would be to be able to work together while becoming increasingly frustrated that they cannot.

Everyone who trains in a profession starts off in Never Never Land. It is specialist concepts, terminology and methods that build the professional skill set. The challenge of being successful in senior roles is one of learning to operate as a management professional, rather than as a professional IT person. You need to spend less and less time on getting your hands dirty and more and more time working with your peers from different parts of the business on solving business problems. Power and influence are drawn from effective communication and working relationships and builds on the existing power base of expert knowledge.

Learning the skills required to leave Never Never Land is an attainable goal. The hardest part is realizing you need to do it and obtaining the resources to learn. You have one of them in your hand.

Essay 4   Finding the right job

Peter Hind
IDC
2001

You can lead a horse to water but you can't make it drink: an old proverb but one which contains highly pertinent advice for the aspiring or incumbent IT manager. *The IT Manager's Survival Guide* explores tactics and techniques to use in the role of IT manager. However, the one thing we cannot address is the people for whom you work. If you establish the best structure for IT will they or will they not drink from its waters?

It is worth noting that there is still a very strong demand for IT workers. *Computer World* on 9 April 2001 reported that 425 000 IT positions in the USA will go unfilled this year according to a study by the Information Technology Association of America. This is in a year noted for its economic downturn. As such, it is worth remembering there are many potential IT positions available. Therefore, the ambitious and motivated IT manager need not be held captive to the failings of his or her business executive. We believe that this state of affairs should give you reassurance that you are not powerless to implement your ideas in the organization for whom you work. Let the business understand the demand for IT staff. You are paid to make IT work. Are they going to back you or not?

However, it may pay to do a little homework before you accept the position of IT manager with a new employer. At the very least this might highlight just what you are letting yourself in for. You will certainly gain an insight into the IT environment you are joining by asking about the IT infrastructure currently in place. It is fair to say that organizations still using Windows for Workgroups and without a standard desktop are likely to be conservative in their application of IT. On the other hand, a business using Windows XP and developing in Java and XML is likely to attach importance to keeping up to date in its IT architectures.

We must stress that neither of these circumstances should be a cause for celebration or alarm in themselves. A very conservative organization might well reflect a company that has been highly successful in leveraging its investment in IT. Alternatively, it might highlight an organization crying out for somebody to galvanize its business systems. Another view is that an organization constantly investing in the latest and greatest might be misguided in thinking that the answer to all its IT prayers always lies in the next release. Conversely, it might also reflect a company in tune with the potential of IT for whom the IT manager is a highly respected strategic partner. The interview process gives you a good opportunity to learn some facts to determine how IT is perceived in that business.

It is then worth while trying to gain some picture of your predecessors. How long did they work there? Why did they leave? How many IT managers has the company had in the last three years? All these questions will give you insights into the organization, its view of IT and the technological approach of its executive. An organization with four IT managers in three years clearly has some difficulties.

It should not be difficult to discover previous incumbents. Several IT publishers maintain a list of IT executives for marketing purposes. A gentle enquiry to the subscriptions manager of one of the dominant IT publications could well reveal a name. Alternatively, your contacts with suppliers might be able to help. They may have dealt with that organization in the past and have a contact name for you to follow.

Once you have made contact with the person why not invite them for a coffee to discuss their experiences in the organization you are considering? While this discussion will give you only one side of the coin it will show your potential employers you are thorough. It will also enable you to ask valid tough questions of them at an interview to see whether they do want IT to work or whether they are just after another whipping boy or girl for the IT manager position. After all, they can continue to pour good money after bad trying to make IT work or they can give you the responsibility to make it happen.

Essay 5 Ask: "What does my company want of me?"

John Oleson
Former CIO and then CFO at John Hancock Insurance. John later joined IDC as
head of the end user research programme IT Adviser. He is now retired and
living in North Carolina
2001

Over the years, a number of CIOs, and in particular new and younger leaders of IT, have committed a series of mistakes that have had a negative impact on the companies for which they work, and in the most egregious cases, they have committed career-limiting mistakes that have led to their early departure "to pursue personal interests".

The most serious failures of the new CIOs are associated with their lack of understanding of the business environment in which they work and the political ramifications of technology options available to them. They fail to assess the attitudes of the CEO, CFO and other top business executives towards the role that top management expects IT to play in the enterprise. They fail to ask the question: is IT a cost centre to be controlled so it does not spend too much, or is IT a means to furthering the advancement of the business through appropriate investments in new technologies?

Most IT executives hope for the latter to be the true attitude of top management, but in a very large percentage of companies the former is the true attitude. When the IT executive fails to determine the true attitude, major problems have developed.

Only about 20% of companies are aggressive in the use of technology for strategic business purposes. Most use technology as an adjunct to individual productivity or as massive data processing machines. In such environments, a new CIO must tread carefully. The introduction of newer technologies needs to be managed in such a way as to win the active support of top management. This support is most often associated with cost/benefit analyses and a hefty ROI from the installation of the new technology. The factors related to the ROI in such companies are conservative, hard dollar savings and documented cost avoidance.

The projection of additional revenue is considered too speculative by top management to be part of the cost/benefit analysis. Premature technology adoption by an aggressive CIO has often led to the loss of management support, the critical factor for the survival of the CIO.

In addition to top management's attitudes toward new technology, the CIO needs to assess the cultural attitudes of employees early in his or her job tenure. The corporate cultural barriers can undermine the CIO's best efforts to introduce a higher rate of technology change or to adopt a new architecture that impacts the way in which people work. The assumption that line managers will be able to increase the speed of technology adoption is flawed. Technology change is always accompanied with some degree of temporary productivity decrease and the bonuses for these managers is closely related to productivity, not to new technology.

The second most serious failure lies in the focus on technology at the expense of business requirements and employee acceptance. This is the flip side of lack of business focus. The CIO who is enamoured of a particular technology, either because he or she is familiar with its use or because the technology is new and exciting, runs the risk of not matching the technology to the real needs of the enterprise, in other words of adopting inappropriate technology. One finds this historically when IBM tried to enter the word-processing business to compete with Wang, which had a much superior product. The old EDP managers tried to force its customers into adopting the IBM solution. This was one of the key drivers of IT decentralization that began in the mid-1980s. A more modern example is found in companies that are early adopters of software version upgrades. The desire of the CIO to be a leading-edge shop can hurt business productivity as systems bugs cause delays from crashes and rework from flawed software.

CIOs must remember that the business of business is to make money, not necessarily to be the first in the use of technology, for technology is only the means to the end, not the end in itself. CIOs who do not remember this are destined to failure.

Essay 6   The trouble with IT projects

John Smyrk
BEc (Hons), MEc (OR) (Monash)
Principal, Sigma Management Science Pty Limited
Visiting Fellow at the National Graduate School of Management, the Australian
National University
2001

Traditionally, the cash crop for the IT professional has been the "IT project". These exercises range from infrastructure (such as hardware upgrades) through to applications systems for the business. Projects involving applications systems have a startling failure rate—often reported to be as high as 90%. A common mistake among IT professionals arises from a confusion between software engineering and process engineering. That makes about as much sense as using the methodologies for building ships as a way of improving a shipping service.

The conventional model of an "IT project"

Two of the key characteristics of an "IT project" are: that its objective is to implement a system and that its project structure is based on a systems development methodology (SDM). The heart of such exercises is the functional specification—based on a list of functions that the application system is to be capable of performing and a model of the data on which those functions are executed. A functional specification is usually assembled by asking the "users" what they want. The resulting list of "user requirements" is matched against candidate "solutions". The "solution" with the best fit will be configured and eventually implemented.

The conventional approach is based on some 40 years of experience—experience that, by any measure, suggests that something is seriously wrong.

Project models and methodologies

The evolution of (two) species of methodology

Today, the world of IT is split into two distinct sectors—those who *create products to sell* and those who *install those products to improve their businesses*. The critical issues faced by firms involved the IT/IT product-development sector concern applications development. These organizations use *software engineering* as the foundation for their projects. Firms in the product-application sector face a different set of key issues—mainly related to the task of enhancing performance by improving core business processes. Over the past decade, a methodology has evolved to deal with projects of this kind. A generic name for this approach is business process engineering (BPE). *Continuous improvement* and *business process re-engineering* are specialist variants of BPE.

Unfortunately, the older *software engineering* methodology has permeated so much of the IT discipline that its shortcomings in product-application are poorly understood—even by IT professionals. The upshot of all this is that there is widespread confusion between *software engineering* and *process engineering*. See Curtis *et al.*[78] for an early paper that recognizes the importance of process modelling, but where, nevertheless, it is seen as little more than an extension of software engineering.

IT projects are those based on software engineering, business initiatives are those based on process engineering. I propose that a major cause of project failure is the use of software engineering-based methodologies for projects whose objective is enhanced process performance.

What has 40 years of SDM experience taught us?

What sorts of difficulties emerge from the use of the *software engineering*-based conventional model? The first problem is that of identifying the users whose needs are to be recognized. Are users people who *use* (that is, *operate*) systems? What about those whose needs are critical but who will never actually **use** the system— in what sense are they users? And if we do take their needs into account are we justified in calling the resulting specification a **user** document?

However assembled, user requirements are often little more than a log of claims. This is particularly true if the IT department holds the budget for the projects concerned. Usually the list of demands on the desired system assembled in this way involves requirements that are:

- incomplete
- mutually exclusive
- technically or commercially infeasible
- irrelevant

Worse still, in the course of the project, the functional specification has an unnerving tendency to move, jump, shift, meander and extend in a fashion that is impossible to contain.

In the end someone just has to decide on a definitive specification—usually a task given to the IT department—regardless of what the users want. As a consequence, it then becomes impossible to get the users to take ownership of the specification—an all too common complaint from the IT professional.

The problem with "IT" projects

So where is the problem?

There are a number of factors that contribute to the present situation. First, there is the role of the vendors of the products being installed. Their view of the world is influenced heavily by the software-engineering orientation of their own product-development activity. In addition to that bias, vendors insist that they sell "solutions". If that were true, then the conventional approach would work because the project would degenerate into "implementing the solution". In reality vendors sell a *product*, the customer then attempts to *utilize* the product in such a way that a solution is realized as an *outcome* (not an output) of the project. The customer and not the vendor is accountable for engineering a solution from the exercise. Claims of selling solutions rather than products should be challenged with the proposition that . . . "there are no IT solutions to business problems".

Second, I suggest that, where projects have not gone well, both the business and IT participants tend to infer that the poor results are due to the incorrect application of the conventional methodology (see, for example, Roberts[79])—instead of jumping to the logical conclusion that the methodology itself is unworkable and shouldn't be used.

Third, "IT projects" are inadequately scoped. Typically scoping begins with one output (the system) which its proponents seek to justify by benefit trawling. Benefit trawling is a mechanism by which beneficial outcomes are treated as "accidental strokes of good fortune that just might happen to us if we get lucky"—instead of being treated as targets for which someone is accountable. If scoping begins with target outcomes, they will frequently include enhanced business performance measured in terms of speed or efficiency. This immediately implies that the core project output is an improved business process—for which the system is simply an enabler.

Fourth, the conventional approach accepts that one can "bolt a system onto an organization", whereas I propose that one can only "bolt a system onto a process". Unfortunately, processes are seen as nothing more than barriers to getting the system in and are often degraded as a consequence—resulting in *a lowering of organizational performance instead of an improvement!*

Finally, the IT function in many organizations holds the bulk of project management experience and it is usually expedient to nominate people from IT as the managers for business projects.

The myth of the "user"

No single concept does so much damage to business projects as that of the user. This is very much part of the software engineering view of the world where developers are building systems for people who will use those systems. The role of the customer is to "use" the product and hence is simply an extension of the product—after all, the product cannot use itself! From the process engineering perspective, however, a member of the staff does not use a system as an end in itself, but as part of a much more important and richer activity—of executing a process.

Directions for change

The reality of the "process agent"

This criticism of the user begs the question "Who then is the corresponding stakeholder in the process engineering view of the world?" Enter *the process agent*. Staff who facilitate and execute business processes are agents of those processes. The user role is incidental and subordinate to the process agent role.

So where should functional specifications come from?

We clearly need to specify the systems that must be configured as part of our business initiative. How do we specify functionality for a proposed application when "asking users what they want" won't work? The logic of process engineering gives us the answer—first the process agents (and other process stakeholders) need to specify the shape of our business process and then derive our functional specification from the demands of the process. In practice, the first step is based on a process flowchart, the second involves mapping that process onto the modules of our selected product. This implies that an application product must be chosen before a full functional specification is available (in violation of conventional wisdom). In summary then, systems functionality is decided by business process requirements, and business process requirements are shaped by the demands of process agents.

The way forward

All projects involving the installation of applications software should be undertaken as business process improvement initiatives (BPIs)—which differ fundamentally from "IT projects" in that:

1. Their goal is to realize target business outcomes, rather than deliver technical "solutions".
2. Their core deliverable is a new process—rather than just an applications system.

Is an IT project ever valid?

An IT project is an appropriate approach to two sorts of exercise: those directed at the creation of a product for the marketplace and those directed at installing IT infrastructure (such as replacing the LAN cables in an office). The first type will employ software engineering methodologies, while the second requires neither software engineering nor process engineering tools.

A generic BPI project methodology

How to replace "IT" projects with business initiatives

To be successful in effecting change requires ongoing vigilance because almost everything project stakeholders see and hear supports the flawed model. In particular, I have found the following principles helpful:

Target process outcomes: Challenge the project objective:

- What processes are being improved?
- How is improvement to be measured?
- What are the target levels of improvement?
- By when will the improvements be realized?
- Who is to be held accountable for the target improvements?

Centre the project on the new process(es): Ensure that the process determines the new system—not the other way around. Of course, the available technology will limit process-enhancement options, but it does this by constraining the design of the new process, not by defining the new design.

Introduce some "political correctness" into project vocabulary: in particular by banning three terms:

- "IT project"
- "Users"
- "Solutions".

A concluding comment

The business community has, for some time now, been extremely unhappy with the value generated by "IT projects". The earlier blind faith in technology and technologists has given way to mistrust and cynicism, but the reaction of business has been largely confined to strategies of punishment—such as threats of outsourcing.

   Unfortunately many in business and IT see that the solution is to be found in simply making the old approach work right next time, whereas the old approach itself is the cause of the problem. The new approach to projects involving IT promotes prosperity through partnership because it recognizes that a meaningful business–IT partnership must be founded on the processes that underpin business—not on the systems that underpin IT.

Essay 7   Make time to grow your IT staff

Kate Behan
Managing Director of Kerandon Pty Ltd and Fellow and Honorary Life Member
of the Australian Computer Society
2001

Along with issues like ensuring good IT governance, achieving business/IT align-ment, giving value for money in IT, and getting projects delivered on time—IT managers also need to be good people managers. Much evidence exists that some IT managers are not very good at this.

Many IT managers claim that their relationships with business management are much better than they used to be. That's great, if it's true. But it's really only going to make a difference if the business/IT relationships all the way down the food chain on both sides are improving. That's only going to happen if you are pre-pared to invest in growing your people (and possibly yourself and some of your non-IT peers).

It's not good enough for you personally to have better relationships with senior executives; the value comes when your staff have better relationships with busi-ness people throughout the organization.

Who's got time for staff development activities? Every successful organization makes time for such activities. If you are not making time for it, then history suggests that you will cease to be working for a successful organization. Most of what you can do in business is easily replicated by others, first-mover advantage does not last long. The one differentiation possible is that your people are "smarter" than those of your competitor. Developing your people is the biggest contribution you can make to your organization.

There are some excellent staff development opportunities and some of the best conferences I have ever attended have been held in recent months. Sending people to seminars and conferences is time consuming and expensive—especially when only one delegate from an organization gets to go. What's the chance that there will be knowledge transfer from the sole delegate to the rest of your organ-ization? If you leave it to chance, it won't happen. So, if you invest in such development, ensure that the one who goes is required to pass on some of the new knowledge to his or her peers. Make time for it, allow time for the newly developed staff member to share that new knowledge and make sure that you are there as well. You might learn really useful things. Depending on the topic, invite some of those business professionals that are major stakeholders in current projects.

A low-cost option is to enrol several of your staff in some distance-education subjects and encourage them to have their own "tutorials" in office time. These can be virtual meetings if your staff are not co-located. Choose the subjects wisely so that your staff can "re-use" work effort as "study" effort. Ten years ago, the Australian Computer Society (ACS) began designing a distance-education post-graduate Certification programme that provides IT professionals with recognition of specialist bodies of knowledge. The most popular specialization for several years was project management. The current "most popular" is e-Business which was introduced in 2000 and has been updated three times since. There's also a specialization for current and budding CIOs on "Management and Strategy for IT", along with Knowledge Management and Software Development.

As one of the initial architects and developers of the programme I'd like to be able to say that it was a great programme when it was launched in 1993; but I cannot. What I can say is that it is now a great programme. Gerald Murphy, a recognized global expert on workplace-based education, now runs the programme and he has made major improvements. These make the subjects far more valuable to employers as well as to students. I maintain an involvement in the programme as a content developer.

Larry Prusak from IBM's Knowledge Management Institute has been quoted as saying that knowledge management is hiring good people and letting them talk to each other. How often do your staff have time for quality conversations? It won't just happen—you will have to create a need for it to happen. By encouraging your staff to undertake education that develops their specialist IT knowledge, you are making it possible for your organization to gain new knowledge with existing resources.

Organizations who offer staff development have higher staff retention. If you encourage several staff to undertake the same subject, they can meet and have quality conversations as part of their study. They can work on group assignments which can also be current work projects. If you are embarking on major projects like customer relationship management you can also involve non-IT business professionals in these workgroups—enrol them as well. It's a team-building exercise, you'll improve relationships, you'll retain your staff, your organization will increase its intellectual capital—and it does not cost much.

Essay 8   Be responsible. Call "Halt!"

Peter Hind
IDC
2001

On 8 February 1879, the notorious Australian outlaw, Ned Kelly, robbed the Bank of New South Wales in Jerilderie of the princely sum of £2141. This was his second bank robbery and the Australian banks became alarmed that his activities could jeopardize public confidence in the security of the banking system. To bring his exploits to an end they offered a collective reward of £8000 for the capture of Kelly and his gang. This was the highest reward ever offered in the Australian Colonies. In today's terms Kelly stole around $500 000.[kk]

Just over 100 years later the successor to the bank embarked on an ambitious IT project. This entailed the redevelopment of all the bank's IT systems by integrating its myriad banking products and services around a unique customer code or key. The objective was to enable the bank to rapidly assess the significance of each client to its business and to highlight opportunities for promoting new products and services these customers may not be using.

This was a mammoth task. Hundreds of people worked on the activity in locations from Sydney to New York. Unfortunately, things did no go according to plan. Seven years later the bank acknowledged that its dream was unlikely to be fulfilled and aborted the project. Conservatively, it has been estimated that the work cost the organization around $500 million.

Yet despite the fact that it would have taken one thousand Ned Kelly bank robberies before it would have lost the equivalent sum of money, the bank did not feel it was necessary to offer a reward to anyone for stopping this loss!

However, it is unfair for us to single out any one institution alone. The Standish Group reported in 1995 on the estimated likelihood of IT project shortcomings. The research showed that 55% of IT projects were late, 33% were delivered incomplete and 50% came in over budget. Standish concluded that together, failed

---

[kk] £2141 at 4% interest for 123 years and converted to dollars at 1:2.

and challenged projects cost US companies and government agencies an estimated $145 billion per year.[80] The Northridge earthquake in California in 1994 cost $10 billion. This was a major news story. Very little is heard in the mainstream press of the lamentable track record of IT managers in calling a halt to disastrous projects whose cost often dwarfs the impact of this natural disaster.

Surprisingly, given this history of poorly managed waste, business shows ever-increasing enthusiasm for the potential of IT. The research company, IDC, has tracked IT investment in Australia each year since the mid-1980s in its annual *Forecast for Management* survey.[81] The findings reveal that IT investment, as a median percentage of an organization's turnover or operating expenditure, has grown from 1.3% in 1986 to 3% in 2000.[82] Yet this has also coincided with a period of savage business restructuring. Throughout the 1990s the accountant was king. Organizations downsized, rightsized and even capsized to try to save money. Yet the evidence is that IT was immune from the attention of these parsimonious preachers of prudence. There is no evidence that IT managers were any better at drawing attention to out-of-control or wasteful projects.

Investment in IT has remained strong because business expectations from IT are high. The challenge, though, for those in IT is helping business fulfil these expectations, *and* to call out when they are not likely to be met.

If, according to Shakespeare, Richard III was prepared to offer his kingdom for a horse, we wonder what the modern business executive would offer for a responsible and reliable CIO who could be trusted to call "Halt!" when projects head into the red.

PART C
THE MANAGEMENT THEORISTS

This part introduces the novice to extant management theories. It may also serve as a useful *aide-mémoire* to the veteran who is long familiar with the theories. The underlying rationale for including these short essays is that IT managers usually rise to the top on the basis of both sound technical skills and good project management skills, but with limited exposure to the broader field of management studies.

Theorists whose work is represented include:

- Weber
- Jacques
- Pfeiffer and Salancik
- Fayol
- Mintzberg
- Mayo
- McGregor
- Herzberg
- Hilmer and Donaldson
- Strassman
- Moltke

The last name may not be familiar to management theorists. It is included as Field Marshal Helmuth Graf von Moltke was one of the foremost minds on organization and sound practice of his day. Army commanders, from Tacitus to the modern day have analysed and studied sound practice for managing organizations in that least forgiving field. We have much to learn from them. Indeed, Saul[83] observed ". . . when humans undertake change—whether in technology or organization—they usually begin on the battlefield. This may be depressing but it doesn't make it any less true."

This part has been included here because the nature of professional training in the IT field does not usually include any substantive exposure to the body of knowledge on organization and management beyond basic planning and budgeting. I hasten to add IT professionals are not alone in this, and many business specialities, such as accounting, marketing, economics and actuarial studies do not equip graduates with sound management knowledge.

The hope is that in providing these brief insights into the works of management specialists IT professionals may be prompted, tempted or otherwise motivated to broaden their knowledge. Managing people is central to management and managing people is tough. A failure to recognize this and equip oneself for the task will make the job of managing miserable, regardless of advice on sound structure and organization.

The samples in this part should help to point the way and assist the intelligent manager in distinguishing between quick-fix fads—not all as obvious and extreme as corporate tree hugging—and sound hypothesis, analysis, theory and practice.

Weber

Weber's seminal work was published in English as *The Theory of Social and Economic Organization* in 1947. The original German text was published in 1924. His theories, expounded in the 1920s, are still relevant and applicable to many organization structures in IT.

Weber analysed forms of authority and types of organizations. He observed (in 1924) that the bureaucratic model was most suited to modern society because it offered the greatest "technical" efficiency.

Weber held that there were three foundations for legitimate authority, which are linked with organization structures:

1. Rational-legal authority, which is held by an "office".
2. Traditional, where tradition assigns power to the person.
3. Charismatic, where power is granted by character, heroism or sanctity.

More recent work by sociologists has enlarged the concepts of legitimacy, authority and power; however, Weber's model is perceptive.

In *The IT Manager's Survival Guide* we are concerned only with rational authority, which makes a claim to observance of proper practice as part of a corporate group supported by policy and industrial relations legislation.

Weber believed the exercise of legal authority functioned best when the officials were organized under the following criteria:

- They are personally free and subject to authority only in respect of their impersonal official obligations.
- They are organized in a clearly defined hierarchy of offices.
- Each office has a clearly defined sphere of competence in the legal sense.
- The office is filled by free contractual relationship. Thus, in principle, there is free selection.
- Candidates are selected on the basis of technical qualifications. In the most rational case, this is tested by examination or guaranteed by diplomas certifying technical training, or both. They are *appointed*, not elected.
- They are remunerated in fixed salaries in money . . . only in certain circumstances does the employing authority, especially in private organizations, have

the right to terminate employment, but the official is always free to resign . . . the salary scale is graded according to right in the hierarchy . . .

- The office is treated as the sole, or at least the primary, occupation of the incumbent.
- It constitutes a career. There is a system of "promotion" according to seniority or achievement. Promotion is dependent on the judgement of superiors.
- The official works entirely separately from the ownership of the means of administration and without appropriation of his position.
- He is subject to strict and systematic discipline and control in the conduct of his office.

Weber viewed bureaucratic administration as being based on control on the basis of knowledge. He felt the following social consequences flowed:

- The tendency to "levelling" in the interest of the broadest basis of recruitment in terms of technical competence.
- The tendency to plutocracy growing out of the interest in the greatest possible length of technical training.
- The dominance of a spirit of formalistic impersonality—work done without hatred or passion, and hence without affection or enthusiasm. The dominant norm is a concept of straightforward duty without regard to personal considerations.

Weber also noted the tendency to "formalism" in bureaucracies that we often see echoed in the *application* systems development methodologies where formalism is used as a line of resistance to common sense.

This underpinning can be seen in most business organizations today. It is not to deny that IT has thrown up some charismatic organization founders, such as Steve Jobs of Apple. However, they owe their power and authority over staff to the legitimacy of their office, not otherwise.

A manager restructuring his unit would do well to consider Weber's observations in analysing his present structure and designing a new one. He might well also hearken to Weber's view that:

> Experience tends universally to show that the purely bureaucratic type of administrative organization . . . is from a purely technical point of view, capable of attaining the highest degree of efficiency . . . It is superior to any other form in precision, in stability, in its stringency of discipline, and its reliability.

Jacques

Jacques' theory is considerable and detailed, building on his initial work in 1976 and through to his first book, *Requisite Organization* (2nd edition, published in 1996 by Cason Hall, Arlington, VA, USA).

Jacques was Visiting Research Professor in Management Science at the George Washington University, MD (Johns Hopkins), PhD (Harvard), Professor Emeritus of Social Science at Brunel University, England, FRCP, and member of the British Physco-Analytical Society. He has worked with organizations in industry, commerce, public service, the Church and the army.

Jacques observed that most bureaucracies suffered from a universal disease in that "they had too many levels of organization". This disease had the following symptoms and more:

- Excessively long lines of command
- Red tape
- Subordinates bypassing superiors and vice versa
- Too many levels involved in solving any one problem
- Organizational clutter.

These issues are often common in organizations and are reflected in discussions about "who my real boss is" or "who I go to when I have a major problem".

His most critical insight was that there was an absence of any uniform method for determining appropriate levels within an organization. Jacques' major contribution has been to formulate a theory that provides a rationale for hierarchical structure.

His theory is based on time-span boundaries or strata that set out universal levels for structuring an organization. Consequently, he states that for any managerial role it is possible to analyse the organization and define which "stratum" the role belongs to and how many subordinate or superior roles should support it, if any. Another important finding was that there was a consistency in human behaviour that hid beneath the formal organization chart and contributed to the instability of the hierarchical model.

This research showed that everyone below a three-month time span felt the three-month time span manager to be the "real boss", likewise all those between three months and a year felt it was the "year-span" manager, followed by those in 2-year, 5-year and 10-year spans. Thus regardless of the paper structure, this is how the reality was perceived. This model is illustrated in Figure C1.

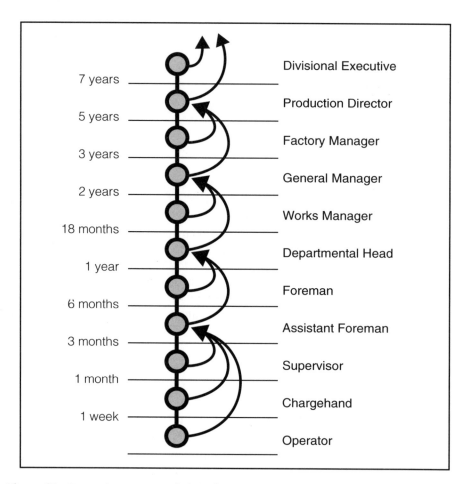

7 years — Divisional Executive

5 years — Production Director

3 years — Factory Manager

2 years — General Manager

18 months — Works Manager

1 year — Departmental Head

6 months — Foreman

3 months — Assistant Foreman

1 month — Supervisor

1 week — Chargehand

Operator

Figure C1—Jacques' structure underlying bureaucratic organization.

As a management theorist Jacques introduced many new concepts including:

- Manager once removed: The manager of a subordinate's immediate manager, and
- Managerial accountability hierarchy: a system of roles in which an individual in a higher role (manager) is held accountable for the outputs in immediately lower roles (subordinates) and can be called to account for their actions.

Jacques' work, which is available in book, audio-visual, software and data charts, is a valuable tool for the rational manager striving to build an IT unit based on logic and service.

Pfeiffer and Salancik

Pfeiffer and Salancik's book, *The External Control of Organizations: A Resource Dependent Perspective* (Harper and Row, 1978) suggests that organization design is largely driven by the external context. This is particularly pertinent to *The IT Manager's Survival Guide*. The external context is often "within the organization" and can be derived in part from Pfeiffer and Salancik's work.

The authors' view is that "to understand an organization's behaviour you must understand how it relates to other social actors in its environment". Likewise, to understand an IT unit's behaviour the same approach can be applied.

Pfeiffer and Salancik dispute the idea that organizations are self-directed autonomous organisms pursuing their own ends, and argue that organizations are other-directed and involved in a constant struggle in this regard. They make a further point that an organization's activities are interlocking and few have the absolute control over their domain, "that is the ability to initiate or terminate actions at one's own discretion". To make matters worse for the purist, these coalitions of various interests sometimes have incompatible goals and preferences. All this should sound familiar to the manager of a typical IT unit, beset by interminable demands, and limited resources.

Furthermore, the authors suggest "scanning" the environment as part of the process of considering structure. They do note that this is often done at a superficial level and most organizations follow the easy course of using readily available data that was gathered for other purposes—such as financial returns. Unfortunately, this is true and it is for this reason *The IT Manager's Survival Guide* lays much emphasis on discovery.

In summary, Pfeiffer and Salancik argue that organizational (read IT units') behaviour is determined through the design of organizational environments (read "the rest of the business").

Indeed, one classic observation by the two authors is that "among the few social scientists who have not neglected environmental design as a way of affecting organizational behaviour are economists. Their basic model presumes that persons seek their self-interest, and therefore, environments must be so structured that in seeking their own interests, individual actors also behave so as to increase social welfare." In this context social welfare might be better interpreted as "common wealth".

Pfeiffer and Salancik make two final observations of particular note in the context of this book.

> Behaviour is a consequence of the context confronting the organization. The design and change of organizational behaviour, therefore, can profitably be approached from the perspective of analyzing and designing the context to produce the desired activities.

That is, in essence, the thrust of this particular work.

Second, they observe that humanists, such as Maslow and McGregor:

> predicted the demise of the bureaucracy as an organizational form. In a climate of social values that stress participation and democracy, bureaucracies with their centralized structures and control are anachronistic. With a more skilled and more educated work force, with increasingly sophisticated technologies, the prediction has been professional, rather than bureaucratic, organizational forms would emerge.

These views conflict with the work of Weber and others, but it is not clear whether what was predicted has emerged, or that it works much more efficiently.

Fayol

Fayol, H. *Administration Industrielle et General,* Dunod, Paris, 1916

Fayol was the first of the modern management writers to propound a theoretical analysis of what managers have to do and by what principles they have to do it; an analysis which has withstood half a century of critical analysis.

Fayol's book was originally published in 1916 and it is remarkable to read the work and reflect how many of the recommendations he propounded are just as relevant today.

Fayol suggested fourteen principles for management, and each is briefly described in this essay.

Division of work

"The object of division of work is to produce more and better work with the same effort". Fayol observed—as did Adam Smith before him—that with fewer things to concentrate on, a worker would do those few things better and faster. He acknowledges this is not always true and that one can reach a point of diminishing returns. Nevertheless, the observation has stood the test of time despite multi-skilled teams and group-work approaches.

Authority and responsibility

Fayol observes that these go together. His seemingly cynical view that ". . . responsibility is feared as much as authority is sought after" rings true, as does his statement "fear of responsibility paralyses much initiative and destroys many good qualities".

Unity of command

This is defined as a principle that a subordinate should receive orders from one superior, and only one superior. Once this principle is violated then authority and responsibility is undermined. He cautions against the dangers of shared command, bypassing the chain of command and poor demarcation of scope of command. The essay on Jacques and his stratum theory of management provides some deeper insight into this pernicious problem.

Unity of direction

This is the simple, correct, and often overlooked principle that there should be "one head and one plan for a group of activities having the same objective". Experience has shown that organizations often have a number of poorly coordinated plans, administered by various executives, sharing the same objective. Observation suggests this phenomenon of "department" or "divisional" plans developed in isolation seems to be increasing rather than decreasing.

Subordination of individual in the interests of the organization or general interests

Often expressed as "In the national interest" or "In the interests of the business . . .", this principle propounds the view that the welfare of the whole must take precedence over the welfare of individuals.

Remuneration of personnel

Fayol states "It should be fair and, as far as is possible, afford satisfaction to the personnel and the firm (employee and employer)". He went on to review and analyse methods of payment, including time-rates, job-rates and piece-rates. These are worth reviewing in connection with bonuses and profit sharing to discover more appropriate ways of remunerating various classes of IT staff, depending on the work and appropriate motivating factors. Fayol showed remarkable insight in this area in 1912.

Centralization

It is difficult to improve on Fayol's own words.

> Like division of work, centralization belongs to the natural order; this turns on the fact that in every organism, animal or social, sensation converges towards the brain or directive part, and from the brain or directive part orders are sent out which sets all parts of the organization in movement. Centralization is not a system of management good or bad in itself . . . it is always present to a greater or lesser extent . . . the question of centralization or decentralization, is a simple question of proportion, it is finding the right degree for a particular concern.

It would be difficult to find a more balanced view today when the arguments for and against decentralization rage, particularly in the field of IT.

Scalar chain

This is more commonly known as the chain of command from CEO to the humblest worker. Fayol noted, as does Jacques, "It is even at times disastrously lengthy in large concerns, notably in governmental ones". Fortunately, Jacques has provided a basis for determining the appropriate length of the chain. Fayol, however, also stresses the need for what he called "gangplanks" to allow people of corresponding levels in different departments to interact directly and not to have to rely on a tortuous communication up one chain and down another when lateral communication would suffice.

Order

"A place for everything and everything in its place" goes the well-known saying, and Fayol subscribes to it, extending it to "a place for everyone and everyone in his place". Fayol was not referring to physical place, for example "at your desk", but more to the view there should be a structure to meet the business objectives and it should be complete and organized. He makes the observation that tidiness is not orderliness, and a library that is clean and tidy but does not have the books indexed and organized is useless. This point often seems to escape managers with a fetish for "tidiness".

Equity

Fayol stressed the importance of equity and equality of treatment of all people within the organization, and the need for all employees' aspirations to be taken into account in the business. This, remember, in 1912!

Stability of tenure

The vast majority of IT people would subscribe to his view: "Time is required for an employee to get used to new work and succeed in doing it well." Fayol notes the importance of stability in the organization and observes that the stable, reliable, knowledgeable mediocre manager may be more valuable than the high-flying fly-by-night who does not know the people or the job.

Initiative

Of this he says "Thinking out a plan and ensuring its success is one of the keenest satisfaction's for an intelligent man to experience". Fayol stresses the importance of encouraging initiative and the need for managers to occasionally forgo some glory and let it fall instead on their subordinates.

Esprit de corp

Of this Fayol says divide and conquer the enemy is fine but "dividing one's team is a grave sin against the business". He stresses the importance of coordination of effort, and using each person's skill to best advantage and rewarding merit "without arousing dissension, bitterness or jealousy". Fayol states, in 1912, that he would "forbid all communications in writing which could easily and advantageously be replaced by verbal ones because it is usually simpler and quicker to give verbal instructions". He points out that the differences and misunderstandings in a conversation can be quickly cleared up while they grow bitterer in writing. All recipients of email "flames" take note!

Fayol's writing seems as fresh today as when it was penned nearly a century ago. Indeed, it is surprising how many "new fads" are little more than Fayol's principles dressed in new clothes.

Mintzberg

Mintzberg H, *The Nature of Managerial Work*, Harper & Row, New York, 1973

Mintzberg questioned much of the received wisdom of the management theorists. His studies and those of his peers looked beyond the theory and observed managers at work and their diaries. He shadowed managers from CEOs to foremen and supervisors and came to the conclusion much of what was believed about management was folklore. His observations follow:

Folklore: "The manager is a reflective, systematic planner."

Fact: Study after study has shown that managers work at an unrelenting pace, that their activities are characterized by brevity, variety and discontinuity, and that they are strongly orientated towards action and dislike reflective activities.

Folklore: "The effective manager has no regular duties to perform."

Fact: In addition to handling exceptions, managerial work involves performing a number of regular duties, including ritual and ceremony, negotiations and processing of soft information that links the organization with its environment.

Folklore: "The senior manager needs aggregated information, which a formal management information system best provides."

Fact: "Managers strongly favour the verbal media—namely telephone calls and meetings."

Folklore: "Management is, or at least is quickly becoming, a science and a profession."

Fact: "The managers' programmes—to schedule time, process information, make decisions, and so on—remain locked deep inside their brains."

Mintzberg explains and justifies his facts in an articulate and engaging way in his work. Having attacked the myths, he then turns to give a basic description of managerial work. Mintzberg believes managers have three roles: the interpersonal, the informational and the decision roles. The manager then undertakes a number of activities within those roles:

- *Interpersonal role.* In this role the manager acts as a figurehead or ceremonial role—welcoming the new, farewelling the departing, lunching with the important and attending the small celebrations that take place within the workplace. The second task of leader is the hiring, firing, motivation, approving, training and deployment of his own staff. In his liaison task the manager spends time with his peers and relevant outsiders. Mintzberg and others monitoring managers at work suggest that approximately 45% of time is spent with peers, another 45% with people outside their unit, including external suppliers and only 10% or so of their time with their superiors.
- *Informational role.* Mintzberg observed that the effective manager is the nerve centre of communication of his organizational unit. "He may not know everything but he knows more than any other member of his staff." Mintzberg also noted: "The manager does not leave meetings or hang up the telephone in order to get back to work. In a large part, communication is his work." In the informational role the manager also acts as a monitor, scanning his environment, collecting gossip, hearsay, speculation and reading—but mostly verbal information gathering. The manager also has to disseminate information passing formal and informal information, including "privileged" information to his subordinates and peers. The third task is that of spokesman where the manager represents the company to others, such as suppliers, regulators, customers and shareholders.
- *Decision role.* Mintzberg suggests the manager has four tasks in this area: entrepreneur, disturbance handler, resource allocater and negotiator. These are explained as follows. As an entrepreneur "the manager seeks to improve his unit and to adapt it to the changing environment". Mintzberg noted that senior executives might be managing as many as fifty projects at once with this aim in mind. As a disturbance handler, the manager is in reactive mode, often dealing with external issues such as supplier, labour unions or serious customer complaints. Mintzberg said of the third decision role, that of *resource allocator,* "To the manager falls the responsibility of deciding who will receive what in his organizational unit. Perhaps the most important resource the manager allocates is his own time. Access to the manager constitutes exposure to the unit's nerve centre and decision maker".

Mintzberg's work provides some interesting considerations for IT managers including the observation "And when subordinates are out of convenient verbal reach of the manager they are at an informational disadvantage".

Mintzberg also discussed a means towards more effective management and believed three specific areas were a concern:

- Finding systematic ways to share privileged information.

- Dealing with both superficial and serious issues and ensuring those serious issues got the appropriate attention and analysis of the broad picture.
- Finally, taking control of his own time and turning obligations to his advantage and turning those things he wishes to do into obligations. Mintzberg noted that others initiated 68% of contacts with senior managers.

Clearly Mintzberg's work and his later writings on strategic planning and other areas are a rich source of learning for aspiring IT managers. The problems that Mintzberg described face you, the manager and your subordinates in management roles, however lowly. These need to be considered in the context of this book.

Mayo

Mayo E, *The Social Problems of an Industrial Civilization*, Routledge, London, 1949

Elton Mayo was one of the great early analysts of the way physiological and psychological changes affect worker productivity. His work is included in this book as it provides the novice manager with a deeper insight into the puzzling and ephemeral nature of team motivation.

One trigger for his work was the perplexing studies of worker productivity in the Hawthorn experiments in the late 1920s. These studies had revealed that worker productivity went up when conditions were improved, and continued to improve even when conditions were worsened or returned to normal. Mayo's observation was that the trigger for improved performance was "What actually happened was that six individuals became a team and the team gave itself whole-heartedly and spontaneously to the experiment".

Mayo believed, and I think correctly, that the problems of management are complex and evolutionary. His impression was that the new industrial civilization that had formed over the past century had profoundly changed the environment for both workers and managers. One key response, as he saw it, was for managers to focus on "the organization of teamwork—that is, of sustained cooperation". It is worth noting it is team*work* that Mayo emphasized, not mere "teams".

He felt (at the time) that this aspect of management was wholly neglected, and while the effective application of science and technical skills would improve effectiveness, it would not improve efficiency without sustained cooperation from the work groups applying the science and technology.

Mayo's view that as the social structure of civilization had been profoundly changed by scientific, engineering and industrial development we had changed from an "established" to an "adaptive" social order. For managers, and especially supervisors, the problem was acute. No longer did a supervisor work with a team of people who had known one another for years, but with "a group of individuals that forms and disappears almost as he watches it".

But Mayo perceived the problem to be even worse for the individual worker of whom he said: "He has suffered a profound loss of security and certainty in his actual living and in the background of his thinking." This was extraordinarily insightful for the early part of the last century. Mayo's insight did not stop there as he also discussed the need for workers to achieve a degree of emotional release by talking through difficult experiences. He was among the first business theorists to point to the importance of also paying attention to personal situations in judging worker performance.

Perhaps the most critical observation he made was that ". . . the age-old human desire for persistence of human association will seriously complicate the development of an adaptive society if we cannot devise systematic methods of easing individuals from one group of associates to another". The manager planning to restructure his IT unit would do well to heed the warning in this statement.

Mayo went further and noted that each unit in a business formed its own "customs, duties, routines and even rituals, and management succeeds (or fails) in proportion as it is accepted without reservation by the group as authority and leader".

A lesson for us in *The IT Manager's Survival Guide* is to beware the delusion that we can, as managers, impose a structure or process without the support and cooperation of our and other work teams.

Another lesson, pertinent to issues in IT management was that ". . . experience showed that articulate complaint, only rarely, if ever, gave any logical clue to the grievance in which it had its origin". The caution here is to ensure that we diagnose the real problem we are trying to solve in creating an IT service structure to deal with business problems. The injunction is to ensure we diagnose the real problem before we respond to the supposed issue or problem.

In summary though, Mayo's greatest contribution is his view that organizing teamwork, that is, developing and sustaining cooperation, was a critical management task. *The IT Manager's Survival Guide* gives support to this view while never underestimating the difficulty in organizing teamwork between IT and other business unit colleagues.

McGregor

McGregor D, *The Human Side of Enterprise*, McGraw-Hill, New York, 1960

McGregor's seminal work explored what he termed *Theory X*: a traditional view of direction and control, and *Theory Y*: the integration of individual and organizational goals. McGregor pointed to three assumptions which underpin the traditional view; namely:

- The average human being has an inherent dislike of work and will avoid it if he can.
- Because of this human characteristic dislike of work, most people must be coerced, controlled, directed, threatened with punishment to get them to put forth adequate effort towards the achievement of organizational objectives.
- The average human being prefers to be directed, wishes to avoid responsibility, has relatively little ambition, wants security above all.

McGregor noted that these assumptions underpinned the bulk of management literature at the time (and still do!). He further noted that they have led to organizational principles based on these quite negative views of human nature.

He does not dismiss these assumptions as totally false. He properly observed that *Theory X* provides an explanation of some human behaviour in industry. "These observations would not have persisted if there were not a considerable body of evidence to support them." The flaw he identifies is that they are only partially true in explaining human behaviour. He notes that while the "carrot and stick" works well in certain circumstance, "man works for bread alone when there is little bread". However, McGregor suggests that once our basic needs are satisfied, we then seek self-fulfilment. Maslow also expresses this view in his now well-known "hierarchy of human needs". McGregor believes that when basic needs are fulfilled our need for self-respect and self-actualization begin to dominate. In short, once wages meet our living needs, we want more from management than wages.

McGregor summarized this, observing "The philosophy of management by direction and control—regardless of whether it is hard or soft—is inadequate to motivate because human needs on which this approach relies are relatively unimportant motivators in our society today. Direction and control are of limited value in motivating people whose important needs are social and egoistic." In other words, the old ways that smack of paternalism, viewing the "masses" as passive and indolent and organizing them as you would children, is passé.

McGregor argues for the adoption of *Theory Y*: the integration of individual and organizational goals to move beyond this point. The motivators underpinning *Theory Y* are:

- The expenditure of physical and mental effort in work is as natural as play or rest.
- External control and threat of punishment are not the only means for bringing about effort towards organizational objectives. People will also exercise self-direction and self-control in the service of objectives to which they are committed.
- Commitment to objectives is a function of the rewards associated with their achievement. (Noting these may not be material.)
- The average human being learns, under proper conditions, not only to accept but also to seek responsibility.
- The capacity to exercise a relatively high degree of imagination, ingenuity and creativity in the solution of organizational problems is widely, not narrowly, distributed in the population.
- Under the conditions of modern industrial life, the intellectual potential of the average human being is only partially utilized.

Clearly, these assumptions imply very different management practices from those associated with *Theory X*.

McGregor noted that: "They are dynamic rather than static: they indicate the possibility of human growth, and development; stress the need for elective adaptation rather than for a single absolute form of control." Indeed, they infer that poor performance is the failure of management rather than of the employee.

McGregor coined the concept of integration of the organizational and individual goals. This concept is based on the belief that individuals can see they can best achieve their own goals by directing their best efforts towards the success of the enterprise, in contrast to the earlier bureaucratic-industrial "command and control" model.

He also stressed that *Theory Y* does not imply abdication or soft management practices. He correctly observes that *Theory Y* will not be easy to implement, and the process of getting people to exercise self-direction and self-control following decades of instructions "to work hard and follow orders".

Later research indicates that some workers may feel very uncomfortable with the *Theory Y* approach. Those who espouse the idea of personality types might argue that there are a body of people, perhaps even predisposed to certain forms of employment, who prefer a command and control environment. The converse is also clearly true.

The IT Manager's Survival Guide accepts the concept of type in the workplace, and believes the best form of management will incorporate some of both *Theory X* and *Theory Y*.

Herzberg

Herzberg F, *Work and The Nature of Man*, World Publishing Co, New York, 1966

This essay on Herzberg is included because he challenged orthodox views on motivation and corporate shibboleths such as policy, interpersonal relations and working conditions. His views are relevant to IT and go some way to explaining the success of unconventional methods and motivation.

Herzberg's work concentrated on motivation, and regardless of how well we plan, organize and schedule our IT unit, poorly motivated staff will bring it all undone. Herzberg believed five factors dominate *job satisfaction*:

- Achievement
- Recognition
- Work itself
- Responsibility
- Advancement.

Conversely five major dissatisfiers are:

- Company policy and administration
- Supervision
- Salary
- Interpersonal relations
- Working conditions.

It is important to note that he pointed out that the opposite of job satisfaction was not necessarily job dissatisfaction, rather it is no job satisfaction, that is, the absence of satisfaction rather than the presence of dissatisfaction. This concept bears thinking about as Herzberg points out some things may have unipolar responses as opposed to bipolar responses.

Critical to understanding Herzberg's viewpoint is the fact that the things which lead to job satisfaction are related to the job itself. Those things, which are dissatisfiers, are those things related to the *environment* within which the job is done.

Thus we have two sets of needs at work, those which motivate through satisfaction and those to avoid demotivation, that is, if they are in order they will not demotivate, but their presence does not motivate. Herzberg coined the term *hygiene factors*—synonymous with the medical meaning of "preventative and environmental" to summarize the group of things that lead to dissatisfaction.

Herzberg's study goes deep into these issues and he implicitly supports the concept of type in the workplace. That is, some employees may be "motivation seekers" and some "hygiene seekers". Herzberg does not suggest that a person is one or the other, rather that one of these aspects of personality will dominate.

His key concern is that managers who are driven to focus on "hygiene factors" as the key to organization performance instil these same characteristics in their subordinates. The issue this raises is that "hygiene seekers" are precisely the type of individuals who will let the company down in a crisis. His reasoning is that during an emergency those things that make up the set of hygiene factors are of least concern and most likely to be ignored.

Herzberg's summation at the end of this chapter in his book is repeated below.

> If we accept that one of the most important functions of a manager is the development of future managers, the teaching of hygiene motivations becomes a serious defect to the company. This, I believe, is one of the major implications that motivation-hygiene theory has for modern management practices. . . . The superior who is a hygiene seeker cannot but have an adverse effect on management development, which is aimed at the personal growth and actualization of subordinates.

Managers of IT units, ever concerned with policy and process, may do well to remember these words.

Hilmer and Donaldson

Hilmer FG and Donaldson L, *Management Redeemed*, Free Press, Sydney, 1996

Fred Hilmer was Professor of Management at the Australian Graduate School of Management and a director of several companies. His co-author, Lex Donaldson, is Professor of Organizational Design at the University of New South Wales, Australia.

Hilmer and Donaldson believe that too much of the writing and practice of management is centred on fads, and too little on careful, sustained professional process. Fads they debunk include:

- Flattening the structure—the argument against hierarchy.
- The action approach—act now, think later.
- Techniques-based management, such as portfolio planning, value-based planning, niche strategies, total quality management, benchmarking, re-engineering and gain-sharing.
- The corporate clan—the happy corporate family culture.
- The directors to direct.

They acknowledge that there is truth in these concepts but that unless we manage based on hard, clear thinking we will lurch from one silver bullet to the next.

In debunking these myths Hilmer and Donaldson offer chilling evidence of management's readiness to unquestioningly accept falsehood, speculation and poorly researched ideas as sound management practice. More so, they warn against the silliness of assuming that one of many characteristics of a successful firm is the key to their success. They point out that success is built upon myriad decisions and thousands of actions that have formed the organization and continue to sustain it. Hilmer and Donaldson are firm in their view that "The best managers are relentless in the pursuit of facts and reality and in their commitment to, energy and skill in leading people to achieve well-defined and considered goals."

They state that if managers wish to be perceived as professionals then they need to start behaving like professionals. "The essence of management is the skilful application of sound and proven ideas to particular situations facing managers, not dogma, jargon or quick-fix fads." They continue:

The knowledge falls into three groups; learning the core disciplines, applying a number of disciplines to problems, and acquiring skills. The core disciplines include data analysis—the dreaded math and stats—economics, organizational behaviour, accounting, finance, marketing, law, and possibly political science. Applied subjects built on the core include corporate strategy and policy, change management, new product development, information systems, technology management, human resource strategy, operations, international and comparative management, and marketing strategy. Key skill areas include—writing, presenting, listening, interviewing—negotiation, numeracy and technical literacy, and interpersonal and leadership skills.

This essay is included to remind the manager that this guide does not offer a simple solution to the issue of IT management. Rather, it seeks to make a contribution to a body of knowledge which already exists on management and organization and which is touched on in the other essays in this part of the book.

Strassman

Strassman PA, *The Politics of Information Management*, Information Economics Press, New Canaan, CT, 1995

Strassman, unlike the other theorists represented in this part, wrote specifically on the subject of IT management. His career includes Director of Defense Information (US Government), visiting professor at the National Defense University in Washington and a research fellow in Business Innovation.

Two of his books, *The Business Value of Computers* and *The Politics of Information Management*, make a valuable contribution to improving IT management techniques. This short summation of his work will concentrate on his contribution to the concept of policies or principles for managing information systems.

Policy development is, in Strassman's view, core to the effective management of IT. His focus is not the minutiae of pedantry but the creation of broad-sweeping constitutional policies that guide the organization in the acquisition, deployment, management and use of information systems. Strassman makes the point that "Policy (from the Greek, to display or make known) defines organization, power and accountability" and that "corporate policies are the equivalent of public law". He argues that "defining governance and business alignment—the strategic processes—must always take precedence in all information management planning . . .". He points out that many strategic elements will influence information management and that the most difficult of these will be to establish information governance policies.

He urges that the model of the US Constitution has much to offer as a guide to scope and depth: "It represents a point of view that addresses the governance of complexity by concentrating only on the fundamentals, while leaving everything else for resolution by means of a due process wherever that is appropriate." Students of Moltke will see many similarities in Strassman's views.

He urges that whenever we develop a constitution for IT, we also develop a comprehensive checklist of who is responsible for what—an accountability and responsibility statement—to make disputes brief and governance simple. He argues that we need a constitution because "complex organizations require complex rules to avoid enthusiastic chaos". This constitution, he argues, should articulate fundamental principles that have a horizon of many decades.

He offers a prototype constitution that sets out the goals, the corresponding IT goals, principles (which can be tested for conformity), and which cover such areas as the responsibilities of the enterprise, business levels and information management policy boards, systems managers, operating managers, planning and finance units, users, decentralization, staff development, systems design, technology advancement, re-use, risk management, security and others.

While the task may seem awesome, Strassman's model only takes 20 pages of a large-typeface textbook and could provide a suitable framework for managing a department as large as the US Defense department's IT services!

Strassman's work also extends to cover examination and views on re-engineering, process improvement, leadership and a number of other issues of importance to managers. However, it is in the field of policies and principles that his contribution has brought about enthusiastic responses from the executives who manage enterprises. Chapter 8 of this book is devoted to the concept of principles and owes much of its genesis to the ideas first promulgated by Strassman in 1995.

Moltke

Hughes DJ, *Moltke on the Art of War*, Presidio Press, Novato, CA, 1993

Field Marshal Helmuth Graf von Moltke (1800–1891) was one of the foremost military minds of his day. His theories on warfare provided the foundation of organization and management of the German army from the mid-1800s to 1945. This essay is included as a stimulus to managers to look beyond the limits of orthodox management theory in seeking solutions to issues. Military theory and strategy is readily accessible and can provide deep insight into sound management and leadership practices. It is worth bearing in mind that errors of judgement in the field of battle are somewhat more terminal than in business.

This essay contains a broad set of extracts from an edition on Moltke's theories. The intention is not to summarize his theories but instead to show the richness and sweep of his thinking about strategy, leadership, organization, and communication which form the basis of running any organization.

Moltke was firmly of the belief that "negative thinking" was a serious issue for managers. We have all had to face those who can give a thousand compelling reasons why something will not work, and who never offer a constructive suggestion on how to make something work. Of them, Moltke said:

> In every headquarters there are men who demonstrate with great perception all the difficulties attending the proposed enterprise. The very first time something goes wrong they prove conclusively that they had "told you so". They are always right. Because they never counsel anything positive (much less carry it out), success cannot refute them. These men of the negative are the ruination of senior commanders (*Heerführer*, p.77).

The manager undertaking a restructure and reorientation of his IT unit should expect to find some of these "negative men" among his team.

Referring to the subject of objectives Moltke made the perceptive comment that:

> one must distinguish between the *object of the war* and the *object of the operation*. Put simply, the object of the war may be to acquire territory while the objective of an operation may be to destroy a battalion of the enemy.

It behoves us to consider this aspect of focus in organizing our IT units and the objectives and sub-objectives that drive the reorganization.

Objectives are usually associated with strategy, and Moltke's view of strategy was:

> Strategy is a system of expedients; it is more than mere scholarly discipline. It is the translation of the knowledge to the practical life, the improvement of the original leading thought in accordance with continually changing situations. It is the art of acting under the pressure of the most difficult conditions (p.124).

Note that Moltke is saying that strategy needs to accommodate an unfolding reality, not that it is "fly by the seat of your pants".

He underpins this view with his thoughts on achieving these goals. "A firm decision and persistent execution of a simple concept lead most certainly to a goal" (p.172). Jack Trout, author of numerous books including one entitled *The Power of Simplicity*, would most certainly agree.

Moltke was also perceptive concerning the obstacles that stand in the way of achieving goals:

> No calculations of space and time guarantees victory in this realm of chance, mistakes and disappointments. Uncertainty and the danger of failure accompany every step towards the goal, which will not be attained if fate is completely unfavourable.

Moltke, however, also stresses—as does Fayol and Jacques—the critical importance of proper communications:

> Continuous communication between command authorities and units is for the cooperation of all towards a single goal . . . The issuing of orders (*Befehlsertheilung*) must observe official channels as far as possible, not only in operations [normal times] but also in battle [emergencies]. Bypassing an intermediate authority destroys its effectiveness and causes it to appear superfluous.

If you are tempted to read *Moltke on the Art of War* you will find his analysis of historical examples of poorly executed strategies and successful campaigns invaluable. They serve as a prompt to analyse our own business issues and the failures of others with rigour and objectivity, that we might learn from them.

I encourage you, when studying management theory, to step outside the "management bookshelves" and include psychology, sociology, and military works in your reading.

Appendix A   Yukl's *specific behaviours for managing relations*

Guidelines for supporting

- Show acceptance and positive regard.
- Be polite and patient, not arrogant and rude.
- Bolster the person's self-esteem.
- Provide assistance with work when needed.
- Be willing to help with personal problems.

Guidelines for active listening

- Maintain attention.
- Avoid overinterpretation.
- Avoid judgemental responses.
- Try to suspend biases and preconceptions.
- Use restatement.
- Show empathy.
- Use probes to draw the person out.
- Encourage suggestions for dealing with problems.
- Synchronize interaction.

Guidelines for developing

Mentoring

- Show concern for each individual's development.
- Help the person identify skill deficiencies.

- Provide helpful career advice.
- Encourage attendance at relevant training courses.
- Provide opportunities for skill development on the job.
- Encourage coaching by peers.
- Promote the person's reputation.
- Serve as a role model.

Coaching

- Help the person to analyse his or her performance.
- Encourage and guide efforts to improve performance.
- Provide support and encouragement.
- Hold practice sessions under realistic conditions.

Guidelines for recognizing

- Recognize a variety of contributions and achievements.
- Actively search for contributions to recognize.
- Recognize improvements in performance.
- Recognize commendable efforts that failed.
- Don't limit recognition to high-visibility jobs.
- Don't limit recognition to a few best performers.
- Provide specific recognition.
- Provide timely recognition.
- Use an appropriate form of recognition.

Guidelines for rewarding

- Find out what rewards are attractive to people.
- Identify relevant aspects of performance to reward.
- Explain how rewards are determined.
- Distribute rewards fairly.
- Give rewards in a timely way.

Guidelines for managing conflict

Problem-oriented procedures

- Identify specific reasons for conflict.
- Identify shared objectives and values.

- Encourage disclosure of real needs and preference.
- Consider a range of acceptable solutions.
- Try to identify additional benefits.
- Avoid resolving issues separately.
- Check to ensure mutual commitment to an agreement.

Relations-oriented procedures

- Express concern for improving relations.
- Remain impartial and show acceptance to both parties.
- Discourage non-productive behaviour.
- Explore how the parties perceive each other.
- Ask each party to suggest ways to change.
- Schedule a follow-up meeting to check progress.

Appendix B   Business initiative proposal

Monitor Agent Performance

Business owner:	Ted Warton
Title:	Manager—B2B Relationships
Owning department:	B2B
Affected departments:	Marketing
	Contract management
	Legal

Description

To partially automate the collection of data on agency performance by automated recording of response and acquittal times on both periodic and special maintenance jobs.

Current situation

Agents currently fill in a form that is posted or faxed to our office. Information on job activity is often illegible, late and sometimes of doubtful veracity. It is difficult to identify and reward high performers or cull those who are ineffectual. An estimated $345 000 per year is paid as a reward to poor performers because of inaccurate reporting.

Issues

- Limited automated collection of current service provision.
- There is considerable latency between service deterioration and action.
- Information capture on services is often labour intensive and gross.
- Form and media limit service information distribution and re-use by our company.

Proposal summary

The proposal is to use a computer system to collect data recorded on individual agents' call-management systems to automate our measuring of their performance. This will then be extended to PDA linked systems to expand the scope of measures when and where appropriate. Ideally measures should be reviewed to ensure that they are consistent with new capability.

Objectives

- Improve speed and comprehensiveness of agency monitoring.
- Reduce cost and effort in data gathering on performance.
- Ensure rewards are paid for actual performance.
- Make reaction to poor service delivery timelier.

Strategic alignment

The project supports the business goal: "Use technology to manage our distribution arm more effectively and efficiently". It also supports the B2B model defined in our Enterprise Architecture. (See Architects Report).

Proposal requirements:
- Create appropriate performance measures that take advantage of the new system.
- Negotiate access to agents' performance data.
- Develop system to collect the data automatically after hours.
- Develop a system to analyse data each night.
- Include automated alert of significant negative deviations.
- Tracking and resolution of negative deviations.

Extend monitoring capability through later issue to agents of PDAs with wireless capability.

Benefits

- Productivity: Reduction in cost (FTE) to both ourselves and agents in monitoring and reporting.
- Efficiency: Rapid response to significant deviation that protects our customer base.
- Customer: More effective and efficient delivery of maintenance and support service to our customer.
- Financial: Nett of savings estimated at 10 FTE per year offset by a cost of $515 000 investment in year one with an ongoing cost of $100 000 per year is estimated to realize $3 800 000 over five years.

BTOPP

Business

- Market opportunity opened by outperforming competitors and having verifiable "better than competitor" service achievements. Market research indicates we may gain between 5% and 7% additional market penetration worth valued at $2.2m over five years.

Organization

- Restructure B2B department to take advantage of automated measurement and save two FTE.
- Restructure contract management and save one FTE.
- Over eighteen months blend contract management and performance measurement groups.

Process

New/changed processes

- Manage agent performance (changed).
- Extract agent data into Xylog monitoring system.
- Operate computerized monitoring system (new).
- Refresh agency agreements to reflect change.
- "On-line" monitoring of agents when PDA links available (new).
- Manage Performance Issues (changed).

People

- Agent motivation to accept change to automated measurement.
- Staff change to react immediately to apparent service failures.
- Role description and remuneration modifications for B2B and contract staff.

Beneficiaries

Accountable	Capability	Impact	Measure
B2B	Improved accuracy reporting	Lower wrongful commissions	Dollar spend on commissions
B2B	Improved accuracy reporting	Cull poor performers	Fewer agents make more calls
B2B	Automation of manual tasks	Reduced workload	Number of staff compared to current
B2B	Improved latency in measure reporting	Faster reaction to poor performance	Reduced customer complaints
Contract management	Verifiable data on performance	Strength in contract review	Reduction in disputes at termination
Legal	ditto	ditto	ditto

Technology

Identified systems

- Agent Performance Level Monitoring
- Contract Management Interface
- PDA Diary System Monitor (Stage 2)

Identified data stores

- Agent Performance Measures

Change management summary

Who	When	How	Action
Agents	New measures set	Changed recording	Training and incentive programme capture new data
Agents	Implementation	New end-of-day procedures	Training and reward system for percentage hits
B2B	Now	New business processes	Assign BPR to team
Contract management	Implementation	Monitoring and renewal cycles	Review business processes

Proposal scope

- Level 1 and Level 2 agents.
- Measures of performance on maintenance calls and emergency calls only.
- This proposal does not allow for other forms of performance measurement.
- Geographic area of metropolitan Sydney and Melbourne only.

Scale

- Level 1 agents   212   Candidates for additional rewards
- Level 2 agents   417   Marginal performers
- Internal users   11   4 B2B, 4 Contracts, 2 Legal, 1 Marketing

Current measures

- Time to respond to customer call   2 hours from placement
- Time to repair category one faults   30 minutes
- Time to repair category two faults   60 minutes

It is unclear whether these targets are met in practice with the current after the event manual recording on daily work manifests.

Release strategy

- Define appropriate measures with agents
- Obtain and analyse existing agent electronic data (on diskette)
- Introduce automated collection and monitoring for level one agents
- Extend automated collection and monitoring to level two agents
- Extend to PDA wireless information gathering post-2003.

Potential solution

The Mantic Agency Monitoring system available through Prologic Limited seems to offer appropriate functionality at the right cost.

Assumptions

- There will be no legal impediment to collecting data from agents.
- Agents will in the main cooperate with the proposal. (Estimate 10% will complain).
- Agents can be educated to leave their systems in "answer" mode to allow automated collection of over 80% of agents each night.
- Required data set and processing needs are small.
- A standard report-writing tool (e.g. Congas or SAS can be used).
- The application uses an existing DBMS licence.
- Data conversion of agent information is not complex.

Expected costs

Item	Stage 1	Stage 2	Notes
Server	75 000	25 000	Stage 2 upgrade
Desktop	10 000		Upgrade existing
Agent PCs	25 000	20 000	Upgrades and PDAs
Modem	15 000		Agents
Printers	5 000		1 × Legal 1 × contracts
Software	125 000	100 000	Includes analysis
BPR costs	150 000	50 000	
Retrenchment costs	60 000	25 000	See savings
Implementation	25 000	25 000	Agent training
Other—Incentive scheme	100 000	50 000	

Risk assessment and contingency

Risk	Probability	Contingency plan
Agents reject concept	Medium	Establishing new contracts in advance of major investment in system
Agent data is difficult to convert	Low	Obtaining and analyse agents data sets now
Software package unsuitable	Medium	Review project viability

Appendix C   Thorpe's 4 Rs

John Thorpe recommended the preparation of a report card based on the 4 Rs. He suggested that "questions inspired by the following list be posed to a cross-section of executives, project managers, business group heads and other employees".

Are we doing the right things?

- Does your organization have a clear vision and strategy? Are its strategic drivers well communicated and understood throughout the organization?
- Are the outcomes and benefits expected to be delivered by initiatives and projects in your organization clear and credible?
- Are committed funds often not spent due to project delays or poor budgeting, while other potentially valuable opportunities wait in the wings?
- Are investments made in small projects at the expense of business transformation programs?

Are we doing things the right way?

- Do you have processes in place to ensure that the 4 Rs are addressed?
- Do you have principles in place that guide all programme/project decisions?
- Is there alignment/synergy between current programmes/projects/initiatives?
- Are you ensuring that you are able to deal with future demands?
- Does your organization have technology architecture?
- Are you following architectural principles and guidelines?
- Are proven technologies being used that are compliant with the corporate architecture?

Are they being done well?

- Are there standard processes for designing and managing projects?
- Do you have the required competencies and experience? Is success dependent on factors outside your control?

- Do you have a good track record in applying the right resources?
- Are plans validated? Is risk managed appropriately? Are there established processes in place for monitoring and control?
- What percentage of initiatives are within budget?
- What is the total value of project costs overruns? What is the average delay in project completion? How many projects are cancelled in midstream?

Are we getting the benefits?

- Is the company getting the results expected from its programmes, and projects?
- Are the initiatives required to realize benefits clear, understood and achievable?
- Do all projects have a business sponsor?
- Are adequate and appropriate resources assigned to projects by the business areas affected?
- Are adjustments made to ensure that effort to achieve benefits is sustained when the business environment changes?
- Are the expenditures capitalized if an initiative is stopped prematurely so that value can be salvaged from the work?
- Are the products maintained and supported once they have been delivered so that the business can continue to realize the benefits over time?
- Are commitments to deliver benefits forgotten once the business case is approved and the investment made?
- What percentage of expected benefits are actually achieved?

Appendix D1   Jacques' time span

Note that Jacques published the Time-Span Handbook *for those requiring a full account of time-span measurement, including the measurement of single-task operators and clerical roles at Stratum I.*

Jacques makes it clear in his book that time span measurement is the time it takes to complete a task, for example a project or report. IT people should find this concept simple—apparently non-task oriented workers do not! Jacques' recommendations follow:

> The procedure recommended is simple: See the *manager* accountable for the role. Discuss with him or her, examples of specific tasks in the role. Explore to find those tasks or task sequences with the **longest target completion time**. In doing so, consider routinely occurring tasks, any

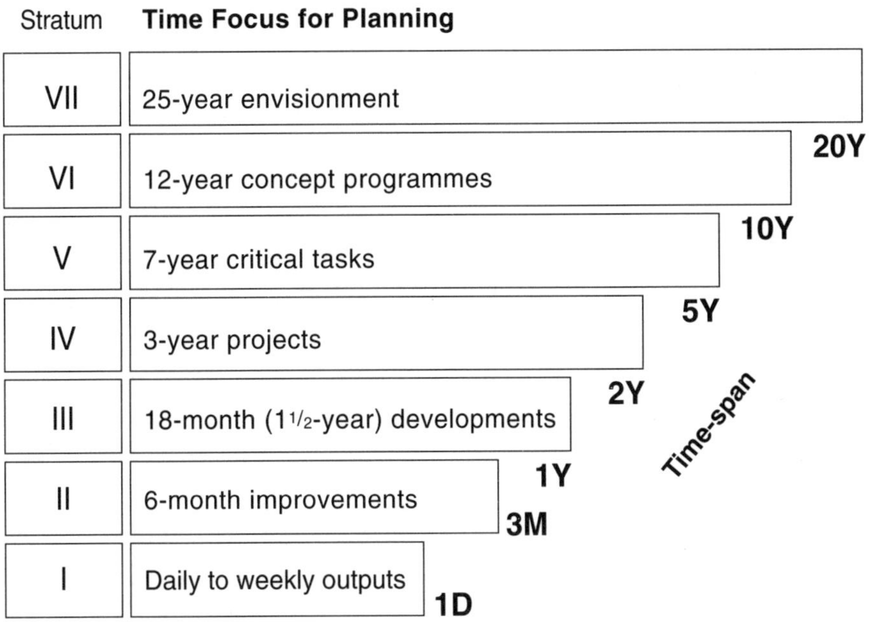

Stratum	**Time Focus for Planning**			
VII	25-year envisionment			
VI	12-year concept programmes			20Y
V	7-year critical tasks		10Y	
IV	3-year projects	5Y		
III	18-month (1½-year) developments	2Y		
II	6-month improvements	1Y		
		3M		
I	Daily to weekly outputs	1D		

(Time-span)

Figure D1.1—Jacques' model for time focused planning.

development projects, and, if the role is a managerial one, tasks concerned with induction and training of subordinates.
- If possible, review the same questions with the subordinate to ensure no tasks are being overlooked.
- When a time-span measure has been obtained, check it with the manager-once-removed, since *for a time-span to be official the tasks assigned by the manager must have been sanctified by the manager-once-removed* in the sense of falling within the limits he/she sets for the intermediate management role.

Jacques gives a number of examples in his text that provides a useful benchmark when comparing your findings to those of other organizations.

Appendix D2   Jacques' complexity measures

The following steps determine the level of task complexity under Jacques' Stratified Systems Theory (SST).

Step One: Formulate the intended output, using task-target-completion time (by-when) as a means of getting precision and clarity in the statement of output.

Step Two: Analyse what work will be required in order to achieve the required output with the planned method. Then ask the following questions about the work:

1. Can the work be done by following an assigned plan to a goal, overcoming obstacles by direct action trial-and-error as you meet them on the way?—*Str-I*.
2. Does the work to be done require the articulation and accumulation of data which are judged significant for the output, and diagnostic judgement based upon linking those data?—*Str-II*.
3. Does the work require the use of serial processing in the construction and choice of plan which balances future requirements against current activity, and holding in reserve other plans which might be brought into play if the selected plan does not work out?— *Str-III*.
4. Does the work to be done require a number of interactive projects to be understood and adjusted each one in relation to the other?—*Str-IV*.
5. Does the work require a continual touch-feel sensing of how changes occurring any-where in the project can impact upon the system to which the project is related, leading to direct actions which can take into account the probable immediate and downstream consequences which cascade through the whole system?—*Str-V*.
6. Does the work require continual screening of the relevant business environment to identify and favourably influence any and all developments there, which might have significance to the problem in hand?—*Str-VI*.
7. Does the work to be done require the development of worldwide strategic options and the creation of business units, by growth, acquisition, mergers, joint ventures?—*Str-VII*.

Step Three: *The level of the project is given by the highest-numbered question which is answered in the affirmative*.

This procedure [of Jacques] is a subjective descriptive process. Jacques says "I do not know of any way, as yet, to measure objectively the complexity of a task or programme. Work with colleagues has been proceeding explicitly for 10 years now to solve this problem, but no solution is as yet in sight. It will be a big step forward if and when we do succeed."

Individual Maturation Bands	Levels of Task Complexity	Organizational Strata	
Mode VII	Construct complex systems	**VII**	CEO COO
Mode VI	Oversee complex systems	**VI**	EVP
Mode V	Judge downstream consequences	**V**	Business Unit President
Mode IV	Parallel process multiple paths	**IV**	GM
Mode III	Create alternative pathways	**III**	Unit Manager
Mode II	Diagnostic accumulation	**II**	First Line Manager
Mode I	Overcome obstacles practical judgement	**I**	Shop & Office Floor

Figure D1.2—Jacques' "Stratified Systems Theory".

Appendix E1 Software inventory

Name:	AKSIT
Age:	1983
Vendor:	AKSIT Dynamics (since liquidated)
Maintenance:	In house—Escrowed Code from liquidation
Type:	Life Insurance Administration
Language:	RPG III
Language generator:	CobGen
Database:	ITAM File
Operating system:	UNIX (AIX)
Server requirement:	IBM AS400 Model 8
LAN bandwidth requirement:	100 10_t
Desktop requirement:	Pentium 100 1GB
Desktop operating system:	Win2000
Size (number lines code):	1 200 000
Number registered users:	100
Number users average:	70
Number users—peaks:	110 (annual marketing drive)
Major periodic runs:	Daily: Day Summary Report
	Weekly: None
	Monthly: Commissions
	New Policy Issue
	New Business Report
	Quarterly: None
	Annually: Year End balances
Special runs (e.g. file compression)	Update Rate Tables

Major functions	Number users	Response	Issue note:
New application	40	2 sec	
Underwriting	10	2 sec	
Manage claim	10	4 sec	(1)
Surrender policy	5	6 sec	
Policy inquiry	20	1 sec	

Notes: 1 This applications module is unstable. Documentation is poor and myriad undocumented changes have been made. Data has been concatenated with technical and business staff experience issues with embedded meaning. RPG programmers are hard to find.
Click on each item for detailed data, e.g. licence number, cost, depreciation, serial numbers, location.

Appendix E2   Hardware inventory

ID:	Utah
Type:	Dell Server Model
Vendor:	Dell Direct
Age:	3 years
CPU:	200 Mhz Pentium
Memory:	128 MB
Disk system:	4 GB
Operating system:	Novell 4.1
Back-up method:	Tape Cartridge
Maintenance:	on-site annual fee

Major peripherals	Brand	Number	Issue notes
BackUp	Systape Drive	1	
Printers	Laserjet 4 to LPT 1	1	
Terminals (Dumb)	None	0	See inventory links
PCs	Dell P100	20	
Other	Fax modem 56	1	

Application	Users	Term Type	Issue Notes
Fax application (FaxIs)	50	PC Pentium	None

Service record—date	Event	Remedy	Issue Note
20-Nov-2000	Tape drive failure	Replaced	None

Notes: This hardware is reliable and adequate for the task.
Click on each item for detailed data, e.g. serial number, location, cost, condition, amortization.

Appendix F   Examples of principles

The following are examples of three principles

Principle 1
Issue: *What guidelines will we issue on procurement of technical infrastructure?*

Options:
    1. Procure on the basis of lowest price.
    2. Procure best of breed.
    3. Procure from a limited number of preferred suppliers.

Preferred: (3) Procure from a limited number of preferred suppliers.
Rationale: Minimizes risks of incompatibility, simplifies integration, controls the range of skillls required and lowers administration costs. Builds better long-term relations with suppliers.

Implications (Positive):
    • We retain the benefits of a homogenous infrastructure.
    • We retain the benefits of bulk purchasing from our preferred supplier.
    • This simplifies procurement processes and allows enhanced electronic purchasing.
 	
Implications (Negative):
    • We may not always pay the lowest price.
    • The range of peripherals may be more limited in the short term.

Approved: **Date:**

Principle 2

Issue: *Will we allow our service providers to sub-contract work?*

Options:
1. No.
2. Yes, unconditionally.
3. Yes, provided the quality, cost, security and service standards are equal or better than specified in Service Level Agreements.

Preferred:
(3) Yes, provided the quality, cost, security and service standards are equal or better than specified in Service Level Agreements, and the service provider takes full responsibility for the sub-contractor and all deliverables.

Rationale:
The service provider cannot be expected to always have every possible skill and resource available at all times. On occasion service demands may exceed the service provider's capacity and capability.

Implications (Positive):
- We enlarge our pool of labour without compromising quality, cost, security or service.
- We are not constrained by the limits of the service provider's staff pool.
- The service provider will be held accountable for delivery through contractual obligations.

Implications (Negative):
- The service provider will incur an overhead in controlling sub-contractors that they may try to pass on.
- We will incur an overhead in auditing invoices and work that is sub-contracted.

Approved: **Date:**

Principle 3

Issue: *Will business units retain the right to fund, develop and manage small projects using their own resources?*

Options:
1. No, the IT unit must undertake all systems development and operations.
2. Yes, business units may retain their current authority.
3. We will examine each project on a case by case basis.

Preferred:
(1). No, the IT unit must undertake all systems development and operations.

Rationale:
One of the drivers for effective and efficient systems is rigorous controls over development and operation. These attributes are compromised by feral IT.

Implications (Positive):
- This should lead to a gradual improvement in the overall quality of systems development and operation in the company.
- Better quality IT should lead to lower long-term maintenance costs.
- Previously hidden costs for IT will be visible and controlled.

Implications (Negative):
- Business units may express frustration and claim delays will occur because of this rigour
- Business units will need to plan and budget for all IT expenses in advance.

Approved: **Date:**

References

1 Bartlett J, *Familiar Quotations*, Little, Brown, Boston, 1919.
2 Scott-Morton M, *The Corporation of the 1990s: Information Technology and Organizational Transformation*, Oxford University Press, New York, 1991.
3 AGSM, *Managing People and Organizations (2000)*, AGSM, Sydney, 2000.
4 AGSM, *Managing People and Organizations (2000)*, AGSM, Sydney, 2000.
5 Mintzberg H, *The Nature of Managerial Work*, Harper & Row, New York, 1973.
6 Yukl G, *Leadership in Organisations*, 4th edn, Prentice Hall, Upper Saddle River, NJ, 1998.
7 Yukl G, *Leadership in Organisations*, 4th edn, Prentice Hall, Upper Saddle River, NJ, 1998.
8 GartnerGroup, *Inside GartnerGroup This Week*, **XV**, No. 38, 22 September 1999.
9 GartnerGroup *Inside GartnerGroup This Week*, **XV**, No. 38, 22 September 1999.
10 GartnerGroup, *The Monthly Research Review*, April 1999.
11 Hugo V, in Goodman T (ed.), *The Forbes Book of Business Quotations*, Black Dog & Leventhal Publishers, Inc., New York, 1997.
12 *Inside GartnerGroup This Week*, **XV**, No. 18, 5 May 1999.
13 Strassman P, *The Politics of Information Management*, Information Economics Press, New Canaan, 1995, p. 46.
14 Strassman P, *The Politics of Information Management*, Information Economics Press, New Canaan, 1995, p. 78.
15 Strassman P, *The Politics of Information Management*, Information Economics Press, New Canaan, 1995, p. 7.
16 Strassman P, *The Politics of Information Management*, Information Economics Press, New Canaan, 1995, p. 84.
17 Strassman P, *The Politics of Information Management*, Information Economics Press, New Canaan, 1995, p. 84.
18 Saul JR, *Voltaire's Bastards*, Sinclair Stevenson (Reed Publishing), London, 1992.
19 McNally J, VicRoads. Personal communication, November 1999.
20 Wilkins MW, Personal communication, October 2000.
21 Tacitus (Jackson J trans.), *The Annals*, Harvard University Press, Cambridge, MA, 1986.
22 Gay CL and Essinger J, *Inside Outsourcing*, Bradley, 2000, p. 27.
23 McNally J, VicRoads. Personal communication, November 1999.
24 Talbot T, *Intep Bulletin*, Issue 95, 10 December 1995.
25 Omerod P, *The Death of Economics*, Faber and Faber, London, 1994.
26 Norley K, Booz·Allen and Hamilton. Personal communication, November 1999.
27 Domberger S and Hall C, *The Contracting Casebook*, AGPS, Sydney, 1995, p. 8.
28 Shakespeare W, *Antony and Cleopatra*, Doubleday, London, 1989.
29 Kepner CH and Tregoe BB, *The New Rational Manager*, Princeton Research Press, Princeton, NJ, 1987.

30 Hughes DJ (ed.), *Moltke on the Art of War*, Presidio Press, Novato, CA, 1993.
31 Kipling R, "The Elephant's Child", in *Just So Stories*, Doubleday, New York, 1912.
32 Kepner CH and Tregoe BB, *The New Rational Manager*, Princeton Research Press, Princeton, NJ, 1987.
33 Kepner CH and Tregoe BB, *The New Rational Manager*, Princeton Research Press, Princeton, NJ, 1987.
34 Kepner CH and Tregoe BB, *The New Rational Manager*, Princeton Research Press, Princeton, NJ, 1987.
35 Aalders R, *The IT Outsourcing Guide*, John Wiley, Chichester, 2001.
36 *Inside GartnerGroup This Week*, **XV**, No. 17, April 1999.
37 Kipling R, "The Elephant's Child", in *Just So Stories*, Doubleday, New York, 1912.
38 Hammer M and Champy J, *Reengineering The Corporation*, Allen and Unwin, New York, 1993.
39 Talbot T, *Intep Bulletin* 95, 10 December 1995.
40 Talbot T, *Intep Bulletin* 95, 10 December 1995.
41 GartnerGroup, Conference Presentation, Sydney, 1999.
42 Thornton N, PA Consulting Group, "Developing business-led outsourcing contracts", Discussion Paper, 1996.
43 Mackay I, *Intep Bulletin* 98, 2 February, Sydney.
44 Wilkins MW, Royal and Sun Alliance, personal communication, November 1999.
45 Mackay I, *Intep Bulletin* 98, 2 February, Sydney.
46 *Gartner Letter*, November 1988, p. 7.
47 Toigo JW, *Disaster Recovery Planning*, Prentice Hall, Englewood Cliffs, NJ, 1989.
48 Hughes DJ (ed.), *Moltke on the Art of War*, Presidio Press, Novato, CA, 1993.
49 Kennedy P, *Preparing for the 21st Century*, HarperCollins, London, 1993.
50 Van der Heijden K, *Scenarios: The Art of Strategic Conversation*, John Wiley, Chichester, 1998.
51 Adams S, *The Dilbert Principle*, HarperCollins, New York, 1996.
52 Pettigrew A and Whipp R, *Managing Change for Competitive Success*, Blackwell, Oxford, 1991.
53 Collins R, *Effective Management*, CCH International, Sydney, 1995.
54 Aalders R, *The IT Outsourcing Guide*, John Wiley, Chichester, 2001.
55 *Inside GartnerGroup This Week*, **XV**, No. 31, August 1999.
56 GartnerGroup, *The Electronic Workplace: The Evolution Continues*, July 1999.
57 GartnerGroup, *The Electronic Workplace: The Evolution Continues*, July 1999.
58 Strassman P, *Politics of Information Management*, Information Economics Press, 1995, p. 302.
59 Thorpe J, *The Information Paradox*, McGraw-Hill Ryerson, Toronto, 1998.
60 Martin J with Leben J, *Strategic Information Planning Methodologies*, Prentice Hall, Englewood Cliffs, NJ, 1989.
61 Mintzberg H, *The Rise and Fall of Strategic Planning*, Prentice Hall, London, 1994.
62 Kerzner H, *Project Management*, 5th edn, Van Nostrand Reinhold, New York, 1995.
63 Lockyer K, *Critical Path Analysis*, 4th edn, Pitman, London, 1984.
64 Zachman JA, in *IBM Systems Journal*, **26**, No. 3, 1987.
65 Spewak SH and Hill SC, *Enterprise Architecture Planning*, John Wiley, New York, 1992.
66 Zachman JA, in *IBM Systems Journal*, **26**, No. 3, 1987.
67 Spewak SH and Hill SC, *Enterprise Architecture Planning*, John Wiley, New York, 1992.
68 Martin J, *Strategic Information Planning Methodologies* (2nd edn), Prentice Hall, Englewood Cliffs, NJ, 1989, and *Information Engineering Planning and Analysis* (Book 2), Prentice Hall, Englewood Cliffs, NJ, 1990.

69 Zachman JA, in *IBM Systems Journal*, **26**, No. 3, 1987.
70 Spewak SH and Hill SC, *Enterprise Architecture Planning*, John Wiley, New York, 1992.
71 Spewak SH and Hill SC, *Enterprise Architecture Planning*, John Wiley, New York, 1992.
72 *Gartner Letter*, November 1998, p. 7.
73 Kuhn TS, *The Structure of Scientific Revolutions*, 3rd edn, University of Chicago Press, Chicago, 1996.
74 Jacques E, *Requisite Organization*, Cason Hall, Arlington, VA, 1998.
75 *Inside GartnerGroup This Week*, **XV**, No. 17, April 1999, p. 2.
76 Tuckman BW, "Developmental sequence in small groups", *Psychological Bulletin*, **63**(8), 1965.
77 GartnerGroup, *IS & IT Management: Using IT for Value Creation and Business Effectiveness*, Report 5601, GartnerGroup, 1999.
78 Curtis MI *et al.*, "Process modelling", *Communications of the ACM*, **35**(a), 75–90, 1992.
79 Roberts T, "Why can't we implement this SDM?" *IEEE Software*, **16**, No. 6, 1999.
80 Standish Group, 1995.
81 IDC, *Forecast for Management*, annual.
82 "IT cost management strategies", *Computer Economics USA*, February 1997.
83 Saul JR, *Voltaire's Bastards*, Sinclair Stevenson (Reed Publishing), London, 1992.

Further reading

The following represents a small number of useful texts for an aspiring IT manager.

Aalders R, *The IT Outsourcing Guide*, John Wiley, Chichester, 2001.

Armstrong M and Murlis H, *Reward Management*, Kogan Page, London, 1996.

Brooks FP Jr, *The Mythical Man Month*, Addison-Wesley, Reading, MA, 1982.

Collins R, *Effective Management*, CCH International, North Ryde, NSW, 1995.

Deal TE and Kennedy AA, *Corporate Cultures*, Addison-Wesley, Reading, MA, 1982.

Domberger S and Hall C, *The Contracting Casebook*, AGPS, Sydney, 1995.

Gay CL and Essinger J, *Inside Outsourcing*, Brealey, London, 2000.

Gilb T, *Principles of Software Engineering Management*, Addison-Wesley, Wokingham, 1988.

Jacques E, *Requisite Organization*, Cason Hall, Arlington, VA, 1998.

Hammer M and Champy J, *Reengineering The Corporation*, Allen and Unwin, New York, 1993.

Hilmer FG and Donaldson L, *Management Redeemed*, The Free Press, Sydney, 1996.

Hughes DJ (ed.), *Moltke on the Art of War*, Presidio Press, Novato, CA, 1993.

Isachsen O and Berens LV, *Working Together*, Institute for Management Development, San Juan Capsitrano, CA, 1988.

Kepner CH and Tregoe BB, *The New Rational Manager*, Princeton Research Press, Princeton, NJ, 1987.

Kerzner H, *Project Management*, 5th edn, Van Nostrand Reinhold, New York, 1995.

Lockyer K, *Critical Path Analysis*, 4th edn, Pitman, London, 1984.

Martin J, *Strategic Information Planning Methodologies*, 2nd edn, Prentice Hall, Englewood Cliffs, NJ, 1989 and *Information Engineering Planning and Analysis* (Book 2), Prentice Hall, Englewood Cliffs, NJ, 1990.

Mintzberg H, *The Rise and Fall of Strategic Planning*, Prentice Hall, London, 1994.

Myers K and Briggs I, *Gifts Differing*, CA Consulting Psychologists Press, Palo Alto, CA, 1980.

Pugh DS (ed.), *Organization Theory*, 3rd edn, Penguin Books, London, 1990.

Saul JR, *Voltaire's Bastards*, Sinclair Stevenson (Reed Publishing), London, 1992.

Schwartz P, *The Art of the Long View*, Currency Doubleday, New York, 1991.

Schuster JR and Zingheim PK, *The New Pay*, Jossey-Bass Inc., San Francisco, CA, 1996.

Scott-Morton M (ed.), *The Corporation of the 1990s: Information Technology and Organizational Transformation*, Oxford University Press, New York, 1991.

Spewak S and Hill SC, *Enterprise Architecture Planning*, John Wiley, New York, 1992.

Strassman P, *The Politics of Information Management*, Information Economics Press, New Canaan, 1995, p. 46.

Strassman P, *The Business Value of Computers*, Information Economics Press, New Canaan, 1995.

Thorpe J, *The Information Paradox*, McGraw-Hill Ryerson, Montreal, 1996.

Toigo JW, *Disaster Recovery Planning*, Prentice Hall, Englewood Cliffs, NJ, 1989.
Tozer J, *Leading Initiatives*, Butterworth-Heinemann, Melbourne, 1997.
Trout J with Rivkin S, *The Power of Simplicity*, McGraw-Hill, New York, 1999.
Ulrich D, *Human Resource Champions*, Harvard Business School Press, Harvard, MA, 1996.
Van der Heijden K, *Scenarios: The Art of Strategic Conversation*, John Wiley, Chichester, 1996.
Weill P and Broadbent M, *Leveraging the New Infrastructure*, Harvard Business School Press, Harvard, MA, 1998.
Zachman JA in *IBM Systems Journal*, **26**, No. 3, 1987.

Readings on enterprise architectures

Boar B, *Constructing Blueprints for Enterprise Architectures*, John Wiley, New York, 1998.
Britton C, *IT Architectures and Middleware*, Addison-Wesley, New York, 2000.
Goodyear M (ed.), *Enterprise System Architecture*, CRC Press, New York, 1999.
Spewak SH and Hill SC, *Enterprise Architecture Planning*, John Wiley, New York, 1992.
Cook MA, *Building Enterprise Information Architectures*, Prentice Hall, Upper Saddle River, NJ, 1996.

Readings on outsourcing

Aalders R, *The IT Outsourcing Guide*, John Wiley, Chichester, 2001.
Domberger S and Hall C, *The Contracting Casebook*, AGPS, Sydney, 1995.
Gay CL and Essinger J, *Inside Outsourcing*, Brealy, London, 2000.
Greaver II MF, *Strategic Outsourcing*, ANACOM, New York, 1999.
Halvey JK and Melby BM, *Information Technology Outsourcing Transactions*, John Wiley, Somerset, NJ, 1996.
Karpathiou V and Tanner K, *Information Technology Outsourcing in Australia*, RMIT, Melbourne, 1995.
Klepper R and Jones WO, *Outsourcing Information Technology, Systems and Services*, Prentice Hall, Englewood Cliffs, NJ, 1998.
KPMG, *Outsourcing Best Practice Guidelines*, HMSO, London, 1995.
Lacity MC and Hirschheim R, *Beyond The Information Systems Outsourcing Bandwagon*, John Wiley, Lacity, NJ, 1995.
Mylott III TR, *Computer Outsourcing, Managing the Transfer of Information Systems*, Prentice Hall, Englewood Cliffs, NJ, 1995.

Readings on strategy

Hughes DJ (ed.), *Moltke on the Art of War*, Presidio Press, Novato, CA, 1993.
Martin J with Leben J, *Strategic Information Planning Methodologies*, Prentice Hall, Englewood Cliffs, NJ, 1989.
Mintzberg H, *The Rise and Fall of Strategic Planning*, Prentice Hall, Englewood Cliffs, NJ, 1994.
Ohmae K, *The Mind of the Strategist*, Penguin, New York, 1982.
Schwarz O, *The Art of the Long View*, Currency Doubleday, New York, 1996.
Thorpe J, *The Information Paradox*, McGraw-Hill Ryerson Ltd, Montreal, 1996. The *Information Paradox* was not written as a strategic planning text yet the ResultsChain™ method which is described in this book seems to provide a sound method for driving and documenting strategic plans.

Index